JEWISH EMANCIPATION

AND

SELF-EMANCIPATION

JEWISH EMANCIPATION AND SELF-EMANCIPATION

JACOB KATZ

5746   1986

THE JEWISH PUBLICATION SOCIETY

PHILADELPHIA · NEW YORK · JERUSALEM

ACKNOWLEDGMENTS

"Jewry and Judaism in the Nineteenth Century." From *Journal of World History* IV (1958), 881–900.

"Religion as a Uniting and Dividing Force in Modern Jewish History." From J. Katz, ed., *The Role of Religion in Modern Jewish History* (Cambridge, Mass., 1975), 1–17.

"Judaism and Christianity Against the Background of Modern Secularism." From *Judaism* XVII (1968), 3, 299–315.

"The Influence of Religion and Society on Each Other at the Time of the Emancipation." From *European Judaism* I (1966) 1, 20–29.

"The German-Jewish Utopia of Social Emanicipation." From M. Kreutzberger, ed., *Studies of the Leo Baeck Institute* (New York, 1967), 59–80.

"Emancipation and Jewish Studies." From *Commentary* LVII (1974) 4, 60–65.

"The Jewish National Movement." From H. Ben-Sasson and S. Ettiger, eds., *Jewish Society Through the Ages* (New York, 1971), 267–283.

"The Forerunners of Zionism." From *The Jerusalem Quarterly* VII (1978), 10–21.

"Situating Zionism in Contemporary Jewish History." From *Forum* 44 (1982), 9–23.

"Zionism and Jewish Identity." From *Commentary* LXVII (1977) 5, 48–52.

"Zionism vs. Anti-Semitism." From *Commentary* LXVII (1979) 4, 46–52.

"Israel and the Messiah." From *Commentary* LXXIII (1982) 1, 34–41.

Library of Congress Cataloging in Publication Data
Katz, Jacob, 1904–
    Jewish emancipation and self-emancipation.

    Bibliography: p. 167
    Includes index.
    1. Jews—Emancipation—Addresses, essays, lectures.
2. Jews—Cultural assimilation—Addresses, essays,
lectures. 3. Zionism—History—Addresses, essays,
lectures. I. Title.
DS147.K367 1986   956.94'001   85–23699
ISBN 0–8276–0261–8

Designed by Terri Siegel

CONTENTS

Jewish Emancipation and Self-Emancipation

Introduction

Emancipation and Self-Emancipation, the two headings under which the articles in this volume are subsumed, occurred in this order historically and were conceived of by contemporaries as mutually exclusive. Emancipation was the slogan that served Jews in England and on the Continent, starting in the late twenties of the nineteenth century, as a battle-cry in their struggle for legal and political equality. By the seventies of the century this struggle seemed to have been crowned with definite success except for Russia, where concessions on the part of one tzarist government were followed by their revocation by another. Yet at the end of that very same decade, reaction set in to the Jewish success achieved in the West, notably in Germany, Hungary, and then also in France, in the shape of the anti-Semitic movement, while in Russia all hope for an ultimate enfranchisement was dashed at the sight of the bloody pogroms in the spring of 1881. It was under the impact of these disappointing events that Leon Pinsker, formerly a staunch and optimistic champion of the idea of Jewish emancipation in Russia, came forward with his "Autoemancipation." The thrust of his pamphlet, written in German, was an appeal to Jewry in East and West alike to become aware of the futility of the endeavor to achieve a lasting solution of the Jewish problem by an emancipation granted by the European states. The solution should instead be sought in the foundation of an independent Jewish commonwealth—an anticipation of the idea of political Zionism, propagated a decade and a half later by Theodor Herzl.

Although in its original context the idea of self-emancipation was pitted against its antecedent, I think it will strike the reader of the essays presented in this volume that in historical perspective it far from signified absolute denial and abandonment of emancipation. First, in contrast to exponents of self-emancipation like Pinsker and Herzl, who were outsiders of Jewish society proper, certain insiders preceded them in propagating the idea of establishing a Jewish state, not out of disappointment with emancipation, but rather perceiving such a state as its natural consummation. This is the theme of my essay on "The Forerunners of Zionism." Some of the other studies show that the striving for self-emancipation did not necessarily entail the rejection of all emancipation stood for. Besides the struggle for civil equality, emancipation also meant the transformation of Jewish society from a tradition-bound community into a modern variation. This modernizing tendency was adopted by the exponents of self-emancipation. The transition from one phase to the other is thus revealed as possessing a dialectical character, self-emancipation being a partial denial and partial incorporation of emancipation.

This characteristic holds true even more of the expected results of the change-over. The initiators of self-emancipation thought they had diagnosed the cause of anti-Semitism and found its remedy. As some of the essays presented here show, Jewish self-emancipation may have transmuted the scene of the struggle for Jewish rehabilitaion, but it has not succeeded in obviating its necessity. The "anomaly" of Jewish existence has deep historical roots; its rectification can come about only as a result of long-term historical processes. The juxtaposition of these two phases of modern Jewish history, emancipation and self-emancipation, can illuminate this possibly disillusioning—but, precisely because of this, necessary—insight.

Jacob Katz
The Hebrew University of Jerusalem

PART
I

EMANCIPATION

Jewry and Judaism in the Nineteenth Century

SOCIO-HISTORICAL SURVEY

1

The beginning of the nineteenth century ushered in a new epoch in Jewish history. This change affected the social, political, religious and cultural aspects of the traditional pattern of life. The history of the era in question may find its analogies in the course of the three millennia of Jewry's past, but actually it stands without exact parallel. Up to the last third of the eighteenth century, Jews were always recognizable as a clearly defined social unit, distinctly set apart from the community at large in whose midst they had settled. Their religious traditions with the attendant institutions, rites, and symbolic expressions created for the adherent an exclusive sphere. The social segregation that resulted from adherence to their own religion was brought into even sharper relief by the fact that this religious tradition had elements as well as forms of expression typical of a national culture. Some holidays and religious symbols were not only designed to manifest transcendental concepts of the creed; they also served for observant Jews as reminders of their national past and of the messianic future that would bring redemption to the world and a reunion of Israel in the land of the ancestors. The records of tradition, viz. Bible and Talmud, were always taught in the national tongue of yore, i.e., Hebrew, or the cognate Aramaic, which had been adopted early in ancient times. Elements of this language, including the concepts, mental images and mode of thinking induced by it, penetrated, particularly through the medium of study at all ages, into all the vernaculars of the Jews, so that the Jewish community developed a particular brand of dialect that was apt to accentuate its segregation linguistically; in some cases this deviation from the locally customary mode of speech created a jargon.

The preservation of this religio-cultural singularity was, of course, dependent on the political restriction of the Jews, which for centuries had been in force as the accepted policy in all Christian and Mohammedan countries. This attitude towards the Jews, which had become an unchallenged tradition, rendered them direct subjects to the respective political power. The discrimination from which Jewry during all these centuries suffered more than other disadvantaged groups in the community consisted of their being deprived of any claim or right to stay at their place of birth or residence. Residential and commercial permits had to be petitioned from and paid for to the potentates. These circumstances make it clear why also from the economic aspect the Jews occupied a peculiarly restricted position. Nowhere did they participate in all branches of local economic life. Only commerce and finance, sometimes a few of the trades, and of the professions only medicine at best, were accessible to them. The configuration of all these elements and traits results in the portrayal of a distinct social unit that is at variance with its environment in all essential features.

The description sketched above of the tradition-bound Jewish community and its adjustment to the life of the respective national hosts has to be borne in mind primarily as historical background against which the development of Jewry took place in the course of the nineteenth century. Yet actually this description holds true for a large part of this minority even throughout the century. According to the accepted demographic estimate, there were about two and a half million Jews at the end of the eighteenth century. At the end of the nineteenth century there were about ten and a half million—a rate of increase that in percentage exceeds all other European peoples for this period. This rapid multiplication of Jewry was not equally distributed among all its parts. Of the two and a half million at the end of the eighteenth century, one million, or forty percent, were Jews in the Orient (in the large Turkish Empire and North Africa). Of the remainder, a million and a half lived in East and Central Europe. The number of Jews in overseas countries was insignificant. This picture, however, is entirely changed by the end of the century. Whereas the number of Oriental Jews remained about the same, European Jewry constituted about 80 percent as the result of their rapid national increase. The remaining million, or 10 percent, lived in America, to which country during the second half of the century, particularly after 1880, the first waves of Jewish mass immigration were directed.[1]

The distribution of the Jewish population in the various European countries has to be taken into consideration for a true appreciation of these demographic facts from the socio-historical aspect. Special attention is to be paid to the fact that out of eight million Jews in Europe, five million lived in Russia. In this empire the great events of the century caused some political and social repercussions, but no new social order emerged from them. The major part of European Jewry remained in the religio-cultural and socio-political segregation described above. The change at the beginning of the century affected only the position of the Jews in Western Europe and the United States. Of course, the revolution that took place with regard to the position of Jews living in the leading countries of civilization had its bearing, if not immediately, upon the fate of Jewry all over the world. This also justifies the tendency of historians to pay particular attention to events occurring in Western countries.

The change that occurred in the position of the Jews in Western countries may be briefly summed up: the heretofore conditionally admitted residents, in most cases also locally restricted to Jewish quarters, became full-fledged citizens of the respective states. In the second or third generation at the latest, these new citizens became extensively adjusted to the customs of their respective bourgeois societies, thus creating a new type: the German, French, or English Jew. This metamorphosis is in no way the result of an internal Jewish development, but rather the effect of political and social changes that took place in these countries. The first signs of relaxation in the relation of the Jews to their surroundings appeared at the latest in the last third of the eighteenth century, as a result of acute and growing criticism levelled against the prevailing rigid class structure of the state and the class stratification of society. This critique called the segregation of the Jews an anomaly and therefore condemned it. The proponents of this criticism were the bourgeois intellectuals in France and Germany, who also witnessed the first acquaintance between Jew and non-Jew, in which direct personal contact led to unreserved fraternization and fellow-feeling for their common interest in the promotion of cultural values. The meeting and resultant life-long friendship between Moses Mendelssohn (1729–1786) and G.E. Lessing (1729–1781), which produced so much mutual inspiration, may serve as the best example. In these critically minded circles of intellectuals the concept of integrating the Jews into the community at large was molded. This concept was then associated with the claim for Jewish equality within the framework of the prospective federal union of states. Here the wish for Jewish assimilation in culture and custom finally found expression. Just as in other areas of social transformation, here also ideology proved a driving force, although it could not serve as a guide for developments to follow; for the actual change did not, as in the conception of the intellectuals, take place as a victory of rationality over traditional prejudice. The absorption of the Jews came rather in the wake of the wider political and social changes that resulted from the French Revolution, the aftermath of which lasted until the middle of the nineteenth century. The new order, based on the direct relationship of the citizens to the state, could not possibly suffer in its midst autonomous Jewish communities with their singular rights and restrictions. Thus the delegates to the French National Assembly were entirely consistent when pointing out that the state faced the dilemma of either recognizing the Jews as equal citizens, or expelling them from French territory. Since for humanitarian reasons the expulsion of the Jews was hardly acceptable, the only alternative was to confer equality upon the Jews as citizens. The logical consistency of the argument had to combat biases and prejudices that had been cherished and nurtured for centuries. Hence the National Assembly, which had proved so change-happy throughout, had to postpone until shortly before its dissolution the official announcement of granting equal citizenship to the Jewish subjects of France (September 27, 1791).[2]

The same spectacle was repeated in the course of the century by the various legislatures of the European states. The advocates of a consistent interpretation of the modern idea of a state claimed equal citizenship rights for the Jews. Reactionary elements, prompted by prejudice and old familiar notions, tried to impede the course of this development. After many fights, advances, and reverses, the principle of granting universal right of citizenship independent of religious persuasion prevailed. The most important dates in the ups and downs of this development are: the Prussian Edict of Emancipation (1812); the revocation of rights obtained in German lands in the wake of the Vienna Congress (1815); and the removal of the Christian faith clause from the oath for public officials in England by an act of Parliament (1858). With the achievement of citizenship rights in the Austro-Hungarian Empire (1867), in the newly founded German Empire (1870), and in Switzerland (1877), the historical process of Jewish emancipation came to a successful conclusion in Western Europe. Citizenship rights had implicitly been guaranteed to Jews in the United States by the American Constitution (1790).[3]

The new historical situation, which, in spite of the intellectuals' ideological anticipation, took the majority of Jews by surprise, confronted the Jewish community with unprecedented tasks. The practice of newly attained political rights required of them cultural and social adjustment. This situation made it incumbent upon them to completely master the language of the community at large and to modify their traditional mode of living. Their ancient, tradition-bound institutions had to be changed, tempered, or forgone entirely. The history of Jewish education and its institutions may well serve here as a characteristic example. The talmudic schools and academies (yeshivot) which up to now had fulfilled the educational functions, disappeared within two generations. In their stead emerged Jewish schools that emulated the schools of their surroundings in almost every respect, or else the idea of a separate Jewish school was dismissed in favor of entrusting the education of Jewish youth to the public schools. This step led to the exclusion of the specifically Jewish elements of tradition that for many centuries had molded the spirit and character of the people. We shall see in the second part of our survey what attempts were made to ensure for the Jewish community a kind of conscious self-identification and to uphold their historical moorings without impeding their blending with the contemporary non-Jewish environment. In any case, one may speak of a process of disintegration at the beginning of the nineteenth century, as far as the Jewish community is concerned. Many contemporaries welcomed this process and gladly promoted it. For the sake of historical justice we are bound to say that this affirmation was not merely motivated by utilitarian reasons.

The assimilation-happy Jews, as one might call them, always found an idealistic rationalization for the amalgamation with their environment. Mendelssohn already felt that his friendship with non-Jews constituted a triumph of pure humaneness.[4] The admission of many other Jews to the circle of men of letters was hailed by enlightened Europeans as a humanistic accomplishment. Later on, particularly under the influence of prevailing ideas to which the average citizen was prone, nationalism in each country became an assimilatory element. The simultaneous appearance of modern nationalism and the emancipation of the Jews is no historical coincidence. The modern state and modern society precipitated both trends at about the same time. The newly emancipated Jews joined the nationalistic movements enthusiastically. Joyously they rallied to the call to fight for national liberation and nationalist revolutions in France, Germany, Poland, and Hungary. In retrospect we may see today that their ready and easy joining of the nationalist ranks was meant to legitimate their newly granted political rights. However, subjectively the nationalistic idea of their respective country of adoption was genuinely cherished, and their sacrifices for it were joyously offered.[5]

Socialism, which served for many as ideological and social medium for assimilation, also gained adherents. The socialist movements of the nineteenth century attracted many Jews and imbued them with sympathy and readiness to struggle alongside the socially disabled. In this case too we have to distinguish between the objective historical forces at play and the subjectively expressed rationalizations. Jewish socialists shared the desire of their non-Jewish comrades to serve in the cause of bringing social salvation to the world. The fact that they found at the same time a solution for the problem of their own social adjustment remains incidental, a post facto sociological observation.

The necessity of an assimilatory element, which would safeguard the legitimacy of the Jew's fusion with his environment as called for by the new situation, makes it clear that his problem of adjustment was of a social nature. Indeed it was rather a complex problem. The social disabilities under which he had suffered for generations, and from which he had just been unexpectedly rehabilitated, did not put the Jew at ease naively to enjoy the newly granted rights. Complete inner and outer adjustment could hardly be achieved within a short span. Even Jewish freethinkers preserved certain typical traits in their thinking and bearing, often even in their appearance. He who did not entirely sever his relations with the religious congregation remained in his Jewish consciousness moored to certain sentiment-charged symbols. The self-consciousness of a minority facing a majority that requires constant self-justification never did disappear entirely. The majority could only be expected to demonstrate its good will by showing consideration for existing differences, without overlooking them. The concept of typically Jewish traits was never forsaken even in circles that showed a most sympathetic and favorably inclined attitude. Radical assimilation, a utopian dream that envisioned Jewry's complete absorption by its environment, thus solving the "Jewish Problem" for all times, never stood a real historical chance. In reality, the nineteenth century solved the political aspect of the problem by granting emancipation to the Jews, thus substituting the social aspect of the problem for the political one.

The Jews became even more disillusioned by their inability to assimilate completely when they looked at the historical circumstances. On the basis of the new political situation, Jewish and non-Jewish advocates of the emancipation came to expect and even prophesy an occupational recon-stellation of the Jews. They believed in particular that the newly granted right to acquire and hold real estate would induce some Jews to engage in agriculture, to become peasants and farmers. Such plans, however, lacked the sociological prerequisites. The widespread urbanization characteristic of the nineteenth century in general made no exception of the Jews. As a matter of fact, more than in any previous times the Jews now became metropolitans and megapolitans, a signal feature of demographic changes during this era. Nor did the concentration of Jews upon certain vocations, trades, and professions disappear. Economic freedom of choice, which, as a matter of principle, took effect in the countries of emancipation, broad-ened the vocational distribution of the Jews insofar as it afforded them a wider choice in the various branches of industry and commerce, particularly however in the professions. It has to be borne in mind that many such new opportunities only developed in the course of the emancipation period as a result of general social and economic evolution. However, agriculture, mining, and the military are occupations traditionally held by certain social strata and therefore, with rare exceptions, they offered little attraction to the Jews. In fact, these occupations were not even made available to them. Hence the vocational redistribution of Jews in all the respective countries shows little change during the age of their emancipation. This stability, in turn, facilitated their identification and promoted their cohesion to a large extent.[6]

Perhaps an even larger obstacle in the way of complete assimilation was the fact that emancipation affected Jewry only in some of its respective countries of settlement. In the nineteenth century Russia's five million Jews, a quarter of a million Jews in Rumania, and a million Jews in oriental countries were not engaged in a struggle for their political rights but in defending their personal security and economic existence. According to the theory of radical assimilation, the cohesive bonds with Jews in other countries should have become severed as soon as the Jews of certain coun-tries enjoyed political equality. In fact, however, Jewish solidarity proved itself a real social force during the nineteenth century, beyond all national and territorial boundaries. On the occasion of the Damascus Blood Libel

(1840), when confessions were extorted from Jews by means of torture, the greatest notables of French and English Jewry, A. Crémieux and M. Montefiore, personally intervened, and were acclaimed by Jewry all over the world and highly commended by liberal public opinion throughout the civilized countries; they were received in audience by the Sultan and gained acquittal and rehabilitation of the innocent accused. Since then, the responsibility of Jewry in the several countries of emancipation for the fate of their brethren anywhere in the world has become an accepted fact. This feeling of solidarity found its organizational expression in the founding of the Alliance Israélite Universelle (Paris, 1860).[7] This and many similar organizations had been active throughout the century in obtaining political rights for the Jews in countries that had not yet granted them full citizenship (e.g., at the Berlin Congress, 1878), and also in raising the social and cultural level of backward communities in Eastern Europe and oriental areas.

From the ideological aspect, the sentiment of Jewish cohesion transcending boundaries of state and territory did not imply any Jewish national base or aspiration. Actually, the readiness to come to the assistance of any Jewish community in another country that was in need or suffering, went hand in hand with the readiness to adjust themselves to their environment, with their devotion to the duties of their state, and with their passionate participation in the political and cultural life of their adopted country. The problem that presented itself in this attitude of dual loyalty was vaguely felt but rarely subjected to conceptual analysis. Only here and there were voices heard demanding for the solidarity of world Jewry a firmer basis in the form of a nationalistically tinted ideology with politically oriented objectives. Up to the eighth decade of the century, such ideas were sounded mainly by traditionalist thinkers, who regretted the disintegration of the time-honored pattern of life and, with reference to their messianic faith, championed the cause of a Jewish national revival on the historic soil of the ancestral homeland. The course of the dialectical development that leads from large-scale assimilation to Jewish nationalism has been demonstrated by the leading socialist Moses Hess. In his *Rome and Jerusalem* (1862), he expressed a surprising endorsement of Jewish nationalism, advocating resettlement in Palestine like one of the traditionalists. Such opinions, however, were hardly favored with any attention up to the sixties, and if at all considered—ridiculed, and if taken seriously—bitterly combatted. These nationalistic aspirations were denounced as jeopardizing the prospects for emancipation during the entire period of the struggle for it. When the struggle reached its successful conclusion in the West, the time for a synthesis seemed to have arrived. After 1860, organizations were already actively engaged in colonizing Palestine. In 1870, the executive of the Alliance Israélite Universelle in Paris approved a resolution to establish an agricultural school in Palestine. These precursors of the nationalist movement could hardly have accomplished anything significant, had it not been for the onset of anti-Semitism as a social reaction in the eighties. The anti-Semitic wave of 1880 in Germany, the Dreyfus Affair of 1894–99 in France, and similar phenomena in Austria and Hungary are largely to be explained as a result of domestic developments in the respective countries, resulting from political differences and social tension. However, all these anti-Semitic movements took their point of departure from the fact of the Jews' incomplete assimilatory process. The existence of singular Jewish traits, the narrow occupational distribution of the Jews and their feeling of solidarity, all provided material for the demagogue to justify Jew-baiting and hate-mongering, and to prove that Jewry constituted an ever-alien and insoluble element within the national body. The radical anti-Semites were not merely satisfied to present these theses as a moral defamation but drove the matter to a programmatic conclusion: the emancipation of the Jews had been a historical mistake and must be rectified by revocation. Anti-Semitism manifested itself in social tensions in the West, whereas in the East, for example Russia and Rumania, where emancipation had at best merely been set on paper, the anti-Semitic wave brought on economic restrictions, expulsions, and pogroms.[8]

The anti-Semitism of the eighties took the Jews in the West by surprise. Signs of social exclusiveness toward the Jews, which had not been wanting in former days, were now dismissed as passing relics of outmoded prejudice. However, the expressions of brutal hate and vile defamation called for a profounder interpretation of the phenomenon. Jewish public opinion in the West found its comfort by and large in the illusion of progress, which in any case had been an integral part of the liberal bourgeois ideology. These circles now attempted to combat anti-Semitism by means of rational enlightenment of the opponents. But in Russia and Rumania, where the very existence of the Jewish masses was endangered by anti-Semitic threats, the Jews resorted to emigration. Since this part of Europe contained a large Jewish population, the consciousness of national cohesion was felt much more acutely than in the West, and so there was a greater inclination to interpret events from a nationalist aspect. As a matter of fact, beginning in the eighteen-eighties an outspoken nationalist movement took shape, which set as its objective the reintegration and regeneration of national Jewish life upon the historical soil of its homeland, Palestine. The first wave of emigration to Palestine coincided with this era. It was characteristic of Western Jewry that although it did not emulate this act, it lent its moral and financial support to it. In any case, the Jews of Western Europe had, after all, also gained some historical experience during the most recent phase of their metamorphosis, which called their attenton to grave problems of Jewish existence in the immediate environment. Nationalist tendencies also revealed themselves here and there in the founding of several organizations and associations. When Theodor Herzl, on the occasion of the Dreyfus affair, arrived at the conclusion—which even to his own consciousness came as a surprise—that the Jewish problem could find its solution only in the establishment of a Jewish state, he found a responsive, if not a radically consistent and aggressive, following in every country where Jews were settled. The function of convoking the first Zionist Congress at Basle in 1897 was to consolidate the already active national forces. Just as the convocation, at Napoleon's behest, of the Sanhedrin at Paris in 1808, which took as its task to bestow its official blessing and religious sanction on the assimilationists, may be seen as the opening event of this epoch, so the Zionist Congress of 1897 may be considered and evaluated as its conclusion. The historian who chooses as his perspective the actual restoration of the Jewish state fifty years later, will see the Zionist Congress of 1897 primarily as a point of departure for the subsequent materialization of the idea that emerged as a resolution and political program from these deliberations. Yet its direct and organic historical significance lies rather in the solemn declaration manifesting the vital urgency of national self-affirmation in the face of a century that had witnessed Jewish degeneration and disintegration. This declaration was made by the consolidation of nationally conscious Jewish forces, appearing publicly before the world, arousing and challenging the Jewish people wherever they were scattered.

RELIGION AND PHILOSOPHY

The historical events described in the first part of this survey, which brought about such a radical change in the position of Jewry at the turn of the eighteenth century, precipitated various ideas in the realm of the spirit, as in the field of religious philosophy and theology, in the results of historical research, and in the social and national ideologies. Heretofore, as long as the Jew was segregated from the surrounding world, being Jewish posed no problem to him. Hence all religious traditions were accepted naively and unchallenged. Aside from a few rare exceptions like Spinoza (1632–1677), even the most distinguished minds found in the study and observance of this tradition their intellectual satisfaction, presenting as it did a world of faith and thought that corresponded to their own perception of reality.

When, however, contact with the larger environment, particularly in intellectual circles, became the rule of the day, their horizon broadened, and spiritual orientation was sought with the help of philosophy and scientific methods. Jewish identity became a problem. The former naive acceptance was now replaced by self-conscious reflection about the religious tradition, its historical truth, its intrinsic value, and its meaning for the present and the future. In this process of intellectual reorientation Moses Mendelssohn (1729–1786) again loomed as the leading figure. The historical situation challenged him with its problem and forced him, however reluctantly, to take his stand. In the beginning Mendelssohn thought it possible to evade the issue. However, when he was asked again and again to state and show cause for his identification with traditional Judaism, he finally felt compelled to present and demonstrate publicly his concept of Judaism and its relationship to other systems of faith and thought. This he did in his book *Jerusalem*, published in 1783, in which he upheld the Divine revelation on Mount Sinai as the source of the Jewish religion. The novel and surprising feature of his concept of Judaism lay in the fact that he limited the content of Sinaitic revelation to a definite part of the religious tradition, namely, ritual laws. The purpose of the Sinaitic revelation was the enactment of the ritual laws. This enactment remained in force for the Jewish people for all times to come. The doctrinal part of the tradition, however, the system of ethics and the tenets of faith, was rationally accessible to all mankind. This dichotomy corresponded to the prevailing philosophy of *Aufklärung*, according to which man could rely on Reason as a guide to arrive at a true creed and valid ethical norms. This doctrine, which became associated in the course of the eighteenth century with the concept of "natural religion," constituted for Mendelssohn a self-evident truth. Therefore he could not credit the Jewish religion with the revelation of metaphysical doctrines, and only the ritual laws were left as the characteristic feature of Judaism. Mendelssohn created with this system a religious platform well suited for his personal position. His loyalty to the traditional way of Jewish life safeguarded his Jewishness. At the same time, however, he had justified his spritual kinship with the non-Jewish intellectuals of his day. Was it not in the spiritual, non-ceremonial realm that all rational religions met on common ground, admitting no differences and granting no priority to the adherents to the Jewish religion? The particular feature of Judaism, the law and the commandments, was destined only for Jewry. Although it was historically unjustifiable, Mendelssohn identified Judaism with the idea of religious non-missionary tolerance. He contended that Judaism had never tried to win any converts to Judaism, nor had it disclaimed salvation for those adhering to other religions. Judaism merely enjoined the Jews to keep the ritual laws, which, in turn, would lead to the pure preservation of a creed rationally accessible to all mankind.[9]

Mendelssohn's concept of Judaism could hardly satisfy the next generation. His theory had equal effect upon Jew and non-Jew by identifying Judaism as a rationally demonstrable faith. Following in his footsteps, the theorists of Judaism in the nineteenth century took their guidance from the rationalist philosophers of the Middle Ages. The mystical trends of the past and present, Kabbalism and Hasidism—the latter flourished in Eastern Europe from the middle of the eighteenth century as a great religious movement—were either disregarded or declared aberrations traceable to alien influences. However, in contrast to Mendelssohn's denial of any revealed doctrines in Judaism, these theorists pressed for the creation of a Jewish system of theology and ethics. The necessity for such a doctrinal system was made stringent by a significant change in the position of the generation succeeding Mendelssohn. To Mendelssohn the unifying bond of the Jewish people was guaranteed by their observance of ritual law, and he could therefore dispense with a doctrinal system. The next generation found itself in a situation in which the observance of the ritual tradition could no longer play this role. Most of Mendelssohn's disciples had already renounced their loyalty to the ceremonial Jewish traditions. Steady social contact with non-Jews had made the observance of the many Jewish customs most cumbersome. The absorption of Jews into the professional life of the environment and their being drafted into the armed forces put practical obstacles in the way of their keeping the laws of their religious tradition. In fact, Mendelssohn's theory provided too weak a basis for the validity of the laws. For if the laws were to serve but as a preservative and educational force for religious truths common to all mankind, this was too cumbersome a way to reach a goal that others could attain by far simpler means. Mendelssohn's exposition of Judaism could easily be used as a vindication for conversion to Christianity; for if the rational basis of all creeds were fundamentally the same, then apostasy lost its dishonorable character that had stigmatized the convert in the traditional view. Many, among them children and disciples of Mendelssohn, undertook this step after his death. They were certainly not motivated by merely rational considerations. The disintegration of the traditional mode of life and the collapse of segregating barriers rendered outmoded their ties with the Jewish sphere of faith and with Jewish clannishness.[10]

This step, however, could not be undertaken by all those who renounced the old Judaism. Many, among them those of independent thought and creativity, abandoned their belief in the traditional tenets and the unconditional observance of the ritual law, yet felt strongly about their being a part of Jewish society and acknowledged the influence of Jewish tradition upon them. This group was groping for a new meaning for their Jewish identity, which resulted in the foundation of a new system of Jewish theology and ethics.

These theological and historico-philosophical attempts of Jewish thinkers in the first half of the nineteenth century were indebted to post-Kantian German Idealism. This holds true not only for the works written in Germany and in German, such as those of Samuel Hirsch (1815–1889), Solomon Formstecher (1808–1889), and Salomon Ludwig Steinheim (1789–1866), but also for the Hebrew writings of Nahman Krochmal (1785–1840) in Galicia. In spite of differences in the structure of their systems, all these thinkers operate on the same premises. They all, expressly or tacitly, dispense with the traditional concept of the historically unique revelation of law or doctrine. For them, Judaism, like any other religion, presents the result of a historical process. Thus the history of the Jewish religion became a free domain for historical research. For Krochmal, as for the historian Heinrich Graetz (1817–1891), who prefaced the study of the historical realia with a historico-philosophical sketch, the philosophical concepts served in fact as a kind of introduction and guiding principle for periodic divisions and a more or less independent presentation of Jewish history. However, the ultimate goal of research and meditation for both the historian and the theologian remained the philosophical vindication of Judaism. The central concept, which played an important function in all these systems, was the concept of the spirit. The unfolding of the conscious self-realization of the spirit constitutes the theological destiny of history. The Jewish thinkers set themselves the task of determining the role Judaism had played in the past and was to play in the future in the course of this development. As may be easily understood, they show marked deviations from the Christian thinkers of their age. The German philosophers, led by Christian doctrines, had assigned to Judaism the function of a transitory stage to Christianity. Even the secularizing historical philosophers maintained this doctrine in their systems, which actually goes back to patristic concepts. According to these theories, there are several stages and phases in the course of the spirit's unfolding and conscious self-realization. In this process, Judaism was assigned a preparatory function. With the emergence of Chistianity, Judaism is treated as a kind of anachronistic feature, which has forfeited its historical function. A Jewish theology dedicated to the vindication of the *raison d'être* of Judaism, even for the present time, had to reject such an interpretation. Moreover, the new Jewish theology, basing itself upon the concepts of Idealist philosophers, reached opposite results. In the historical process of the spirit's self-realization, the decisive role is assigned to Judaism. Judaism contributes the true faith to the world. Although Christianity is recognized as a missionary force for the true faith—herein the Jewish theologian and historical philosophers follow the great medieval thinkers, particularly Maimonides—it is criticized for having made concessions to pagan customs and elements of thought. Thus only Judaism remains to bear the torch of the true faith. As the ultimate end of this process an era was envisaged that would see the triumph of its truth and the breakdown of separation barriers between the religions. However, this ultimate merger was made dependent upon the self-reflection of Judaism and recognition of its mission in the world, as also upon the self-criticism and purification of Christianity. For the present the separate existence and continuation of the Jewish confessional congregation was regarded as justified in spite of political emancipation and social assimilation and integration.[11]

From the point of view of Jewish history one may sum up the achievement of these philosophical systems, whose validity nobody would want to defend nowadays, as follows: At a time when all other ties of the individual to the Jewish community had disintegrated, these systems taught and promoted a consciousness of the peculiar value and meaning of Jewish identity.

Although this new theology of Judaism proved to be a curb to centrifugal trends, yet within Jewry it became the expression of a religious schism: for these theories assumed implicitly or explicitly that the observance of the ritual law, which even Mendelssohn recognized as the criterion of Jewish identity, had lost its validity entirely or at least in the heretofore absolute sense. These new theologians ascribed to the ritual and ceremonial observances the function of mere symbolic expressions of the faith. The time-honored concept according to which the observance of the Law in all its minutiae is the *sine qua non* for the religious justification of the Jew, was considered outmoded.

This theology thus deprived the Jewish religion of its historical basis. Until this point the rabbi's religious authority had derived from his erudition in the Law, his proficiency in the *halakhic* literature. By virtue of his scholarship and wisdom the rabbi was capable of solving any cases of doubt and the problems of the religiously conscientious. With the suspension of any obligation towards the Law in the traditional sense, the *halakhic* literature could no longer serve as a standard in questions of ritual and law. In fact, the theologians were not only divided on the question of how far the ceremonial law was still applicable to certain details, their embarrassment was of a more fundamental nature. Their break with the *Halakhah* deprived them of the source that invests the rabbi with religious authority. In the course of their discussions about ritual and ceremonial questions they continued studiously to cite from *halakhic* literature. These quotations, however, were mostly designed to serve as demonstrations for the still tradition-bound Jew that these new-fangled concepts could also be corroborated from the ancient source material. As far as the conscience of the new theologians was concerned, it no longer felt responsible to the authority of the *Halakhah*.[12]

In the foregoing account, we have not only described the embarrassment of the theologians themselves and the source of their differences, but most of all the contrast between them and the traditionalists. To the latter group belonged foremost the masses of the Eastern European Pale. Also in certain areas in Germany, the traditional mode of living and basis of faith remained in force. Smaller and larger groups of loyalists survived the Age of Enlightenment and the new religious trends. And from the second third of the nineteenth century onward the maintenance of religious observance as a matter of principle was not only defended by tradition-bound loyalists, but even found its literary exponents in modern-trained rabbis, led by S. R. Hirsch (1808–1888). S. R. Hirsch may by all rights be considered the founder of modern Jewish orthodoxy. His mind no less than the minds of his adversaries had also been nurtured on German Idealism. The foundation of his faith remained, however, untouched by the new tendencies. For Hirsch the observance of the laws, of whose divine origin he was deeply convinced, remained the vindication of Jewish identity. The elements of speculative philosophy that he had absorbed served him for the symbolic interpretation of the details of the commandments and for the propagation of their observance. Hirsch was not only a deeply religious, and despite his militant nature, integrated personality. He was also a highly gifted pamphleteer. By virtue of these gifts, he became the leader of circles that either still persevered in the old faith or had been newly reconverted to it.[13]

In the middle of the nineteenth century Jewry presented a religiously divided community, a situation which seemed to defy reintegration. Both sides pressed for a formal schism. Yet there were attempts to mediate. In 1844 a Rabbinical Congress was convoked in Brunswick, which was succeeded by many of its kind in the following years. As a matter of principle, the representatives of all trends were asked to participate in these consultations. There were some who cherished hopes that these congresses would not only reach authoritative decisions on the issues in doubt but would even succeed in resolving the conflicts. These hopes remained unfulfilled. Orthodox spokesmen stayed away. Even the non-orthodox groups did not reach any agreement among themselves. This led finally to a situation in which it was left to the respective communities or individuals to resolve how much of the tradition should be kept, which part was to be deleted, and how the religion was to be adjusted to the *Zeitgeist*. Only the state laws in Central European countries, which required membership in a religious body, prevented the complete disintegration of the Jewish communities. Despite this compulsion, the development led to a downright separation in two countries, in Germany and in Hungary. Fearing the infringement on their way of life by the majority rule of the reform group, the orthodox sector succeeded in securing for itself the right to establish separatist congregations and state organizations. By all indications it appeared as if the religious conflict had divided Jewry into two hostile camps.[14]

The scene of the struggle was, as mentioned, Central Europe. In France, England, Holland, and the United States, although there was no lack of tension and conflict, the schism was glossed over in terms of a compromise (France and England), or resulted without much struggle in the establishment of various differing congregations on a basis of their right for free religious assembly (U.S.). Chronologically speaking, these movements were limited to the half century from 1830–1880, the age of liberalism, when it looked as if external social and political pressure upon the Jewish community was about to disappear entirely. The religious traditions seemed to constitute the sole cohesive force within the Jewish community; therefore, anywhere that the religious conflict over these traditions grew acute, the unity of communal life became disrupted. In Russia, where millions of Jewish masses still lived under the political pressure of the Czarist regime, some of these religious conflicts, imported from the West, also became evident in the forties. Although the advocates of reform here represented only a small minority, their clash with the traditionalists found sufficiently vehement expression in social and literary form. But the cohesive force of external pressure and criteria of identifiability like a common language (Yiddish), folkways, etc., which safeguarded their participation, made them so community-minded that thoughts of separatist divisions hardly arose. Alongside the traditionalists there arose a group of secularists within Jewish society, and besides religious literature, works of secular enlightenment appeared. This social and literary development resulted in the modern nationalism that emerged after the seventies.[15] A movement dedicated to purely religious or theological problems, groping for new foundations with reference to the traditions, did not evolve on the Russian scene. At best we may recognize the *Musar* movement, founded in Lithuania by Rabbi Israel Lipkin of Salant (1810–1883), as an original religious creation of the age. Rabbi Israel, firmly rooted in the traditional creed, was deeply concerned over the disintegration of the religious community, which heretofore had provided the individual with a reliable frame of reference and vouchsafed his traditional mode of life. The new development left the individual, as far as religious backing was concerned, standing on his own. Rabbi Israel tried to promote conscious training in self-discipline and religious awareness for the individual, according a preferential place to ethics. The *Musar* movement saw in the laxity and mechanism of the traditionalists the case for the secularists' defection. Therefore, *Musar* demands constant awareness of all religious values and responsibilities, and a keen sense of the scale of peferences in trivial and important matters alike. Rabbi Israel tried to win disciples in the West, in Germany and France. His influence, however, left its mark mainly in Lithuania, and even there only in those institutions of learning (schools and *yeshivot*) which had been established or affected by his movement.[16]

The second half of the nineteenth century presented hardly any new development in the religious realm. Both the reform and the neo-orthodox trends merely consolidated their positions as established earlier in the century. In Judaism, just as in the Christian environment, interest shifted from the religious to the ethical. In Judaism, however, there was a particular reason for this emphasis. With the resurgence of anti-Semitism Judaism became exposed to defamation on account of its alleged particularistic moral doctrines. Quotations from ancient Jewish literature were cited to prove the validity of moral obligation only among Jews; in their relations with "strangers," Jews were said to be absolved from many or all obligations. Jewish theologians and educators at the beginning of the nineteenth century were aware of this issue. They recognized in the double standard of morality the obverse of Jewish solidarity to which they had been forced under the duress of ghetto segregation. Much effort had been spent at the time of emancipation to eradicate the traces of such opinions and to educate the Jewish community in the conduct of universal ethics. At the time of anti-Semitic resuscitation in the eighties, when the issue was raised again, this process of education had already been brought to a successful conclusion. Hence the Jewish theologians and educators became justifiably highly indignant about the renewed charges. A new literary movement set in, which dedicated itself to the demonstration of the purity of Jewish ethics, in order to combat the unfounded charges, and to strengthen Jewish self-respect and morale. These efforts resulted in more or less comprehensive works on the system of Jewish ethics. The most definite and richly doc-umented compendium of its sort is probably the two-volume work of M. Lazarus (1829–1905): *Die Ethik des Judentums* (translated by Henrietta Szold in 1891: *Ethics of Judaism*). However, these books were written under the pressure of social defamation and by their apologetic tendencies often inflicted injustice upon historical truth. They not only defended the uni-versal character of Jewish ethics in the hoary past, the talmudic period, and the Middle Ages, but often projected into their source material inter-pretations of the essence of Jewish ethics that clearly stemmed from the particular climate of their own age. The century's greatest Jewish thinker, Hermann Cohen (1842–1918), did much to carry the discussion a stage further.[17] Cohen was the founder and leading proponent of the Marburg school of neo-Kantianism, and his ethical system and religious philosophy derive from that source.

In his systematic presentation of the Jewish religion Cohen insisted upon the inclusion of selected historical source material from Jewish lit-erature. Thus he drew abundantly on the prophets, the psalms, talmudic passages, and the writings of Maimonides, the classical representative of medieval religious philosophy. Cohen believed to have thus delimited the essential and perennial elements of the Jewish religion. His presentation therefore served not only as a systematic statement of his position within the trends of the Jewish camp, but simultaneously as a means of combatting intellectual and political anti-Semitism. This philosophical outline of Ju-daism rendered a considerable service to the Jewish intelligentsia as a means of rebuffing the repeated attempts at their conversion, particularly pursued by Protestants. According to Cohen, Judaism was not only con-sonant with the requirements of the modern mind; for him and his follow-ers Judaism constituted the most valid religion as far as modern science, contemporary culture, and the teleological prospects for progress were concerned. Nor did Cohen feel any conflict between his Jewish allegiance and his deep-rooted attachment to German culture and his loyal, though not uncritical, devotion to the German state. Hence he remained an op-ponent of any national Jewish tendency. Political Zionism meant to him treason against the primary message of Jewish religion, particularly against its essential messianic idea, which implied a universal eschatology for all mankind. It is characteristic of this interpretation that Jewish identity is not predicated on the mere fact of Jewish birth, but upon the acceptance of definite doctrinal content.[18]

The move toward Jewish nationalism, which occurred in Cohen's days, aimed at the reversal of the latter concept. For the champions of nation-alism, the doctrinal content of Judaism was at best of secondary importance. Their native identity with Jewry was an indisputable fact, regardless of their personal attitude toward the historical or traditional elements in Ju-daism. This platform was often advocated by the nationalist ideologists, as by the essayist Bin Gorion (Micha Josef Berdyczewski, 1865–1921) and the Hebrew poet Saul Tschernichowski (1875–1943; at a certain phase of his development), who rejected any attachment to Judaism not only in the religious but even in the ideological sense, attempting to substitute for it a kind of Nietzschean cult of power or pro-biblical paganism. Theoretically less pronounced nationalists declared that the identification with the Jewish nationalist movement would be independent of any kind of religious commitment. In this vein Ahad Ha'am (Asher Ginzberg, 1865–1927), ideologist of cultural Zionism, preferred the agnostic who regarded the Jewish concept of God as the creation of the Jewish national genius to the traditionalist who accepted the Jewish nation as a Divine creation. Except for its orthodox wing, which cherished hopes for the national renaissance of the traditional way of life, the Jewish nationalist movement strove mainly for the creation and revitalization of the formal elements of national existence, like Hebrew as a living tongue, secular literature, national history, and the return to the historic homeland. Yet even with regard to spiritual interpretations of Judaism, the nationalist movement made valuable contributions. It was Ahad Ha'am who on the one hand regarded the Jewish religion as outmoded yet upheld his belief in Jewish ethics, which he sought to identify with the aspiration for absolute justice. In fact, there were several attempts to formulate concepts and traits that distinctly mark off Judaism, or rather the Jewish national character, from similar phenomena in other ethnic or cultural groups. Like many other nationalist movements, Jewish nationalism based its political claims on traditions of its national culture; thus even the political orientation effected a strong creative impetus to cultural expression. The problem of Judaism from the religious and ethical aspect, which had been the focus of Jewish movements heretofore, became a rather confused issue with the nationalists' approach to it, as they raised merely formal national elements to the status of absolute values. On the other hand, this orientation inspired a national self-confidence that provided the Jew with a fresh and promising approach to his own identity problem, for nationalism emancipated the Jewish theoretists from the compulsion for apologetics. Taking his Jewish identity as self-evident instead of as presenting a moot problem to himself, he regained his inner balance and freedom. Now it was possible for him to face and take all that had been handed down to him by former generations without running the danger either of losing his ties with this past or of having personally to accept the traditional mode of living.[19]

As a spiritual force, however, the national idea only became effective at a time that lies beyond the scope of this survey. As a matter of fact, nationalistic forces have only recently come fully into play. In their present process of passing into history, they are still beyond the historian's ken.

Religion as a Uniting and Dividing Force in Modern Jewish History

2

At the dawn of the modern era, when the first signs of a change in Jewish destiny became apparent, many predictions were made by perceptive observers concerning the nature of this change. The first to indulge in this kind of prophecy seems to have been Voltaire. In the supplement to his *Essai sur les moeurs et l'esprit des nations* (1761), while discussing the lot of the dwindling number of Gypsies in Europe, he drifted into a comment on the Jews. The Gypsies are losing ground, said the great writer (who was at the same time also a historian and one of the first modern anthropologists), because of the diminishing need for the professions by which they used to make a living: magic, fortunetelling, and the like. Reasonableness and enlightenment being on the increase, people were spurning the Gypsy's services, leaving him no profession on which to thrive.

> The same catastrophe could befall the Jews: when the society of man is perfected, when every people carries on its trade itself, no longer sharing the fruits of its work with these wandering brokers, the number of Jews will necessarily diminish. The rich among them are already beginning to detest their superstitions; there will be no more than the lot of a people without arts or laws, who, no longer able to enrich themselves through our negligence, will no longer be able to sustain a separate society, and, who, no longer understanding their ancient corrupt jargon, a mixture of Hebrew and Syrian, ignorant even of their own books, will assimilate among the scum of the other peoples.[1]

This is a remarkable passage, which I have not found quoted in any of the many treatises dedicated to Voltaire's relations with the Jews.

Voltaire's expectation of the future of the Jews represents a distinct deviation from the traditional Christian one. Christian tradition did forsee the disappearance of the Jews, hoping for their perception of the Christian truth and their ultimate conversion. Voltaire, on the other hand, tacitly assumed that no positive religion would play a part in the life of future society: religion would serve neither as a dividing fence between Jews and Christians nor as the final medium to unite them. Instead, Voltaire conceived of the differences between the two communities in terms of culture and, even more, of economic function—anticipating in a flash the Marxist conception of later days. The central motif of Voltaire's prediction is, of course, his trust in the decisive efficacy of rationalism. By applying their reason, nations would conduct their economic affairs in a way that would obviate the Jews' special function. Jews themselves would experience the beneficial effect of enlightenment; they would be healed of their superstitions, i.e., their religion, and join the community of reasonable people. Those who did not would disappear in the scum of the earth through the lack of justifiable function.[2]

Viewing it from the perspective of the second half of the eighteenth century, Voltaire's prognosis can be said to have been well founded and well argued. Why did this prophecy, like many others based on similar assumptions, fail to come true? For, as we all know, the Jewish community did not become absorbed by its Gentile environment in spite of the deep effect the age of rationalism exercised upon both of them. Were there other factors involved besides religion that perpetuated the cleavage between the two groups, or was the diagnosis of the waning influence of religion on society based upon an illusion?

The role of religion in postrationalistic society is a complex phenomenon. The central term that seems to govern these discussions is *secularization*. This term is used to designate two different concepts, one comprehensive and the other more specific. The comprehensive concept of secularization refers to the fact that in the course of the transition from medieval to modern society many aspects of human life that formerly had been conducted under the auspices of religion—and perhaps even controlled by its institutions—now extricated themselves from its sphere and began to lead an independent secular existence. The retirement of religion from certain spheres of life created, so to speak, an atmosphere of indifference that facilitated the encounter of people from different backgrounds in the pursuit of common goals. I have myself used the term *neutral society* in characterizing the Berlin intellectual circles of the late eighteenth century where Moses Mendelssohn and some other Jews were permitted to move as equals among equals. Later, however, I found it necessary to alter the adjective from *neutral* to *semi-neutral*.[3] Closer study of the Mendelssohn era, as well as of later times, convinced me that the term *neutral* was in need of qualification when applied both to the Mendelssohnian experience and to any other attempts at integration of Jews into non-Jewish society. For neither at the time of Mendelssohn nor at any later time was a complete neutrality even approximately achieved. (With regard to Mendelssohn, by the way, my reservation is now fully substantiated by the most elaborate and enlightening biographical study of Alexander Altmann.[4])

The second, more specific, application of the term *secularization* is also our clue to an important limitation of true neutrality. This application follows more closely the original meaning of the term, namely the expropriation of ecclesiastic possessions in favor of lay or profane ownership—as happened during the Reformation and during Napoleonic times. Historians and sociologists, beginning, it seems, with Wilhelm Dilthey, observed a similar process in the field of culture: concepts, symbols, and all kinds of stylistic elements originating in the realm of religion had been translated into a purely profane context. They began to call this secularization.[5] The process of profanation, sometimes also called de-Christianization, was therefore dual-faceted. When the state severed its ties with the church, it became a secular institution—a precondition for Jewish emancipation. But when, during ceremonies of state, Christian symbols were used—no doubt in order to invest the aims of the state with a religious dignity—secularization in the more specific sense of the word took place. With regard to Jewish identification with the objectives of the state, this second kind of secularization inevitably had a negative rather than a positive effect. When intellectual circles, salons, and societies unaffiliated with any religious institution were created, an avenue for socialization was opened up also for the Jews. But when Masonic lodges, though committed to a purely humanistic set of values, used Christological language to express them and figures from Christian tradition (such as St. John the Baptist) to represent them, this sort of "secularization" operated against the unproblematic inclusion of Jews into society.[6]

Similar self-contradictory tendencies can be observed on the purely intellectual level. Immanuel Kant, for example, developed a system of ethics that presupposed the existence of God—but denied the dependence of morality upon revelation as postulated by Christian, or for that matter Jewish, theology. At a later stage, Kant set out to prove that his autonomous ethics was identical with what had been taught by Jesus and transmitted by Christianity through the ages. Thus Kant lent his secular humanistic teaching a Christian-religious garb, employing in the course of his presentation all the central notions of Christian theology, such as sin and redemption—a clear case of secularization in the second, specific, sense of the term.[7] This Kantian exercise in harmonization is only one of countless attempts to reinterpret Christianity to fit basically worldly philosophies, ideologies, or Weltanschauungen. From the standpoint of a Jewish adherent of any of these, their interweaving with Christian phraseology could only have a deterring effect. In the case of Kant, this was intentional: he stated in unequivocal terms that, unlike Christianity, Judaism could not be reconciled with the pure morality of his system. Indeed, his conclusion with regard to Jews was that, unless they wished to continue their ghetto existence or forgo emancipation, they would have to purify their religion, or rather, found a new one. This new Jewish religion, like Christianity, would be based on the teaching of Jesus (identical with that of Kant), but the Jews would not be expected to follow the interpretation of this teaching as evolved by the Christian Church. They should be free to evolve their own symbolic representation of the ethical teaching, the trappings of the true religion according to their own idiosyncrasies. Thus Kant's conditions for Jewish political and social integration fell just short of a demand for conversion.[8] Other exponents of a secularized Christianity dropped such reservations and demanded—or hoped for—the joining of the Jews to the Christian churches as the only way for their true incorporation into a Gentile state and society.

Although the Voltairian concept of a religiously indifferent society continued to have advocates, it failed to become the prevailing pattern of modern times because, unsuspected by Voltaire, the double-faceted process of secularization was to prevent its realization. The enticement of Christianity as the escape route from the Jewish predicament remained strong as ever, merely changing its ideological justification. It replaced theological and Christological arguments with ethically, philosophically, or culturally oriented vindications. The Jewish community saw itself faced with its perennial rival, Christianity, in a new metamorphosis, namely as a semi-secularized agency of cultural assimilation. At times it seemed more formidable in this guise than it had been in the truly religious thrust of the Middle Ages.

The scene of this new encounter between Judaism and Christianity was mainly the German-speaking countries. In Germany, but certainly not there alone, mighty social factors aggravated the situation. There Jewish emancipation was a long, drawn-out process, the idea of it having been propagated since the last decades of the eighteenth century, but its implementation was only gradually and imperfectly achieved in the course of a hundred years' on-and-off struggle. Many positions in the service of the state, of science, and of scholarship in the universities, much coveted by the intellectually minded, were denied Jews—unless baptized. Another factor was the spiritual disorientation of the Jews, especially of the first generation emerging from the ghetto. For the social and religious disintegration evident in the whole process of secularization that was engulfing European society did not spare the Jewish community. We shall consider later what this involvement meant for the religious unity of the Jewish community itself. Here, we must assess the measure of its influence upon the decisions of those who felt attracted by the prospect of joining Christianity. The situation of the ghetto escapees can, I think, best be characterized by the sociological term *anomie*, introduced by Emile Durkheim: "a state or condition of individuals or society characterized by a breakdown or absence of social norms and values, as in the case of uprooted people." People brought up in the atmosphere of the ghetto—with all its restrictions, discipline, and warmth—were, once they left it, indeed prone to being bereft of social norms and values. No wonder that some of them went the whole length of estrangement and landed in the Christian Church. Indeed, some Jewish contemporaries feared, and some missionary-minded Christians hoped, that the disintegration of traditional Jewish society would lead to the absorption of the greater part of the community by the Christian Church.[9] That this did not happen, and that the breaking away from Judaism, although a cause of great concern and agitation at times, remained within tolerable limits for the existence of the community, was a result of the ambivalent nature of secularization. For, although the motivation and the ideological justification for conversion were secular, the act of transition—of actual acceptance into the church—retained its religious ritual character. Formal baptism (not genuine conviction of the truth of the accepted religion) remained an indispensable condition. Heavy social pressure on the one hand and a measure of cynicism on the other were required to make the deal acceptable. This type of conversion was most common in places where highly attractive rewards, such as the higher ranks of academic positions in Germany, were denied to unbaptized Jews. But whatever the premium, it could not be acquired except at the price of impaired integrity; we know from the life stories of many who yielded, as well as of those who withstood the temptation, the anguish involved in the process of arriving at a decision. This is not to say that there were no convinced Christians among the converted. Dorothea Mendelssohn-Veit-Schlegel became a devout Protestant and then an ardent Catholic. August Neander served the cause of Christianity as a learned and pious church historian, and Julius Stahl as the defender of the idea of a Christian state and the political philosophy of Prussan conservatism. But a closer study of the lives of these and many other converts reveals that they arrived at such Christian conviction and devotion only through a process of adaptation or in the wake of some religious experience after their baptism. The decision to change their religion was taken on rational considerations rather than as the result of a genuine conversion. And even these post facto converts were a rare exception. Much more common was the type who retained his mental reservations vis-à-vis Christianity, such as Heinrich Heine, or who belittled the importance of religion to minimize the moral scruples attached to the change, such as Ludwig Börne. Indeed, we find most of the converts in social circles, among intellecuals in the academic professions and in the universities, where such an attitude was possible; not in the service of the church, toward which converts had strongly gravitated at other times and in other places.[10]

This failure of the German churches to benefit spiritually from the Jewish influx is at variance with what had been achieved in medieval Spain, where many of the converts had become priests, monks, and theologians, some of them using their positions and learning to combat and pressure their "brethren in the flesh." Even more telling is the failure of the German churches in comparison with the success of contemporary France. The Catholic Church of France, especially in the first two-thirds of the nineteenth century, drew a great number of Jews into its orbit to take their place among the important intellectuals. Many of them were not content with receiving baptism but strove for ordination as priests and monks— an unmistakable sign of genuine conversion. I shall mention here only the example of the brothers Theodore and Alphonse Ratisbonne of Strasbourg, whose lives were given much attention by Catholics but ignored by Jews— wrongly so, in my opinion, for failures, no less than successes, of Jewish society belong to Jewish history.

Theodore and Alphonse were the sons of Auguste Ratisbonne, the head of the Strasbourg Consistoire, son-in-law of Naftali Cerfbeer, one of the pioneers of Jewish emancipation at the time of the French Revolution. Theodore, born in 1802, was brought up as a rich man's son, receiving a good secular and a slight Jewish education. Attending a Jewish school in Frankfurt, then serving in the firm of Fould in Paris, he returned to Strasbourg to take up the study of law at the university. There, together with two other Jewish students, Theodore became acquainted with Louis Bautain, a professor of philosophy who, typically for that time, developed a full-scale social and theological doctrine that granted faith in Catholic dogma first and absolute importance. These absolute truths included, of course, the relegation of Judaism to a mere preparatory stage of Christianity. Indeed, Bautain advised his Jewish pupils to return to the synagogue, including the observance of the Law, for as long as they were not prepared to enter the state of Christian grace. Young Ratisbonne followed his master's advice and even became involved in the activities of the Jewish community as the supervisor of the childen's Jewish education, while at the same time maintaining contact with Catholic circles of the revivalist type in preparation for his conversion. The public announcement of the *fait accompli* in 1827 scandalized the community, especially when it was followed by the conversion of two other Jewish disciples of Bautain. All three entered a seminary and became priests. Ratisbonne, officiating in Paris, dedicated his life to the conversion of Jews. His main attempt was directed toward his own rich and widely scattered family, not without some success.[11] But the most famous conversion, and one of the most celebrated by the Catholic Church—that of his brother Alphonse—seemed to occur without his direct contribution.

Alphonse, the youngest of the Ratisbonne sons and twelve years the junior of Theodore, strictly rejected his brother's approaches by declaring himself a secular rationalist Jew. Then in 1842, at the age of twenty-eight and just after his engagement, he passed through Rome and visited the Church of San Andrea, where he experienced a vision of Mary. He prostrated himself and left the place as a changed man. He joined his brother, became a Jesuit, and, with his brother, founded the Convent Notre Dame de Zion in Paris with a chapter in Jerusalem, where Alphonse went and where the order still operates, although now forgoing the evangelization of Jews.[12]

The case of Alphonse Ratisbonne is a cause célèbre in Catholic literature, where, because of the sudden and unexpected change of heart, he figures as a modern Paul. His conversion has also attracted the attention of modern psychologists. William James commented upon it in *The Varieties of Religious Experience*.[13] Considering it as an individual case, detached from its historical background, he could only describe this most startling conversion as exemplifying the mental capacity for sudden and lasting change of the whole personality. We need not quarrel with James, for the psychological explanation may be valid as far as it goes. Still, placed in its historical context as one of many Jewish conversions in the same social circles, the case loses much of its strangeness. About Theodore Ratisbonne, James knew only the bare fact that he preceded his brother in conversion. But Theodore was, as we have seen, not the only one, even in the immediate circles of Strasbourg. Five years earlier, another Alsatian Jew, David Drach, son-in-law of the Chief Rabbi of France and himself a most likely candidate for this post, had turned Catholic, causing tremendous agitation because of his status and his success in taking his children with him against the wishes of their mother. Some years later, two sons of an Alsatian rabbi, the Libermanns, were followed at some distance by two Lehmann brothers.[14] What we encounter here are not individual psychological events but a sociohistorical phenomenon, which must be considered as such.

Unlike the Jews in Germany, Jews in France achieved their formal emancipation almost at one stroke during the French Revolution. Having suffered some reversions at the time of Napoleon, their full political equality was restored under the Bourbon Restoration. Socially and spiritually, however, Jewry—especially the Ashkenazi branch in Alsace, the bulk of the community—remained apart, confronted by traditional antagonism on the part of its immediate surroundings and looked down upon by French society at large. This is not surprising, since the France of the Restoration returned to Catholic traditions, recasting and reinterpreting them to fit new circumstances but still retaining the basic components. One of these components was, of course, the depreciation of Judaism as a lower form of religion and morality, superseded by Christianity. These ideas concerning Judaism were disseminated at that time not only directly, by agencies of the church, but also by the prevailing schools of social philosophy directly or indirectly indebted to the Catholic tradition. It will suffice only to mention such thinkers as Chateaubriand, De Maitre, and De Bonald. French Jews who came into contact with any facet of intellectual life were consistently confronted with this derogatory evaluation of their religion. If they aspired to social integration, they must have felt repelled, finding no group with which to identify so long as they retained their Judaism. The fact of formal emancipation was only apt to aggravate their social and spiritual isolation and even ostracization.[15]

The encounter of the French Jew with Christianity was a much closer parallel to that of the Middle Ages than that of his German contemporaries.

The medieval Jew conceived of the gulf that separated him from the world of the Christians in terms of contradictory religious tenets. Still, when he was enticed to leap over the gulf—subjectively experiencing the conviction of the truth of Christianity—the attraction to do so might well have emanated from the obvious superiority of the surrounding society in all possible respects. To French Jews of the first half of the nineteenth century, too, Christianity might have appeared an integral part of the surrounding culture and society, for such it was believed to be by the majority of the French themselves. The identification with state, society, and culture, which in principle was open to them, but in actuality was as closed and remote as ever, was apt to engender a subjective conviction of the truth of Christianity—the only secure avenue to a role in the coveted overall unity. The psychological vehicles through which this process of identification operated differed from case to case. Some converts, of course, made the decision with rational calculations of the advantages in mind; others followed a more complicated psychological pattern. But I should like to return for a moment to the case of Alphonse Ratisbonne. In spite of his own testimony that until the hour of his conversion Christianity was beyond his range of interest, we may surely assume that a possible acceptance of Christianity had at times occupied his mind. Neither his brother's decision to go this way when he himself was fourteen years old, nor the subsequent discussions that we know to have taken place in the circle of the family, could have left him indifferent. We may believe him when he tells us that he discounted this possibility and successfully suppressed his desire for it— until the moment that desire erupted and carried him away.

What could a minority community do when faced by the danger of absorption into the majority? The first weapon was a condemnation of the fugitives, who were regarded as deserters. True, relations with members of the family or Jewish friends were often kept up by the converts. This was a change from older times, when such leniency on the Jewish side was unthinkable. But the official attitude, strongly supported by Jewish public opinion, was still as severe as ever. Theodore Ratisbonne continued to see and correspond with some of his Jewish relatives, but when he appeared at the deathbed of his father hoping to convert him, the members of the *hevra kadishah* attending the dying man simply turned him out.[16] Jews were naturally reluctant to concede the converts bona fide conviction, suspecting them of having acted from ulterior motives—and in most cases they may have been right, even in France. Indeed, the main argument of the public defenders of Judaism—rabbis, preachers, and writers—did not run on theological or philosophical lines. Rather, it was an appeal for loyalty to the community, which still had to struggle for social and, in most countries, political acceptance. Conversion was branded a dishonoring act even by many like Heinrich Heine, who could not resist committing it. Others, as, for instance, Gabriel Riesser, confessed to having refrained from baptism only out of intellectual integrity.[17]

But reservations on the part of Jews with respect to Christianity also found expression on a higher intellectual level. Just as the long-standing antagonism between Christianity and Judaism continued to operate on the Christian side in spite of secularization, so it did in the opposite direction as well. Despite the newly acquired vistas that Jews were deriving from historical criticism, and a new ision of the future conjured up by religious reform, their negative attitude toward Christianity underwent almost no change. On the contrary, freedom of speech now being the privilege of free citizens, the exponents of Judaism—theologians, philosophers, and historians—gave vent to Jewish resentment against Christianity as though avenging those past Jewish generations who were doomed to silence. While Mendelssohn in his well-known encounter with Lavater was still reluctant to enter into controversy about Christianity, fearing the possible consequences for his underprivileged community, two or three generations later Joseph Salvador in France, Elijah Benamozegh in Italy, and Abraham Geiger, Ludvig Philippsohn, and Heinrich Graetz in Germany openly discussed the role of Christianity in general, and vis-à-vis Jews and Judaism in particular—some of them, such as Graetz, in a most passionate manner. The main thrust of these polemics was to prove the superiority of Judaism in one respect or another, ethical, social, or otherwise. If Kant denied Judaism the right to be called a religion in the sense in which he wished to define religion, Moritz Lazarus set out to prove, as did Hermann Cohen later, that it was Judaism and not Christianity which had anticipated the Kantian ethics. A similar inversion of the positions of the two religions was forcefully defended by Samuel Hirsch as against Hegel. Jacob Fleischmann, in analyzing discussions of Christianity by these modern Jewish thinkers, has concluded that most of them avoided the real issues and that not much clarification resulted from these encounters.[18] This may be the case judging from the vantage point of philosophical penetration and consistency. Historically, however, such polemical rejoinders performed an important function. They lent the Jewish public, and especially Jewish intellectuals, a crutch to lean upon when confronted by the claim of Christianity to be the only morally and intellectually respectable religion.

Fleischmann has observed that all the Jews who were taking part in polemics against Christianity were deeply involved in the religious issues of their time and assumed a critical attitude toward their own religious tradition. In fact, with the possible exception of Benamozegh, not one of them would have claimed to be an Orthodox Jew. While the critically minded exponents of Judaism felt called upon to contest Christianity, the Orthodox seemed to be entirely immune to such temptation, a fact indicative of the deep social and intellectual cleavage between the two groups. The reason for this Orthodox insensibility is easily stated. I have shown in my *Exclusiveness and Tolerance* that toward the end of the traditional period, i.e., the seventeenth and eighteenth centuries, a comparatively tolerant attitude toward Christianity evolved in Judaism, not because of any rapprochement between the two religions but because of the deep divergence between the two societies on both the practical and spiritual levels.[19] This attitude continued to prevail with the Orthodox, possibly even gathering strength in modern times. Orthodox Jews, prevented as they were from intimate contact with Gentiles by their way of life, remained at a social distance from their Christian environment. They conceived of no danger from Christianity and had no reason to diverge from the placid attitude that had developed in preceding generations.

Of course Orthodox Jews deplored the defection of great numbers of Jews to Christianity but, as they observed that conversion in most cases was preceded by the abandonment of the traditional way of life, their wrath fell upon the heads of those whom they held responsible for the disloyalty of Jews to their tradition—the *Maskilim*, the rationalists and the religious reformers. Thus the differing positions assumed toward Christianity by the two camps reveal on closer inspection the deep division that was beginning to affect Jewish society itself. Indeed in the first decades of religious divergency, which began to smolder at the time of Mendelssohn and erupted into the Hamburg controversy in 1819, it looked as if Jewish society would fall into bits and pieces. The Orthodox participants in the controversy referred more or less openly to the history of the schismatic sects of Judaism, hinting that the same fate might befall the Reformers as had befallen the Sadducees and Karaites. Rabbi Moshe Sofer Ha-Hatam Sofer, who became the leading personality of the Orthodox, said in so many words that, were it not for the governmental prohibition against making use of the *Herem* (the religious ban), the rabbis would be duty bound to excommunicate the innovators.[20] As things stood, all they could do was to enjoin separation from the reformists upon the community, and this was done in the strongest possible language. Isaac Hirsh Weiss said of Rabbi Moshe Sofer that he failed to recognize the signs of the times and made a heroic attempt to turn back the wheels of history. But I think Ha-Hatam Sofer must be credited with a correct diagnosis of his times; to the deterioration of tradition in Germany, his native country, and to the first signs of dissolution in Hungary, including his own community of Pressburg, his reaction was not one of accommodation and change but rather of preservation by a conscious enhancement of the tradition. Rabbi Sofer conceived the idea of a culturally self-contained Jewish community at the price of voluntary limitation of its contact with the surrounding world and of the exclusion of members who were not prepared to live up to the strict demands of religious discipline.[21] At the time of the promulgation of this program, the exclusion of the recalcitrants pertained to only a small minority. But things moved quite fast also in Hungary. In his last year—he died in 1839—Rabbi Sofer saw the propagation of Jewish emancipation. Well aware of its implications, he deplored it, but, open-minded realist that he was, he could scarcely hope to avert it. Because of political events—the failure of the 1848 revolution to achieve national independence—the implementation of Jewish emancipation had to wait until the reconciliation with Austria in 1866. Meantime the advocates of emancipation were energetically preparing for it, modernizing education, introducing some measure of religious reform, and planning an overall organization for the whole of Hungarian Jewry. The conservative elements, on the other hand, most of them ardent disciples of Rabbi Sofer, moved in the opposite direction: they carried the idea of cultural asceticism and organizational separation to extremes scarcely contemplated by the master. In 1865, two years before Jewish emancipation in Hungary, an assembly of the most intransigent rabbis proscribed the study of any secular subjects and the introduction of any change, not only in the ritual and worship but even in the external structure of the synagogue or the aesthetic form of the service.[22] The year following emancipation the government convened a conference of representatives of the Jewish communities and assigned them the task of creating an overall organization for all of Hungarian Jewry. It was in the course of this so-called Jewish Congress that the conflict between the two camps led to an open confrontation and to an irreparable breach.[23] No doubt the modernists, believing themselves to be in greater harmony with the prevailing liberal trend, especially in government circles, thought they could control the life of the Jewish communities through the projected organization. They totally underrated their opponents. The lay leaders of the traditional groups, having learned the techniques of organization and political lobbying, provided assistance to the rabbinical leadership. Imbued with the idea of organizational independence as the only guarantee for pure Orthodoxy, the extreme right-wing rabbis refused to cooperate with those not absolutely traditional and observant. When a middle group (headed by Azriel Hildesheimer, of German origin and at that time rabbi of Eisenstadt) failed in its attempt to mediate, it felt obliged to join the extremists, who clearly carried the day. The whole Orthodox minority left the Congress, and the planned organization could be established only for the so-called neological majority. After some lobbying, the government agreed to the establishment of a separate organization for the Orthodox, and later to that of a third for a number of communities, called status quo, which were reluctant to join either of the militant two.

The organizational division between Reform and Orthodox conformed in Hungary to a visible cultural diversity between the two camps: openness toward secular learning, modern education, and so on, on the one hand; a self-imposed exclusion, a kind of voluntary ghettoization, on the other. But the trend toward separation should not be attributed to this cultural gap, for it manifested itself also in Germany and later in England, where the entire Jewish population went through the process of cultural adoption. (In France, it was avoided owing to the governmentally imposed organization of the Consistoire.) In view of the repeated clashes between reformists and traditionalists in many communities, a schism was seen as the inevitable, and also the desirable, solution as early as the thirties by Abraham Geiger, albeit privately.[24] To aid and later to propagate it publicly fell to his former friend and subsequent opponent, Samson Raphael Hirsch. Hirsch concluded his public condemnation of the Braunschweig Assembly's proceedings in 1844 with the remark that no compromise was possible between the principles avowed by the majority of those assembled and those who kept to the tenets of traditional Judaism. The minority, which disagreed with the decisions of the assembly, ought to have demonstrated their disagreement by leaving the assembly, as there is no common ground between Reform and Orthodoxy, and the only way open to both is separation from one another.[25]

As is well known, Hirsch lived up to his principles and, when in 1851 he was invited to serve as rabbi of the Orthodox minority in Frankfurt, he engaged in a long but successful struggle to secure the independence of his community. Now Frankfurt Jewry had been one of the most active in modernizing itself, beginning with the early nineteenth century. The community was headed for decades by radical reformists who showed little patience with those who objected to innovation.[26] The partisans of Orthodoxy may have exaggerated the vexations they had to suffer at the hands of reformist zealots, but the basic facts are historically well substantiated. The current law—the *Gemeindezwang* prevailing in the whole of Germany and beyond—obliged every Jew to belong to the local Jewish community, and the Orthodox could do no more than hope that their special needs would be taken care of by the community. This was the first objective of the struggle. But Samson Raphael Hirsch had a more far-reaching goal. Regarding it religiously objectionable to belong to a non-Orthodox community, he tried to establish his own independent congregation. This, of course, required a change in the law. An opportunity for this arose in 1873, when the Prussian Landtag (Frankfurt had belonged to Prussia since 1866) revised the law governing the relationship of congregants to their respective communities. This law, while it permitted any individual to change from one Christian community to another, gave a Jew only the choice of remaining in his community or opting out of Judaism altogether. The state, following a time-honored practice, recognized only one Jewish religion. It was just this that the Orthodox contested, pointing out the deep division between any two Christian denominations. It was therefore a *Gewissenszwang*, or restraint of conscience, to compel an Orthodox Jew to belong to a religion the tenets of which he denied.[27] This appeal to the liberty of conscience worked. Eduard Lasker, a consistent liberal politician and the only Jewish member of the Landtag, identified himself with the Orthodox point of view and recommended it; the so-called *Austrittsgesetz* became law in 1876.

We may add that such a reference to liberty of conscience had already played a part in the successful struggle of the Orthodox in Hungary to secure their independence.[28] The maxims of liberty may sound strange in the mouths of Orthodox zealots who, had they had their way, would have felt duty bound to enforce the Law upon every Jew. Yet as the conflict between the two Jewish groups was fought out before a non-Jewish forum, ideas current in the non-Jewish world became the terms of reference in the fight. It was the doctrines of liberalism, widely accepted in the sixties and seventies in Germany as well as in Hungary, through which, paradoxically, the Orthodox prevailed against their more modern adversaries. In Hungary, the Minister of Education and Religious Affairs, Baron Joseph Eötvös, the promoter of Jewish emancipation who was responsible for the convening of the Congress, was the outstanding liberal thinker and statesman. The very fact that he wished the Jewish assembly to decide on ways and means for the projected organization reveals his liberal attitude. When, to his amazement, it turned out that the participants lacked basic consensus, he could not possibly reverse his policy and impose the organization by a governmental decree.

There is another connection of the described events with the prevailing liberalism of that time. The external pressure of animosity on the Jewish community reached its lowest ebb in the sixties and early seventies. Whatever tokens of antagonism toward the Jews were still evident could easily be interpreted as residuals of a waning past—only with the emergence of the anti-Semitic movement in the last years of the decade were they recognized as a continuous undercurrent, ready at any time to come to the surface. With their growing sense of social and political security, Jews could afford to risk the disruption of their communal unity. At any rate, the issue of religious identification seemed to be of greater, indeed greatest, importance. No other designation than that of a religious group was available for Jews at that time. The acceptance of Jews into the state in the course of emancipation took place under this stamp. The very wish of the state to lend the Jewish community an organization along with that of the churches demonstrated the classification of the Jews in purely religious terms.

The definition of the Jewish community as a purely religious unit was, of course, a sham from the time of its conception. It was contradicted by social reality and much of Jewish activity. The *Wissenschaft des Judentums*, for instance, included in its inquiry all aspects of Jewish life, secular as well as religious; the reconstruction of the Jewish past by historians like Graetz cultivated a comprehensive Jewish identity. Similarly, the Jewish press—the *Jewish Chronicle* in London, the *Allgemeine Zeitung des Judentums* in Magdeburg, both active from the forties—informed their readers of events of Jewish interest from all countries and quarters, serving as an important channel for overall Jewish identification. Then came anti-Semitism in the West and the pogroms in Russia, followed by the national movement, providing a framework for practical cooperation between conflicting religious commitments.

The national movement revealed from its very beginning a tendency to overcome the differences between the Orthodox and the Reform. Rabbi Yehuda Alkalay, the first forerunner of modern Zionism, who had been active since the 1840s, rebuked both the Reform rabbis and those who opposed them during the Braunschweig convention of 1844. Alkalay wanted to direct the full energy of the Jewish people to restoration of the nation in its ancient homeland and maintained that in a true conception of the destiny of the Jewish nation the difference between the Orthodox and the Reform would simply disappear.[29] As we all know, this prophecy was only partially fulfilled. While the national movement dissipated the conception of Judaism in purely religious terms, it did not succeed in restoring a consensus on what role, if any, religion should play in the characterization of the nation. What happened in Jewish society is similar to what we observed in the Christian world. In spite of the exclusion of religion as a determining factor in state and society, it remained there in two different ways as an important ingredient in the life of the collective. First, religion remained the primary concern for a minority, the Orthodox and the traditional. Second, the traditional elements—the Sabbath, the festivals, the Hebrew language, and, indeed, the very attachment to the ancient homeland—although secularized, derived much of their emotional appeal from the original religious connotations.

Thus, religion continued to operate as an important social agent. Internally, it operated as a dividing factor, albeit not to the extent that it disrupted the overall unity of the community as it tended to do during the era of liberalism. Externally, however, it continued to serve at least as a delineation from the non-Jewish world. For, in spite of the effect of secularization, Jewishness and Judaism, in whatever guise or in whatever redefinition, remained exclusive of any other religion. To be Jewish nationally or to belong to a Jewish community but at the same time to adhere to Christianity, or, for that matter, to any other religion, is an oddity. Jewish religion in an age of secularization serves simultaneously as a dividing and as a uniting force.

Judaism and Christianity Against the Background of Modern Secularism

3

I

Somewhere in the eighteenth century, Christianity and Judaism, like religion in general, began to find themselves faced by an entirely new situation that forcefully affected their relationships with each other. Any proper definition of this situation will have to take into account the term secularism or secularization, a concept implying that, in contradistinction to previous centuries, several areas of thought and action in society had now detached themselves from the control and supervision of religion and its established institutions. Philosophy, science, and art, as well as the economy and the control of state and society, proclaimed their independence and asserted their right to follow their intrinsic trends without any concern for what religious doctrine and authority would permit or recommend.

It is not easy for us to appreciate, in historical retrospect, what this rebellion of the world against God, so to say, meant to the representatives of religion in that age. At times, they became apprehensive that the expectations of the more radical protagonists of secularism might indeed be realized and religion entirely superseded. Some theologians found a ready interpretation for this dreadful prospect. It was conceived as the struggle of the anti-Christ to establish its kingdom—in Jewish parlance, it was regarded as the religious and moral deterioration that, according to tradition, would precede the era of redemption.

What actually occurred failed to fulfill these apprehensions. Neither Christianity nor Judaism disappeared—but both accepted a new and unforeseen role in which much that had previously been regarded as fundamental within both religions, and much that had pertained to their outlooks upon each other, had undergone substantial change. How they accomplished this feat is the subject of this paper—but the description will naturally be presented largely from the Jewish angle and confined to the European scene.

For our purposes, we must first examine those features of secularism which bear directly upon the standing of religion in a secularized society. Not only were certain areas excluded from the domain of religion, but also religion itself became the object of secular scrutiny and criticism. First, the rationalists arose, who measured religion by the yardstick of human reason. Then came historical criticism, which directed its attention backward, to the origins of religious traditions, and thereby, at certain times intentionally and at others unintentionally, undermined the claim of tradition to absolute authority.

From this struggle with both rational and historical criticism, Christianity and Judaism emerged thoroughly changed, and the nature of this change is manifest in the manner in which they now approached each other, as compared with the precritical age. For one thing, their encounter shifted to new ground. This aspect deserves examination in some detail.

In the Middle Ages, the conflict between church and synagogue was concentrated in three main areas: dogma, exegesis, and morals. In the field of dogma, the Jewish doctrine of the absolute unity of God, as opposed to the trinity, was the main point of contention. Next in order of importance in this area is the argument about the advent of the Messiah: whether the event had already occurred in the past or was expected to take place at some future date. Exegesis was concerned with the claim that certain Christological references were contained in the Hebrew Bible. As for the controversy over moral teachings, this resulted mainly from the Christian attack on Jewish morality as having, among other faults, particularistic trends. Of the three main issues, the conflict on morals retained, and may even have increased, its significance throughout the modern period. Dogma still remained of some consequence, while exegetical arguments almost entirely disappeared.

While the old areas of conflict receded, new issues now came to the fore. Which of the two religions conformed more closely to rational criteria? Which was burdened more heavily by mysteries? Such were the questions posed during the Age of Enlightenment. With the rise of Romanticism, the question assumed something of this nature: Which of the two religions is more capable of satisfying the urge for religious emotion? When positivism became dominant, religion appeared almost entirely discredited. Only the moral issue remained as the deciding factor in assessing the relative merits of the two traditions. Was Christianity to be preferred because of its universalistic ethic, or must it be discarded because of its unrealistic demands upon the individual to forgo his just rights, in contradistinction to Judaism, which had, as its point of departure, the insistence on objective justice? The two religions were weighed against each other in other respects as well. Which of the two was the more optimistic; which the more conducive to the development of culture, art, science, etc? Likewise, in the wake of the great social and political upheavals, Judaism and Christianity were held vindicated or condemned as they were held to conform to, or to contradict, the accepted political or social trend of the time.

It is neither possible nor at all necessary to enumerate all the various answers propounded to the queries concerning the respective merits of the two religions. Much that has been written, by both Jews and Christians, will certainly be found subjective and partisan. On the other hand, the close scrutiny of the sources of the two religions from so many different angles, at times performed by first-class minds, could hardly fail to reveal certain valid insights into the real characteristics of the two rival religions. Yet, penetrating as these insights may have been, they would hardly enlighten anyone who is interested not in understanding the two religions, but rather in deciding in which of the two to believe, like the heathen king in Yehudah Halevi's *Kuzari*. Summoned before the heathen king to present their cases, the modern protagonists of the two religions would no doubt be dismissed with a pronouncement such as this: "You both have said many nice things about your own religion and some nasty things about the other, but you have not touched upon what I should like to know—which of the two is the true religion."

Thus it was that, at the threshold of modern times, Gotthold Ephraim Lessing, in his famous parable of the "Three Rings," advised Jews, Christians, and Moslems to abandon the contest as to which of them possessed the true religion; instead, they should compete in demonstrating which religion made its adherents the better human beings. The generations that followed seemed to have heeded his advice, but only partially: they ceased to engage in combat with each other on the question of which was the true religion, but they continued to quarrel, as we have seen, on which religion was superior in other respects.

The conflict of Judaism and Christianity, in their broader *Weltanschauung* rather than in their fundamental doctrines, was the direct result of the process of change induced by the impact of secularization upon religious traditions. Among their own followers, the exponents of religion preferred to speak the language of *Weltanschauung* rather than of religion, and they stressed the beneficial by-products of religion rather than its soul-saving properties. This attitude was characteristic not of liberal theologians alone, but even of Orthodox rabbis who refused to yield a single iota of traditional doctrine and ritual. Reading their sermons, we find them caring more about the general outlook and attitudes derived from religion than about religion itself. The same shift, it seems to me, occurred in most Christian communities as well during the nineteenth century. Confronted by a secularized world, the two religions learned to use the language of *Weltanschauung* when talking among themselves and when debating, or rather quarrelling, with each other.

II

In one respect, however, the Jewish-Christian polemics of modern times preserved their medieval patterns, viz., in allocating the roles of accuser and defendant. The challenger was still the Christian; the respondent, still the Jew. This applies not only to the few concrete instances where Jews were called upon either successfuly to defend, or else to defect from, their faith, as in the case of the Mendelssohn, Lavater, and Sonnenfels controversies to which I shall revert later. The same applies also to other instances in which both the challenges and responses were addressed to no particular destinations. The allocation of the roles was inherent in the situation. If not originally non-missionary in character, the Jewish religion had certainly become so by the end of the Middle Ages. On innumerable occasions, Jews boasted of having no parallel to the Christian dictum: *extra ecclesiam non est salus.* On the contrary, they quoted—as talmudic—a passage only formulated in precisely these words by Maimonides in the twelfth century: "The righteous of the nations have a share in the world to come."[1] This doctrine of toleration, Jews felt, put them in harmony with the prevailing view of secularized society. It certainly fitted in with their lot as a religious minority exposed to the pressures of the religion of the majority, and upon Jewish apologetics fell the task of warding off the danger of defections to the Christian churches—a danger which, in the first two generations after the crumbling of the ghetto walls, had assumed alarming proportions. Not that the Christian message had reached Jewish society suddenly. What had overtaken individual Jews was the temptation to join the ruling majority. Sometimes they succumbed cynically to obtain the tangible benefits conferred by the change of status. At other times, the decision was ideological, representing the acceptance of the evaluation of Christianity as a higher stage of development or some other formulation conceding the superiority of Christianity over Judaism.

Genuine conversions to Christianity did occur at that time—but converts in this category were rare exceptions. M. Drach, son-in-law of the Grand Rabbi of the Consistoire of France and himself a potential future candidate for the position, accepted Roman Catholicism in Paris in 1823. Of course, even in his case it could be argued that his decision was motivated by the attraction of French culture and the desire to enter the high society with which he had had some contact. But such a psychologism would be unfair. Any conversion can be accounted for, in psychological and sociological terms, by external causes. Yet as long as such a decision is explained, even subjectively, by religious experience, one has no right to dismiss the justification as a psychological disguise. Reading Drach's autobiography, one gains the impression that the Roman Catholic faith had overwhelmed him—and with this the historian has to rest content.

As I have said, Drach's case, though not unique, was, however, quite exceptional. Most Jewish conversions of the nineteenth century followed different patterns. The well known cases of Heine and Börne were more representative. Finding their careers hampered by their Jewishness, they decided to accept Christianity. At first Heine's conversion caused him terrifying nightmares, till he succeeded in discovering a formula of justification: his baptismal certificate was his ticket of admission to European culture. Börne compensated for his hatred of the Frankfurt ghetto, his birthplace, with an even fiercer hatred of the petty German rulers and Philistines. Yet whatever reasons were given were all *ex post facto*.

In some cases, however, ideological justifications preceded the final decision to convert. The famous church historian, Johann August Wilhelm Neander, is normally regarded as having been a convinced and even ardent Christian, and rightly so, when judged by his later years. Yet, by looking more deeply into his early life, I have discovered that he became a real Christian, in the Protestant pietistic sense, only much later, as the result of some religious experience. His conversion to Christianity, which he underwent during his student days, was a result of philosophic and historical considerations. Similarly, Julius Stahl, the spiritual leader of Prussian conservatism, developed only gradually, after a period of time, into a Christian philosopher. His acceptance of Christianity upon his entry into the university can be accounted for by, to use a modern term, acculturation in the humanistic Gymnasium of Munich.

The three types of converts described so far confronted Judaism with dangers from three separate quarters, and each had to be dealt with differently. Characteristically enough, and in contradistinction to the Middle Ages, the least concern was roused by the genuine converts to Christianity who, after seeing the "light," sought to transmit their experiences to their "brethren in the flesh." These individuals were often enlisted by the missionary societies to spread, on their behalf, Christological writings among the Jews. At best, these efforts, which, by the way, are still in vogue, were only apt to elicit a smile among Orthodox and enlightened alike, although for different reasons. Not a single French Jew believed that Rabbi Drach had become convinced of the truth of Christianity by discovering correct interpretations of certain verses in Isaiah. They assumed, instead, that Drach aspired to the chair of Oriental languages at the Sorbonne, a position he indeed later occupied. Nineteenth-century Jewish folklore produced its anecdotes reflecting Jewish mistrust of all conversions. These stories attributed the conversions to the enticement of social and political advancement. Though they may do an injustice to one or two individual cases, they prove that within the context of nineteenth-century society such conversions were an anomaly rather than the product of any distinct social or cultural trend.

The conversions to gain materialistic ends have already been noted. Yet the reaction to these occurrences did not provoke any controversy of a religious character. Judgment was passed on the character of the convert, rather than any religious assessment made of his act. Gabriel Riesser summed up the situation best: he himself had been tempted but had withstood the trial; even were one to be convinced of the truth of another religion, he contended, a Jew should never leave the fold as long as his community suffered from political and social disabilities.

The real struggle of Jewish apologetics was with the third type of convert and conversion, where the justification was based, at times, on the moral and philosophical evaluation of Christianity as compared with Judaism. Let us recall once more the issues involved in these evaluations: first, the conformity of religion to rationality, which had made its earliest appearance at the time of the Enlightenment. Here Judaism had the opportunity to score a point, and Moses Mendelssohn proudly propounded that Judaism possessed no tenets out of accord with reason. And Judaism maintained this advantage as long as rationality was accounted a virtue. The scale was tipped in the other direction soon after, however, and Judaism paid a high price for having been associated with rationalism, on the authority of its most distinguished representative. After Schleiermacher's emotion-charged speeches on religion, rationality impaired the reputation of Judaism, and as a result many Jews, among them Mendelssohn's own daughter, joined Christianity as the religion of Romanticism.

Another of Mendelssohn's interpretations of Judaism subsequently produced fateful consequences for Judaism. According to him, Judaism had no special doctrines besides being the religion of reason, the Law alone being its particular characteristic. Here Christians found a vindication of their own tradition, which regarded the Law, and its abrogation by the founder of their religion, as the point of contention between the two. With the infusion of historical concepts into European thinking, this differentiation between Judaism and Christianity as two phases of human development could now be translated into non-theological terms, on a popular as well as a highly philosophical plane. Abraham, son of Moses Mendelssohn and father of Felix, the composer, though he himself remained a Jew, could justify his children's baptism by the simple assertion that previously Judaism had been the religion *"der meisten gesitteten Menschen,"* of the majority of civilized men, while in his own days Christianity had become such a religion. The philosophical parallel to this statement can be found in all the great systems of the philosophy of history—from Fichte to Hegel— all of which, as Nathan Rotenstreich has shown, assigned Judaism the role in the development of human history of being a preparatory stage, to be left behind when the higher stage, represented by Christianity, was reached. The historical approach afforded Christian partisans a new weapon. Their claim to possess a superior system of morals could be substantiated by history, if it is assumed that every later stage represented a higher degree of development.

To all these attacks Jewish apologetics gave their retort, and in some cases even launched their counter-attack. In my book on Jewish-Gentile relations in the Middle Ages and modern times,[2] I have adduced proofs that a tendency toward leniency in evaluating Christianity manifested itself in Judaism during the seventeenth and eighteenth centuries. This attitude was conditioned by the assumption that both parties would now desist from active missionizing. The conciliatory trend reached its peak during the Age of Enlightenment, when it appeared as if Judaism and Christianity had found a common ground in the spirit of rationalism. This attitude changed in the era of semi-emancipation, when the Jewish community found itself the target of more or less active propaganda on the spiritual, political, and social level. Much of the old Jewish "resentment" was thrust into the counter-attack of Jewish intellectuals against Christianity. Nothing was more intensely resented by Jewish apologists than the Christian claim of possessing the higher morality. As the Italian rabbi, Elijah Benamozegh, writing in the '60s of the nineteenth century asserted: "If there is anything that retards the coming of the great day [of reconciliation], it is the superiority which the daughter arrogates to herself over her old parent—Christianity over the religion of Israel—in the matter of morals."

Jewish sensitiveness on this point is readily understood. In the first place, Jewish apologists were aware of the strong Jewish solidarity inherited from the ghetto period, that lent some justification to the charge of particularism. On the other hand, Christian criticism was not confined to the theological plane but served very often as a point of departure for vituperative attacks by anti-Semites. Indeed, the transition and even a combination of both was not unusual, especially in nineteenth-century Germany and France.

The moral issue has remained a continuing bone of contention for generations, sometimes involving historical evaluation. Were the ethics of the Gospels really new, or were they merely a collection of old Jewish dicta transmitted by Jesus' contemporary, Hillel the Elder? The answer to such questions was not merely a matter of social prestige for Jews, the hinge on which the loyalty of certain members of the community may have turned; sometimes, at least as long as the struggle for political emancipation had not yet been successfully concluded, the decision might have led to tangible consequences. The European countries had not accepted the principle of separation of church and state, and so the question arose whether the religion of the synagogue might claim a worthy place alongside the church, which enjoyed official recognition. Writing in Prussia in 1844, Joseph Levi Saalschuetz set out to prove this point. The only real difference between the two religions, he claimed, was the Christian dogma of the trinity as against absolute Jewish monotheism. Messianism, ritual, and moral doctrines, if not identical in both religions, are not so substantially divergent as to justify political or social discrimination against Jews. Saalschuetz gave his booklet the imposing title: *Die Versöhnung der Konfessionen; oder Judentum und Christentum in ihrem Streit und Einklang* (The Reconciliation of the Creeds; or Judaism and Christianity in their Conflict and Harmony).

Reconciliation here did not imply fusion or unity, but the acceptance of each other as equals in state and society.

On a somewhat higher philosophical or rather theological plane, a bid for coexistence was made by a more prominent contemporary of Saal-schuetz, Samuel Hirsch. He was a radical Reform rabbi who, in the 1860s emigrated to the United States because he could not bear the compromising atmosphere of Germany, and in his new home he became the leader of the radical wing of the Reform movement. Yet Hirsch was a philosopher, indeed the most important philosopher that German Jewry produced at this juncture. His conception was an offshoot of the Hegelian school, but he demonstrated his remarkable independence of his master's system, using his philosophical acumen to correct Hegel's theory concerning the relative positions of Judaism and Christianity in the scheme of the evolution of the human spirit. While, according to Hegel, Judaism represented an earlier stage of development, later superseded by Christianity, Hirsch re-garded both religions as representing different but equally valid manifes-tations of divine revelation. Judaism and Christianity are depicted against the background of the paganism of the religions of nature, which they both overcame. Thus, according to Hirsch, Christian exclusiveness was justified as long as it was directed against paganism—but to use this exclusiveness against Judaism was preposterous! Hirsch was ready, then, to accept the much-decried declaration of the Christian church: *extra ecclesiam non est salus*, but with the added proviso: *nisi Judaeis in religione eorum*. Here is the clearest possible formulation of a Jewish-Christian reconciliation based on mutual recognition—Christianity for the Gentiles, for all Gentiles; Judaism for the Jews.

I may mention that the argument of Franz Rosenzweig in his famous twentieth-century philosophical work, *Stern der Erlösung*, follows similar lines. Rosenzweig, too, accepted the validity of Christianity for humanity, but stipulated a special religious status for Judaism. Actually, twentieth-century Judaism has not made any really new contribution to the Jewish-Christian controversy. The social situation remained more or less static, and every Jewish thinker felt impelled to take his stand vis-à-vis Christi-anity, the more so as every systematic exposition of Christianity assumed an attitude of moral and spiritual superiority towards Judaism. Thus, Adolph Harnack's *Das Wesen des Christentums* elicited Leo Baeck's *Das Wesen des Judentums*. Even non-religious thinkers like Ahad Ha'am, the leading phi-losopher of modern Jewish nationalism, felt compelled to define the dif-ference between Judaism and Christianity. As a positivist, he sought this difference not in the area of religion as such, but in their attitudes towards morality. This example, as well as others, vindicates our assertion that the controversy with Christianity is a function of the theory the controversialist subscribes to in his definition of Judaism. The same may be said of Martin Buber's attempt in his *Two Types of Faith*. Buber has, I think, been correctly characterized as a "religious anarchist"—someone for whom the content of the religious act does not count, only its subjective, accompanying attitude being significant. Accordingly, when Buber came to define the difference between the two religions, he ignored their respective contents, but tried to discern it in "two types of faith."

III

All that has been said concerning Jewish-Christian relations up to now has revolved around a *modus vivendi*, a mutually acknowledged coexistence of the two religions. But the secularism described above could also produce a more radical approach, the fusion of the two religions. For if rationalism or historical criticism could prove that the two religions had the same essence, then the wide cleavage between them does not merit preservation. There were people who jumped to such conclusions, especially in the early days of rationalism. Two such episodes have become famous. Moses Mendelssohn was repeatedly approached to change his religion. The first and most famous incident was the approach of the Zurich preacher and writer, Lavater. His appeal was simply an attempt to make a famous Jew see the light of Christianity. The last incident occurred toward the end of Mendelssohn's life. An anonymous writer explained, in a pamphlet addressed to Mendelssohn, why the latter's own philosophy was really inconsistent with his remaining a Jew. Only recently the identity of this anonymous author could be clarified, and this clarification yielded a better understanding of the motive underlying his approach.[3] Mendelssohn thought it was Joseph Sonnenfels, famous as the leading figure of the Austrian Enlightenment during the time of Maria Theresa and Joseph II, who had been baptized in his youth by his father. The author maintained that in Christianity as expounded by enlightened contemporaries Mendelssohn would find what he had discovered in his own rationalistic interpretations of Judaism. The pseudo-Sonnenfels gave a concise description of rationalized Christianity: the adoration of the one, only God, the observance of divine precepts, and the ingathering of all peoples under the scepter of a Messiah of whom the prophets had spoken. It was obvious whom the author referred to as the Messiah, but, significantly, he did not mention this Messiah by name.

We shall see presently why this modification failed to satisfy Mendelssohn. But first let us take up the second instance, the cause célèbre of David Friedländer, a disciple of Mendelssohn who subsequently adopted a much more radical approach. Thirteen years after the death of his master, Friedländer published a pamphlet, at first anonymously but later acknowledging its authorship, in which he suggested that the rich householders of Berlin might possibly convert to Christianity, on the condition that the Protestant authorities would omit the dogma of the trinity from the confession of faith to be pronounced in the act of baptism. Friedländer's offer was addressed to Superintendent Teller, who was known as a rationalistic interpreter of Christianity. Friedländer and his followers were thereby led to believe that their compromise would be acceptable. They were wrong.

Here we can perceive the real forces underlying religion even in an age of rationalism. Rational interpretation may afford the believers and worshippers the assurance that their actions are not inconsistent with reason—but the conclusion does not follow that rational formulations can replace the acknowledgment of dogma, or be the substitute for symbols, ritual, or worship. Hence Sonnenfels' and Friedländer's attempts at compromise were doomed to failure. Teller and Mendelssohn might have been disposed to philosophize on the rationalistic significance of their respective religious dogmas, but they were not prepared to barter their religion away for quasi-rationalistic equivalents. This also implies the failure of any attempted fusion of the elements of various religions. Sonnenfels hinted at possible mutual concessions by Christianity and Judaism, thus paving the way for hoped-for reconciliation. But Mendelssohn immediately sensed that such concessions would be only the prelude for the merging of Judaism into Christianity. Such a "deal" could be accepted only by someone seeking a pretext to overcome his inhibitions against unconditional conversion—and this was what Friedländer was looking for. Mendelssohn, who took his Judaism seriously, and Teller, who was committed to Christianity, rejected any such compromise outright.

IV

This consideration leads us to form a realistic assessment of the whole trend of reconciliation which produced so much discussion but no real, tangible results. In theory, the differences between the two religions could be dismissed as negligible—but to accept the consequences would have meant to combine the two communities and fuse their modes of worship. Any practical attempts would have aroused deep-rooted aversion, well explained by the psychology and sociology of religion, on both sides. I can best illustrate the point by an example of Jewish-Christian practice taken from traditional times: Samuel Abuhab, a Rabbi of Venice in the seventeenth century, records a tacit agreement between Christian ownership and vice versa. Now, a crucifix stood in front of every Christian home, while every Jewish entrance had its *mezuzah*. When a dwelling changed hands, and the new owner was of a different religion, the departing owner would take care to remove his religious symbol before the new owner would take possession and affix his symbol. Thus the crucifix and the *mezuzah* may have known of each other's existence, but they never met under the same roof. The symbols were mutually more exclusive than their owners, those who venerated them, since Jew and Christian did come together under the same roof, not only for business purposes but at times even socially. In the sphere of religious experience, however, they could scarcely meet, since they each responded to different symbols, not only visible but conceptual as well. This state of affairs still persisted in the eighteenth and nineteenth centuries, when the contacts of the two communities, in other spheres of life, increased in frequency and intensity. The more that neutral spheres of life emerged, the greater became the opportunities for common Jewish and Christian activities, but neutrality between the two religions is almost a contradiction in terms.

Many Jewish scholars, from Samuel Hirsch to Martin Buber, have, as it were, reclaimed Jesus for Jewish history and his teachings for Jewish theology or ethics, maintaining that he did not in any essential way depart from the original Jewish doctrine. But it has never occurred to a Jewish community to include on such a basis some part of the New Testament in its canon, or to add Jesus' name to the list of prophets or Jewish sages in the context of prayer or meditation. Any such attempt would create a scandal, and the community concerned would very soon find itself outside the Jewish fold. On the other hand, speculations of scholars on such historical appropriation passed almost unnoticed. Of course, the absorption of a part of the New Testament or Jesus' name would have meant turning them into a Jewish symbol. Symbols, however, have their own historically conditioned individuality and cannot be adapted at will to premeditated conceptions.

True, the history of religion knows of syncretistic combinations of religions, but such occurrences were the products of more primitive conditions, where the process of fusion could continue, so to speak, unobserved by the actual participants. In the sophisticated atmosphere of the eighteenth and nineteenth centuries, fusion could be the result only of conscious effort, and thus the chance of success was very small indeed. When in the '40s of nineteenth-century Germany radical Protestants and Catholics established the so-called *Freigemeinden* and severed their connections with their previous religious establishments, their leaders declared their congregations open to Jews as well, and some Jewish individuals do seem to have joined. Yet the whole phenomenon proved abortive.

There is only one example of a quasi-religious association where neutrality paved the way for Jewish participation, but even here Jews were burdened by inherent problems and difficulties. I refer to Freemasonry, which, when it originated in eighteenth-century England, accepted the principle of the Deistic creed, the belief in the one God, leaving "particular opinions to the brethren."[4] This seems to furnish an ideal situation for the possible absorption of Jews and Christians in one common association. Some Jews did, indeed, become members of the lodges in England, France, and Germany about the middle of the eighteenth century. But the vicissitudes of Jewish participation in Masonic fraternities is an intricate story, still untold. I have devoted some years of study to the problem and can here briefly indicate the main lines that touch upon this paper. The crux of the matter is that the Deistic rationalism of the Masonic associations did not preclude the need for symbolic elements. The Freemasons were eclectics. They accepted symbols from various sources, some Jewish—the Temple of Solomon, for instance, becoming one of Freemasonry's central symbols. Still, the founders were Christians, and so they introduced many of the symbols of their own religion, to which they sometimes gave a Deistic interpretation. Thus St. John, for instance, became a type of patron of the entire Masonic order; the Bible, a symbol of the association. In most countries the oath was taken on the Gospel of St. John. A Jew, on entering the lodge, might have found some elements of his own religion there. Yet he also encountered much of the other religion. Either an exception had to be made, in his case, and he would be allowed to take the oath on the "Old Testament," for example, or otherwise he would have had to reconcile himself to accepting the Christian symbolic elements. The latter course rendered him suspect as an unprincipled individual, and his admission to the lodge could then be opposed on the grounds of a deficiency existing in his moral character. Indeed, this problem concerning the Jew in Freemasonry has never been satisfactorily resolved.

One example exists of an offshoot of Freemasonry that occurred at the end of the eighteenth century, the Asiatic Brethren in Vienna and other German-speaking towns, where a syncretistic ritual of Jewish and Christian elements was created with the avowed intention of absorbing Jews and Christians into one spiritual association. Here Jewish and Christian symbols, festival dates, and rituals were deliberately mixed together so as to satisfy both sides. Interestingly, the Kabbalah served as a *tertium quid*, a binding element. Of course, the Kabbalah is Jewish in origin, but, as is well known, certain of its elements have been carried over into Christian circles. Nonetheless, this whole association was short-lived. The Christian participants, at least, resented the Judaizing tendency, and the venture soon breathed its last.

To become an unrestricted association embracing Jew and Christian alike, the Masonic fraternity would have had to transform itself and omit every symbol reminiscent of Christianity. This did indeed occur in post-Revolutionary France, not out of consideration for the Jews, but as a result of the conflict with the Roman Catholic Church. French Freemasonry became a secular anti-clerical institution—later even tolerating atheism. Here it was possible for Jews to join without any mental reservation, but this association was completely outside the realm of religion. In other countries, especially Germany, Freemasonry retained Christian elements in its ritual. Nevertheless, not only secularized Jews but even certain modern rabbis aspired to membership in Masonic lodges. These individuals obviously felt the weight of the problem of having to participate in a service where Christian symbols played a part. We know how some of the rabbis solved their problem. Here we renew our acquaintance with Samuel Hirsch, who was not only a member but also rose to the rank of *orateur* of the Luxembourg lodge. We have observed above that as a philosopher Hirsch evolved a system in which Jews and Christians were reconciled, to the exclusion of all other religions. As a Freemason he combined Christianity and Judaism and preached, so to say, this doctrine of combined religion in his lodge. His book, *Die Humanität als Religion*, is a collection of Masonic sermons, which, strangely enough, has never been recognized as such. We have reason to devote some attention to this work, for it reveals how a possible combination of the two religions may be achieved by purging both religions of their specific, individual content. The doctine of original sin in Christianity and the significance of religious observances are flatly rejected. Yet even apart from the content, one can sense the strangeness of Hirsch's undertaking. As I put it elsewhere[5]:

> It is one thing to subject Judaism and Christianity separately to philo-sophical analysis and find that they possess elements in common. It is another to preach the doctrine of a single religion combining the sources of both. In his later book Hirsch does not appear as a philosopher. There he assumes the role of an authoritative teacher—a function imposed on him by his office of *orateur* to the lodge. Here, then, the two religions are not dealt with separately. The sources are quoted side by side: "Moses said—and so Jesus said—." The book is replete with such expressions, as if the author were preaching simultaneously to a Jewish and a Christian audience. Indeed, this is what Hirsch was doing, speaking in the very special surroundings of the lodge, which consisted of Christians and some Jews. I doubt whether any parallel to Hirsch's book exists in the vast literature in which Judaism and Christianity are compared.

We have also to assess the consequences of any undertaking such as Hirsch's. A reconciliation of the type he proposed implies the exclusion of all other religions not parties to the covenant; and, indeed, Hirsch restricted his Freemasonry to Christians and Jews alone. Thus Hirsch, who fought against Christian exclusiveness, was ready, theoretically, to impose the same restrictions against the adherents of other religions. This is the in-evitable consequence of any reconciliation between Judaism and Christi-anity on the basis of their common tradition. Thus it happens that any possible Jewish-Christian reconciliation would raise not only religious but also other issues, moral or humanistic. For anyone truly committed to universalism would recoil at any reconciliation effected at the expense of all outsiders. Here, Leopold (Yom Tov Lippmann) Zunz may be cited as an example. We have no knowledge of Zunz's attitude towards Hirsch's philosophy—but the latter had a precursor in the person of Solomon Levi Steinheim, and from what Zunz had to say about Steinheim's *Die Offen-barung als Lehrbegriff der Synagoge*, we can gauge what attitude Zunz would have adopted vis-à-vis Hirsch. Steinheim regarded Judaism, by virtue of its revelation, as the denial of all other religions, with the possible exception of Christianity insofar as it retained elements of Judaism. On reading the work, Zunz confided to a friend: "I cannot agree to this cleavage between revelation and paganism. Instead, I see only the emanations of the same world spirit everywhere. (Contrasts, perhaps even contradictions, in the world of phenomena, which, however, are reconciled by philosophy.) Away with present-day, exclusivistic hostility! It almost seems to me that, despairing of any positive content in Judaism, one contrasts it with non-Judaism, e.g., an apple tastes the opposite of a non-apple! . . ." This was the opinion of someone deeply rooted in Judaism, yet, at the same time, equipped with the critical acumen of a great scholar of history.

V

In summing up and perhaps drawing some conclusions at the same time,[6] it might be best to return to our starting point. Secularism has affected the role played by religion generally and, in particular, changed the position of the religious denominations. It did not, however, succeed in ousting religion nor in effacing the particular characteristics of the two religions whose interrelation we have been considering. The historical cleavage between Judaism and Christianity outlived the attempts at reconciliation that followed in the wake of secularism. These attempts, of course, were at no time backed by the whole Jewish or Christian community, nor were they indicative of the views held by their respective intellectual exponents. The bulk of the Jewish community, it is true, had become less fervently attached to Judaism, though without losing its reservations towards Christianity. Jewish thinkers, too, did not always tend toward a reconciliation; on the contrary, some of them stressed the differences between the two religions, seeing in the denial of Christianity by Judaism the latter's *raison d'être*.

This attitude has at times been questioned as being an altogether negative one. But I am not at all sure that this is a valid or a just criticism. It is true that few Jewish thinkers could present a complete theory in terms of a well-defined system to justify adherence to the ancient faith. One of the results of secularism was that it undermined the dogmatic foundations of religion by fostering a rationalistic method of criticism. But Christianity scarcely fared better in this respect. It, too, had to forgo the claims to a compehensive *Weltanschauung.* It, too, became largely apologetic.

The inability to rely exclusively on its tradition does not, however, imply the abandoning of religion altogether. History and many other branches of knowledge teach us that the source of religious commitments lies deeply embedded in the nature of man and that its rational justification is a secondary phenomenon. Therefore the lack of rational justification is not tantamount to a withering of the religious urge or attachment. This is why religion retains much of its power even in the teeth of secularist criticism that had discounted much of its rational justification. If religion is no longer the mainspring or inspiration, it is still part of the life of individuals and certainly of the group. But it has to rely, instead of on the vital impulse and creative impetus, on notions and symbols inherited from the past. The present may go about religious tradition selectively, but it cannot afford to discard it. Elements of the ancient tradition, ideas and visible symbols are still the best stimuli to which contemporary religious sensibilities respond. This being so, the future of religion is contingent on the cultivation of elements in the religious tradition rather than on their effacement.

There is, however, no surer way to obliteration than blending symbols or ideas that, by their historical connotations, are inimical to each other. The symbols of the Christian and those of the Jewish religion are such mutually exclusive elements. Communal worship of Christians and Jews, attempted in certain places, leads perforce to the omission from both religions of what was most meaningful to both communities. On the other hand, retention of controversial symbols may so inhibit reaction as to countermand the very purpose of communal worship.

From the specific Jewish standpoint, additional apprehensions are raised. There is no point in glossing over the fact that Judaism, not only in the numerical but also in a very special historical sense, is a minority religion. Judaism withstood the temptation to follow the Christian majority who accepted the Jewish religion as a basis for their faith but gave it an interpretation of their own. Jewish opposition was maintained in the face of the relentless claim that Christianity had superseded it and that Jews should accept the conclusion of logic, the result of exegetics, and all the judgment of history. Though the arguments changed, the claim was not waived. If in recent times some Christian thinkers and institutions have tried to omit from an exposition of their system a vindication of Christianity at the expense of Judaism, it is to be doubted whether this would prevail with Christianity at large. The expectation of the ultimate conversion of Jewry is too deeply ingrained in the Christian system for an ejection as a result of intellectual considerations. This, though genuine, may turn out to be ephemeral. There is good reason to believe that the Christian claim will reappear in the course of time. The merging between the two communites may well expose the Jewish minority to an overwhelming vindication of Christianity or result in a gradual adaptation to the religion of the majority.

Judaism has maintained itself as a minority religion by fierce resistance, compensating for deficiency in number by intensity of rejection. If it is to continue in these days of secularism, it cannot afford to relinquish a method that, if not always the most appealing, has stood the test of time. It is easy for Christians to declare that, in view of the overwhelming power of secularism, the adherents of the two religions would do well to overlook their differences and join forces. This may sound most plausible in Gentile ears. Relying on Jewish historical experience, however, we should rather heed the apprehension voiced by Moses Mendelssohn that a too intimate union might end in the majority absorbing the minority religion.

The Influence of Religion and Society on Each Other at the Time of the Emancipation

A general discussion of religion and society presupposes that there is a give and take between these two fields, but in my particular subject, the influence of religion and society on each other at the time of the Emancipation, the influencing effect appears to be in one direction only, for according to the generally accepted theory, the social factor at this time outweighed the religious. Reform [Judaism], which is the classical manifestation of the religious aspirations of the time, is governed by the social assimilation of which it is itself an expression.

Before we can answer the question of whether or not this theory is in fact correct, we must try to define the positions of both Judaism and Christianity at the time of the French Revolution and in the one or two generations before and after it. It seems that the position of religion during these generations was itself fixed by a third factor, the intellectual factor. In the final analysis the most prominent characteristic of the period was the ascent of the rationalistic current, and the reaction to it in the form of the irrationalism of the Romantic movement. To a very large extent, rationalism undermines the very foundations of religion, whereas the irrationalism of the Romantics reconfirms it. Although this view is essentially correct, it would be much too simple to say that the rational and the romantic are two ideological movements that stand outside the sphere of social processes. The truth of the matter is that these two currents of thought are so intertwined with the social and political movements of the period that at the same time they are both an expession and cause of events in the social and political fields. If we were to say therefore that religion was influenced by both rationalism and romanticism, we should have said in effect that both social and ideological currents forcibly influenced the shaping of religion's image at that time.

If this is true with regard to the Christian religion and Christian society, then it is even more relevant to Judaism and its followers. The *Haskalah* (Enlightenment Movement) affected the Jewish community from within via renewed contact with the outside world, but the *Haskalah* itself certainly cannot be seen only as an intellectual discipline for it brought with it political and social aspirations, hopes for citizenship of the state in which the Jews were living and for social integration into the immediate surroundings. These intellectual and social currents came together and were caught up into the Jewish religion on the way. The majority of that generation, however, saw Judaism as the main obstacle to obtaining social and political integration, and it is small wonder that the rationalistic critics, who wanted to change the status of the Jew in society, attacked Judaism first.

The rationalist criticism of religion is directed against Christianity and Judaism, but occasionally, with Voltaire for example, even the arrows pointed specifically at Christianity can reach their target only via the living flesh of Judaism. In order to raze the walls of Christianity, Voltaire singles out biblical Judaism against which to hurl his slingshots, with the calculated intention of bringing down the whole edifice by destroying its foundations. In addition, deists, atheists, and Christians join in this criticism of Judaism which at the outset is rational rather than historical. Similarly, the criticism is directed not against the principle of faith so much as against the practical side of Judaism, i.e. against the *mitzvot* (divine commandments) and the whole special way of life that is governed by them. From an aesthetic point of view Jewish observance seemed repulsive and the Jewish way of life faulty. Faced with the current theory that the principal commandments of the Mosaic law, and even more those of Rabbinic Judaism, were given to differentiate this nation from others, the whole of practical Judaism, like some outdated relic, is doomed. Thus at a time when there is a longing to remove the barrier that distinguishes the Jewish community from its environment, this practical Judaism is considered to be not only meaningless but also harmful and destructive to those who hope for social improvements.

To this criticism of ritual Judaism is added a faulting of the Jewish ethic: A community that by adherence to its religion becomes closed within itself, is unable to behave in a proper and respectable manner to the stranger, who is not included within its framework. The critics substantiate their arguments by pointing to Jews who have been found to be swindlers, usurers, and even robbers and embezzlers. These proofs receive the stamp of authenticity by use of the premise that misdeeds by Jews are not co-incidental but rather develop from their law and their moral code, which are in turn a result of their ritual and social self-containment. Much of what is said by rationalistic critics is taken from the detractors of Judaism in Christian and even pre-Christian times. Nevertheless there is a change in content, and so all the more in results. The change in the content is due to the fact that the rationalists sometimes link together their opposition to religion in general and their hatred of Judaism and the Jewish people in particular. The rationalist viewpoint obtained an objective standing for these accusations against Judaism, a status they did not have when used by the representatives of Christianity. This is the reason why rationalist criticism had a better chance of appealing to the Jewish *maskilim* (those Jews who identified themselves with the aims and methods of the Enlightenment), especially at a time when the practical conclusion of the critics was not to the detriment of the Jews, but rather for their good. An example of this is the criticism of Christian Wilhelm Dohm, whose main purpose was to suggest a reappraisal of the civil standing of the Jews, but according to him this reappraisal was dependent on the removal of faults, conditioned in some respect by the Jewish religion and the ethics it proclaimed.

Among the Jewish *maskilim*, Mendelssohn was almost unique in that he answered this criticism with his own, affirmative opinion concerning the practical *mitzvot;* but on the subject of the ethics of the Jews—if not that of Jewish ethics—his answer was given in weak language. He certainly did not blame the deterioration of the self-containment resulting from Jewish observance, but he acknowledged that cultural and linguistic separatism was likely to become an ethical stumbling block. The majority of the Jewish *maskilim* accepted this criticism against the practical side of Judaism, and Dohm himself, who was a personal friend of Mendelssohn, predicted without any hesitation that Mendelssohn's pupils would listen to their teacher in all but one thing, namely, adherence to religious ritual. And this prediction was more than just a guess, or the wishful thinking of Dohm, who had himself drawn away from the positive side of Christianity. And this is not all that we find in the 1780s, for the Jewish *maskil* who had broken away from practical Judaism was by now diffused in all the big cities of Germany—Berlin, Breslau, Königsberg. Most of the followers of Mendelssohn regarded his philosophy as a valid starting point for discarding some more or less important parts of the tradition rather than for justifying it in its entirety.

The justification of religious observance did not, however, seem an integral part of the rationalistic outlook. The Jewish *maskilim* therefore were prone to identify themselves with the criticism of their religion. Immediate contact with the non-Jewish members of society weighed heavily on the Jewish way of life, and the acceptance of non-Jewish circles as the reference group with which to identify themselves opened the road for a negative evaluation in the contemplative sphere. Not only are theories that would abolish the practical side of Judaism re-uttered by Jews, but, worse than this, the negative aesthetic evaluation of everything whose source is in the Jewish tradition becomes widespread. It is exactly because the aesthetic evaluation is like a reasonless judgment that it discloses the identification of Jews with non-Jewish circles. Even where social contact with the outside world has not yet materialized, the aspiration for identification transfers the scale of values from outside the Jewish community to within it. Aaron Horin, for example, living in the city of Arad in Hungary, and having no contact with non-Jewish rationalists, nevertheless identifies himself with their aesthetic evaluation and omits the chant signs for the reading of the Torah in the synagogue because they seem to him to be incompatible with good European taste. For the same reason he asks the members of his congregation to remove their head-coverings during prayers, as this does not agree with the ideas of European society concerning the way in which to show respect. It is in matters such as this, in line with principles of religious tradition itself, but in themselves without fundamental importance, that the direction of the interdependence between religion and society makes itself known. It seems that our first premise, that the effect of influence is in one direction only, is confirmed; society influences religion, and not religion society.

Nevertheless, Judaism has, even at this time, a staying power far greater than at first sight seemed to be the case. The critical theories went far beyond the abandonment of Jewish observance and the adaptation to Christian criteria. The logical conclusion when followed up consistently should have been the complete abandonment of Judaism and subsequent attachment to the Christian camp, and many members of both the Christian and Jewish communities did indeed arrive at this very conclusion. The adoption of Christianity, which is a recurring phenomenon amongst the Jewish community during the whole period of the Diaspora, has new paths opened to it at this time, and, in a way, it has been made easier, at least from an intellectual point of view. In the same way that the *Haskalah* split Judaism by its criticism, so it also split Christianity and presented it with those principles through which it was possible to harmonize itself with the claims of rationalism. Conversion to Christianity lost much of its accepted meaning, namely as a change of heart and acceptance of principles of faith that contradicted those of Judaism; now it became possible to identify conversion as a change from one system of worshipping God to another, to a better and more enlightened system of worship.

This change can be exemplified from the life of Moses Mendelssohn himself. As is known, Mendelssohn was challenged in 1769 by the author-priest Lavater that he should either change to Christianity or refute the proofs as to its truth, which were included in the book by the French author Bossuet. The intention, despite the fact that rational proofs were referred to, was for him to accept Christianity in all its details and essentials, its dogmas, and the mystical elements that it contained. For Mendelssohn it was easy to answer with a firm no—which was nothing but a declaration of his belief in Judaism and his inability to accept the Christian dogmas. Mendelssohn was challenged again, thirteen years later, to take the step from Judaism to Christianity. This new challenge was included in an anonymous pamphlet that appeared in 1782, which caused Mendelssohn to write his great book *Jerusalem*. Scholars did not know the identity of the pamphlet's author and so did not pay too much attention to its contents, but what is certain is that the author appeared as one of the leaders of the Enlightenment of the period; that in fact his challenge to Mendelssohn to convert to Christianity does not include the request that he identify with the Christian dogmas nor with its mystical side either. The step can now be taken at a much smaller intellectual price; the Jewish *maskil* has nothing more to do than to identify himself with the fundamentals of the Deistic faith, which, according to the view of the anonymous author, are also the fundamentals of Christianity—and of course it was well known that the Jew, Mendelssohn, held to his Judaism as a religion whose fundamental principle was none other than the faith in pure monotheism.

But it is not our concern to see how Mendelssohn is rescued from his attack. It is sufficient for us to focus upon the unity of the religions, which was one of the axioms of rationalistic teaching and which brought to maturity the challenge to transfer from Judaism to Christianity. This possibility found a place in the hearts of Jews, and there is no doubt that many of the converts to Christianity in this period explained their step to themselves by a theory of this sort. The attempt by David Friedländer to bring the whole of the Berlin congregation over to Christianity, by means of fixing with representatives of the church conditions and restraints in the declaration of faith, is the clearest evidence of the fact that the enticement penetrated very deeply into the Jewish community.

Rationalism, however, is not only the pill for sweetening the conversion. If we look further afield, to the generations after Mendelssohn, we find parallel paths, and the common factor amongst them is that none of them demands acceptance of the burdens of traditional Christianity in its fullest sense, and even less genuine conversion in the sense of change of heart and spiritual rebirth. The Christian church was satisfied in the main by a formal declaration of faith, and there were certainly converts to Christianity whose declaration was no more than lip-service, while their mental argument was that of personal benefit, and even this somewhat cynically, as the famous examples of Börne and Heine demonstrate. But not all those who converted without conviction did so for the sake of profit and personal benefit alone. There are middle types who lean on whatever theory eases the changeover and protects them from the necessity of being drawn into cynicism. One reason was the theory of the basic unity of all religions, and another the new roads that were opened up with the rise of the Romantic movement, through which Christianity could wrap itself in philosophical and historical dress. Young Jews, educated in the high schools by Christian teachers, were sometimes ensnared by the teachers' religion, which was no more than a mixture of religious enthusiasm with historical and philosophical dolling-up and a more or less admitted lack of attention to the Christian dogmas. It was enough for pupils to be impressed by these teachers' sweep of knowledge and depth of thought, and to compare these with what they found in the Jewish community at the same time, for them to become convinced of the superiority of Christianity over Judaism. It is true that this conviction came with the social reward that through a change of religion they were rescued from the community into which they were born, which was still far from enjoying an equal standing in the state. However, the calculation of these interests was not necessarily acknowledged at the time of the decision and it cannot be said that this decision disqualified the character of the man who made it.

Julius Friedrich Stahl and Johann August Wilhelm Neander, who converted to Christianity in their youth, did so it would appear without reservation. However, neither of them had a genuine Christian conversion. Stahl converted to Christianity only after he had been refused admittance because of his Judaism to the University of Munich, and of Neander we know that he only converted as a result of being drawn after his teachers and friends at the high school in Hamburg—and they were Christians in the philosophical and cultural meaning of the word. Only years after the conversion did he become a believing and enthusiastic Christian. In any event, the subjective identification of both Stahl and Neander was an honest step, and because of this they were able to become fertile and fertilizing forces within the Christian social framework, Stahl as a political ideologist and Neander as a theologian and scholar of church history.

The process of defection from Judaism, which was one of the most outstanding features of the period, is considerably more complicated than at first meets the eye. However, the compass of this falling away was not nearly as great as historians, with Graetz in the forefront, imagined. In distinction to the generation that preceded the *Haskalah,* where the defection was from the edges of the Jewish community only, the main significance of the present process was that it struck at the ruling class and even at prominent and outstanding personalities. The whole of the enlightened class in Judaism, which had been rescued from the framework of traditional Judaism, entered the ring and were brought face to face with the attractive power of Christianity. The accepted approach in our historiography is to see those who left Judaism and those who clung to it as two camps separated fundamentally, the one of weak-charactered people who were easily enticed, the other of mighty men who stood firm under trial—but this view has no justification at all. What remarkably characterizes the period is that all the members of social stratum, equal as to position, education, intellectual and human attainment, are caught in a state of seduction and subsequent decision—and part of them go right and part of them go left, some of them defect from Judaism while others hold fast to it.

And so we arrive at an appreciation of the staying-power of the Jewish religion at this period; for all those who were tried but not seduced were witnesses to some spark that yet remained to that same Judaism that was now reviled by everyone. And who was sure of the generation, who was not tried? Even Mendelssohn, whose position was both proud and unequivocal, admits that in his youth he examined the two religions, the one against the other—and decided in favor of Judaism. In my opinion, one must regard his testimony as genuine autobiographical witness. Even though Mendelssohn shows no sign of doubt concerning Christianity, or exceptional wrestling with it, there was an examination on the intellectual plane that preceded the trial which came to him from outside. There was nothing more natural at that time than the situation that one who left behind the accepted stereotype in Judaism, whether by deed or in thought, should be immediately caught up in the dilemma "Jew or Christian?" The middle position that adopted neither Judaism nor Christianity, did not yet exist, but was formed in actual fact by the stand of those who, despite their estrangement from the accepted stereotype of Judaism, still decided to remain within its fold. Except where the biographical testimonies are sufficient, we are not in a position to say what caused this positive decision, and such cases are few in number. An emotional link with the biological source, a childhood obligation to the stereotype of Jewish life, a strong attachment to loved members of the family—these certainly made a contribution, but without doubt the contest also had an intellectual and ethical side to it. Not everyone was able to ignore the sting that rested in the Christian dogma, either when dulled by a rationalist theory or when softened by philosophical wrappings in all their variety. We hear from Spielding, one of the Christian leaders of the Enlightenment in the Berlin of Mendelssohn's time, that a Jewish doctor confessed to him that he would be prepared to accept Christianity if only it would give up the belief in the trinity, and the doctor added that a large number of Jews in Berlin thought similarly. The central Christian dogma served, therefore, as a hindrance to christianization. This was, as a matter of fact, the last restraint for Friedländer when he turned to superintendent Teller with his strange conditions that the adult Jews of Berlin should not have to admit the fundamentals of Christianity literally. Similar causes were working also with Gabriel Riesser who—in contradistinction to the opinion of his biographer, who thought that he had never been tempted by Christianity because of his determined character—wrestled in his youth with the seduction of conversion, but overcame it. Riesser was from the second generation of those who grew up in a home with a *maskil* father and thus was free of the burden inherited by the majority of those who came out of the ghetto. In his case, therefore, the changeover to Christianity was unlikely to be involved with a multitude of psychological barriers. His decision was conscious and extremely clear, and its reason lay in the intellectual depth of his thinking, which did not allow him to affirm with his lips that which he could neither acknowledge nor believe in in his heart.

By no means do we know the measure of involvement in the problem of all the personalities or the method of their escape from it, and it strikes me that there are still some surprises in store for us with the publication of some hitherto unknown sources. We have an outstanding example of this in the life of Zunz. Certain hints were given by him that he owed his faithfulness to Judaism to Grillen, namely, to an obligation without any actual reason. However, the publication of his letters and those of his friends some years back by Nahum Glatzer reveals that Zunz did in fact, during his youth in Berlin, consider the possibility of becoming a Christian, and for a considerable time his decision was left hanging in the balance until finally he decided—but without the possibility of accounting to himself as to the reason for his choice.

Seen against the background of Jewish history of past epochs, what occurred in the Jewish community at the end of the eighteenth century, and in the first half of the nineteenth, appears as a contraction of Jewish life resulting from its involvement in temporary temptations. We shall, however, reach a more moderate evaluation if we can realistically imagine the historical situation in which influential people were forced to make a decision. All of those who were active in fashioning the image of Judaism at this period were rescued from the chains of traditional Judaism and found themselves, as it were, in a movement of ever-increasing withdrawal. It was not possible to guess *a priori* where any one of them would go, and, as we have seen above, many of them continued past the boundaries of Judaism itself. In any event, those who did halt on the way saw merit for themselves in this fact, and if the decision had come to them from some acknowledged experience, then it became a source of inspiration to them in their work and in the adoption of their position.

The first result of this situation was that among those who stopped short before conversion, there evolved a new attitude towards the enticing qualities of Christianity. The Christians who were engaged in studying the Jewish question even in the Romantic period—and there were many in the circles of politicians, public figures, writers and theologians—stuck to the accepted image of Judaism received from the period of the *Haskalah*. Both by those who sought their political good and by their opponents, it was put to the Jews that the fate of Judaism was fore-ordained, and that it would disappear from the world inasmuch as it was nothing but a fossilized remnant from earlier ages. Only very slowly did a Jewish position arise that was able to deny and refute these claims. And it seems, strangely enough, that those who were themselves at some time or another the nearest to being absorbed by Christianity became those who were most ready for action against it. It is impossible to understand or appreciate the works of Zunz, and even Graetz and the systems of Samuel Hirsch and Formstecher unless they are seen against this background.

This is an innovation compared with the period that precedes rationalism. As I have mentioned elsewhere, a kind of tolerant relationship with Christianity was created in the Judaism of the seventeenth and eighteenth centuries and it is interesting to note that Orthodox circles in the nineteenth century continued with this line by emphasizing the common basis of Judaism and Christianity. At the same time, modern researchers and thinkers, who were involved in the struggle between the two religions in a most vital way, revealed the contradictions between them and came to grips with Christianity by way of either historical description or philosophical analysis. It is even possible to say that some of them did Christianity an historical injustice, but in any event they placed before it an independent Jewish position for which the time was ripe.

The experience of having undergone temptation and returned to Judaism was decisive for those who had been tempted when they took up their position as Jews on the question of Judaism. The halt in the withdrawal from the old created, in the best of those tempted, an incentive to redefine Judaism in new ways and gave them a critical position with regard to the old and the traditional. In the first place, the means of discrimination between that which was seen fit to be preserved and that which was condemned in the old form were taken from the store of ideas of the Enlightenment, and, from the Romantic period onward, from the ideas of critical history. Moral strength was needed by those making the decision, and this strength was drawn from the consciousness that Judaism had for a long time been dragged into the whirlpool of dissolution and that in its old form it had, because of both the attacks that came from outside and the criticism from within, no hope for revival. Every attempt at reconstruction, even if it did not intend to do more than preserve the minimum, seemed like a rescue operation.

Because of this, the work of the founders of the science of Judaism and the first Reformers can be seen, at least from a subjective point of view, as a positive act, a sort of building on heaps of ruins. We are able to reconstruct the atmosphere in which these groups came together in Berlin and Hamburg, and see that their primary experience was one of rediscovery of the vitality of Judaism after it had been abandoned and neglected. Those who attended the Reform synagogues of Berlin and Hamburg felt the experience of return in repentance which, even if it did not exactly bring them back to the bosom of the old faith, did nevertheless save them from estrangement or complete apathy. The words of the preachers that were heard at these meetings imitated in their form the Christian sermon in use at that time, but their intention and aim were the disassociation from absorption into the Christian community and the creation of a new religious framework in Judaism. There is no doubting the truth of the reports that come from various sources that in these first years of Reform both the leaders and the led reached a spiritual height that could have been both satisfying and encouraging to the hope for a genuine revival. From Hamburg we know that one of the preachers used to preach without any preparation and speak according to the inspiration of the moment, so that his words might have a more basic quality. An experiment of this sort is not possible except in a place where the emotional and religious tension has reached such a degree that it gives strength to the expression of feelings and ideas without intermediaries.

A revitalized atmosphere of tension like this is not able of course to continue for any appreciable length of time, and it did not in fact persist for more than a few years. To those who participated in it, it gave strength to stand up to their opponents from the old camp, who judged and excommunicated them in the name of the authority of the old Judaism. The historical fertility of the experience was dependent on whether those who proclaimed the new system would be able to produce from their midst not only people who would be inspired for a short period but also a religious authority of some sort or other able to set itself up against the authority of traditional Judaism. With greater or lesser clarity the problem of authority troubled those who aspired to Reform Judaism during the whole time of their activity, and I have already mentioned that rationalism and historical criticism provided the means of distinguishing between what was worthy to be retained and what was destined to be forgotten. With these two tools it was easily possible to draw distinctions between the principal and the subordinate, between that which was original in Judaism and its accretions. Such distinctions were often made by those who knew what they were talking about, but more often by half scholars whose aspiration for change caused them to find support in the tradition for present necessities. However, there was no lack of hypocritical characters who pretended that their emendations were supported by the accepted method of interpreting the tradition, while among themselves they had long since disclaimed its authority.

The real question, however, was not one of retaining or rejection, but rather, according to what religious authority it could be achieved; and in this question was realized the limit of the hopes for renovation. Even in theory the exponents of Reform were not able to make a clear distinction between the permitted and the forbidden, the wanted and the unwanted. For the distinctions between Biblical and Rabbinic Judaism, the original and the added, the national and the religious, were not able to stand the test of careful consideration and strict logic. After two thousand years, traditional Judaism was much too complicated to give the chance for differentiation among its various and differing elements. However, even if they had been able to do this from an intellectual point of view, it would not have helped them. If, for example, they had managed to arrive at a sound conviction to the effect that such and such fundamentals were biblical, original, religious, and so forth, this would not have constituted a sanction from some religious institution of authority in which those of the general public who were concerned would have been able to find an honest salve for their consciences. Religious authority of this sort was never found, nor, incidentally, was a central charismatic personality who would have been able to give the decisions such force that no one would have been able to query them. In contradistinction to the *Haskalah*, which found a leader for itself in the personality of Moses Mendelssohn (not someone who put himself at the head but who was recognized as an exemplary figure), the Reform movement had many initiators, advisers, and litigants, but no single qualified and acknowledged leader. The absence of such a leader was strongly felt and was occasionally expressed explicitly. When, for example, the movement acquired the name of Reform or Reformation, the comparison was made with the Christian Reformation. Where was the Jewish Luther who would accomplish the Reformation? Ehrenberg, Zunz's teacher in his younger days, laid great hopes on his gifted pupil and appealed to him in one of his letters "Be our Luther!" But Zunz's talents, big though they were, were not of the sort of Luther's, and after participation in the creation of the revitalized atmosphere in the Reform synagogue of Berlin, he withdrew in favor of work in the area of education and research. In such a way he was able to supply material to those who aspired for renovation, but he was not able to be their qualified leader.

To tell the truth, the matter did not depend on individual talent. The Reform movement, even though it came into being at a period when the time of rationalism in Europe had passed, was not free from the influence of the latter, nor was it able to free itself. Jews, more perhaps than Christians, were wont to stick to the way of rationalistic thought because it opened up for them the road from the old Judaism and the ghetto to the European Enlightenment and the surrounding society. And in any case, even in European society there is no denial of the achievements of rationalism, even where there was a change of attitude to it, and the Romantic movement, as well as the philosophies that resulted from it, did not return the world to any honest religious simplicity within which the rise of a new religious authority would have been possible. If Reform—in the sense of a renewal of religious authority resurrected from a foundation in the tradition—is at all possible in a religion such as Judaism, then it came some generations too late.

In the period of Reform only Samson Raphael Hirsch spoke with full religious authority, and undoubtedly in his youth he also went through the process of cutting himself off from the old Judaism, but we have no idea how far his thoughts and considerations went. In any event, the restoration was much more acute for him than for his friends, and he remained critical of the modes that were widespread in the old Judaism. Nevertheless he accepted the authority of the *Halakhah* (Jewish Law) and based on it the claim for a practical Judaism in the modern conditions of society.

By the sheer strength of his personality, and with ideological means of persuasion with which he equipped himself, through contact with the modern spiritual streams, he succeeded in attracting a circle of believers. In this case religion helped to create a new social framework which, sometimes with extremism and fanaticism, drew apart from the general Jewish community and achieved religious authority but only at the price of the surrender of the unity of the Jewish community even in outward appearance.

With respect to the majority of the Jewish community the binding power of *halakhic* authority was no longer felt, but the inability of the Reform movement to replace it with another authority left Judaism dissolute and broken open from all sides. From this point on it was possible to identify Judaism with every social or political aspiration of the individual or the group, and the religious institutions themselves submitted to the influences of, imitation of and social adaptation to, the surroundings. What was stated at the beginning of this article is therefore correct, namely, that in the reciprocal relationship between religion and society, it was society whose hand was uppermost.

Despite this, religion is not without some staying power, for those who did not exchange Judaism for Christianity, or who did not disown all religion publicly and intentionally, continued to adhere to some of its customs and institutions. This loyalty, whatever the subjective cause of its continuation may be, was sufficient to distinguish its proponents as a religious minority in the society of the majority; a few Jewish symbols were sufficient to serve as a shield against complete identification with the surrounding society, and its religion.

Consciousness of Jewish uniqueness was preserved and guarded against complete assimilation. If religion ceased to fashion the life of the community, it certainly continued to contribute at least to its existence. And no social influence could be more salient than this.

The German-Jewish Utopia of Social Emancipation

I

German-Jewish history has received heightened interest lately, in the wake of German Jewry's fate at the hands of the Nazi regime. The calamity of course affected the Jews throughout Europe; but the destruction began in Germany, and only step by step were the other communities drawn into its orbit. The historical reasons for the destruction must be sought, first and foremost, within the confines of German-Jewish history. Hence, it is well understandable that historians have directed their attention to the German-Jewish *past*, expecting to find there the answer to the terrible riddle of the present. Paul W. Massing's book on the anti-Semitism of the Second Reich indicates by its very title, *Rehearsal for Destruction*, that the seeds of the catastrophe had been sown two or three generations before its actual occurrence. Similarly, Eleonore Sterling's *Er ist wie Du*, which deals with anti-Semitism in the first half of the nineteenth century, also reflects the experience of the present generation in its treatment of the historical past. In contrast to these genuine efforts at historical inquiry is the pretentious rambling of Hannah Arendt in her *Origins of Totalitarianism*, wherein the author claims to have found a predetermined historical law which necessitated the catastrophe.

The underlying assumption of such presentations is that events can be sufficiently explained by their antecedents. I confess that I cannot share the assumptions of such a philosophy; and in this case, I cannot believe that the Hitler catastrophe was predetermined by latent forces in German or Jewish history or in the combination of the two. These reservations, however, do not mean that I would deny the deep impact that certain events exert on the mind of the historian when he comes to examine ones that have preceded them. After the long interfusion of German and Jewish history dissolved under such frightful circumstances, it is natural that we should again have a look at its beginnings. We are certainly more apt to detect signs of deficiency and failure in the history of emancipation and assimilation than those historians who regarded these as the starting point of an everlasting symbiosis.

I intend to concentrate on one point only: I believe that the incongruence of incipient emancipation and assimilation can be detected by a close scrutiny of the data of that time alone. My contention is that, from the very beginning, the initiators of a possible assimilation, or as it was called at that time, amalgamation, fostered exaggerated expectations of a Utopian character. Now when I speak of a "German-Jewish" utopia, I mean one conceived by Jews of Germany and Germans themselves. On both sides, those who favored the integration of Jews into German society envisaged it happening to a degree that could never have materialized. Thus, mutual disappointment, as well as criticism and even discrimination, was the natural result.

II

Let us first determine the areas of life to which the expectations of integration pertained. First, there was the sphere of legal rights and obligations connected with citizenship. Second, there was the prediction of a new occupational distribution. Third, there was the hope for an uninhibited and unqualified access of the minority to the society of the majority.

All these points were clearly conceived of by the two greatest promulgators of the hoped-for change: Christian Wilhelm Dohm on the non-Jewish side and Moses Mendelssohn on the Jewish. Both Dohm and Mendelssohn denied being reformers; their disclaimer was justified if we take "reformer" to mean one who intends to implement his ideas by the forceful disruption of the prevailing conditions and traditions. Neither Dohm nor Mendelssohn would have supported such an insinuation; rather, they both relied on the beneficial effect of reason upon society and thought that they had already observed some results in their own lifetime. The ultimate result they conceived was a radical transformation of society; for they each accepted the tacit assumption that the entry of Jews into the society-at-large would presuppose changes in the structure of that society itself.

This combination of restraint and radicalism is especially manifest in Dohm's recommendation for the granting of civil rights to Jews. He wished to see Jews granted citizenship in their countries of residence where, hitherto, they had lived only as aliens with well-defined claims and obligations. Once they ceased to be aliens, they would attain an equal footing with all other citizens, for religion, according to Dohm, ought to play no part in establishing claims of a civil character. This was the ultimate expectation;

however, for the immediate future, Dohm did impose some restrictions. For instance, he would hesitate to grant a Jew the right to become a state officer. He arrived at this compromise of his theories because, for the time being, he was forced to accept the privileges of the established estates upon whose support he counted. But, relying upon the reforming force of reason, he believed that these privileges would eventually be willingly surrendered by their holders; and in Dohm's image of the future society, Jews were to be established as citizens with no curtailment of their rights whatsoever.

The general impression given by Dohm's book at the time of its appearance in 1781 was that of an overall recommendation of civil rights for Jews. It was regarded as such by Mendelssohn, who reflected Dohm's ideas in his own statement on the subject. At the end of his life, Mendelssohn made public what until then must have been a silent hope, the thought that Jews might be accepted as full citizens in their respective countries. Mendelssohn, however, even more than Dohm, clearly based his expectation on the assumption that a radical change in the structure of the state itself would come about. He unreservedly accepted the idea of the separation of church and state as first propounded by John Locke and others. Dohm's book, and some other events, were only indications for Mendelssohn that the time for the realization of this idea was approaching. Measured by the reality of that time (the 1780s), this amounted to no less than blindly putting one's faith in the rightness of an idea.

For just in this respect, developments in Germany took a different turn from that conceived of by these early thinkers. During the period of emancipation, separation of church and state was not accomplished anywhere. Where formal equality of Jews and Christians before the law was achieved, this meant rather to equate Jewish religion with Christian denominations. By granting Jews civil rights, the state also granted Jewish organizations a certain status, either as overall organizations for the Jewry of an entire country or at least for the Jews of an individual community.

Strangely enough, this incongruity between the original ideas and their actual implementation was overlooked, or perhaps even covered up by later promoters of emancipation, who continually regarded themselves as implementers of the original ideas, when in fact they changed the terms very substantially. Gabriel Riesser, the great fighter for emancipation in the 1830s and 1840s, did not base his demands on the principle of church-state separation. Already in his first pamphlet, with which he made a public appearance, Riesser recorded with great satisfaction the announced intention of the French Parliament to pay the salaries of rabbis as it did those of Christian clergymen. The ideal had become the equality of church and synagogue, not the separation of church and state. In this sense, Bruno Bauer's criticism of Jewish aspirations was not without some justification. He indicted the Jews for not demanding rights themselves on the grounds of purifying the state from any connection with religion—in Bauer's mind, the only valid basis for such a demand.

We may conclude that the aspiration for political emancipation had definite utopian elements. It was utopian for Dohm and Mendelssohn to suppose that the separation of church and state could be achieved through the effects of reason on a society in which the rights of the church were so deeply ingrained. Even more utopian was Riesser's thought that in spite of having relinquished the idea of the separation of church and state, organized Jewish religion could attain the same status as the historically established churches. In fact, the representatives of the church in Germany had never given up their claim to superiority, and nothing was resented more than the Jews' daring to criticize the church or Christianity. Jewish religion continued to remain a pariah religion, and this could not but have affected the social status of its adherents.

III

The immediate practical objective of the legislation that was meant to change the Jews' status in the state was the granting of the formal rights of citizenship. But in terms of the social philosophy on the basis of which the change was conceptualized, the change was meant to include the Jewish role in economic life as well. It was in this field that, especially in Germany, a most radical shift was formulated and recommended. Originally, no doubt, Jews had been admitted to a country because of their usefulness in a business or financial capacity. When the idea of accepting them as citizens began to be propagated, their exclusive attachment to one occupation began to be regarded as an anomaly in need of rectification. This rectification was sometimes even taken as a *pre*condition for full acceptance as citizens.

Even before Dohm's recommendation, the idea of transferring Jews into manual work and agriculture had been proposed by some enlightened writers. In Dohm's own plan of reform, the shift from trade to other occupations was a major factor. The assumption that Jews would be capable and willing to take up other occupations derived from a belief in the essential oneness of human nature. The contrary assumption, that Jews took to trade because of a particular inborn bent in that direction, was discarded as presumptuous. Rather, the legislation that had imposed restrictions upon Jews in their choice of occupations was held accountable for their one-sidedness. Once the cause—the restrictions—was removed, the effect—one-sidedness—would likewise disappear. Dohm did not explicitly ask whether Jews would then take to *all* possible occupations, high or low; but the details he did consider imply a positive answer. He certainly assumed that Jews would become not only owners of estates and freeholders but agricultural laborers as well. The same would apply to handicrafts; Jews would be drawn into all these spheres of activity like other human beings. The existence of a possible inclination against certain occupations would, as mentioned, have been discarded on principle. And as for religion, Dohm maintained that in the long run religion would adapt to the needs of economic activity and would not impede occupational mobility.

Why, we may ask, was such a shift thought not only possible but so desirable? The answer is that the giving up of trade, especially the petty business of peddling, was regarded as a precondition for moral rehabilitation. That the bulk of Jews were morally defective, and even corrupt, was taken for granted; and this, once again, demanded an explanation. Here too, an indigenous Jewish inclination was discarded, as was—graciously—Jewish religion. Thus, the occupation to which Jews had long since been doomed was made responsible for their moral deterioration. We have here a combination of prejudices: against trade, which in Germany was not regarded as a very honorable occupation, and against Jews as a group. Trade was held to be unproductive and conducive to moral transgressions, and this prejudice clung naturally to the Jews, who, as a group, indulged exclusively in this morally dangerous occupation. For this reason, the shift to other fields of activity, and especially to handicrafts and agriculture, was regarded as the means to recovery and rehabilitation.

Mendelssohn did not share all these assumptions; being himself engaged in trade, he did not think it unproductive, and he spoke up even in favor of the peddler. Even this kind of trade, he maintained, is productive in that it provides the population with commodities and buys up superfluous products. But as for the moral danger involved in trade, particularly when exercised by Jews among non-Jews, he seems to have shared the misgivings of his contemporaries. He also accepted the historical explanation for Jewish one-sidedness as being the legal restrictions imposed upon Jews. Mendelssohn certainly desired an enlargement of the field of activity and expected it to come about with the removal of restrictions. In this context he formulated his famous epigram: "They bind our hands and then reproach us for not using them."

Thus, supported by the authority of both German and Jewish ideologists, each society tried to live up to expectations. The agencies of non-Jewish society were the individual governments, which, if they did not grant full civil rights in their respective countries, at least altered the regulations pertaining to the economic activities of their Jewish inhabitants. The legislation in the last decade of the eighteenth century and the first three decades of the nineteenth contained provisions whose declared object was to divert Jews from trade, particularly peddling, cattle-dealing, and the like. This aim was to be achieved either through outright prohibitions or through the offer of a reward—such as free choice of residence or even citizenship—to those who chose the desired activity, especially agriculture.

Among the economic experts and men of practical politics there were only a few who doubted the wisdom of the theory that the current vocations of the Jews were indeed harmful. The Bavarian economist Rudhart was one of the few; during the discussion in the Landtag of Württemberg in 1828 on the eve of the Emancipation Act, one member spoke against the intended amendments of the law which would divert Jews from their traditional occupations. These men maintained that the petty trader made use of many products which, economically, would otherwise be a dead loss. And if the peddler sold the peasant a commodity that the peasant could not otherwise find, it was all to the economic good; for it incited the peasant to increased productivity. These remarks, however, were in opposition to the generally accepted theory that such trade was morally suspect, since it led the buyer into wasteful spending and the seller into reprehensible business practices.

Traces of this theory are recognizable in the legislation of most German countries, with the notable exception of Prussia. There, the law of 1812 gave the Jew the unrestricted right to choose his own occupation, except for taking up state office.

The agencies in Jewish society that dealt with occupational redistribution were the Jewish communities or some voluntary organizations specifically established for the purpose. In some localities, as for instance in Baden, the communal organization, established on a state-wide basis, undertook to divert Jewish youth from the traditional occupations. The *Oberrat* trained young Jewish men in agriculture and tried to place them in apprenticeships. This was undertaken in most places by voluntary Jewish associations in cooperation with state authorities. From Alsace to Hungary there was no community of any standing that did not have such an institution. The members were recruited from the enlightened, who were the driving force behind the movement; the financial burden was carried by the well-to-do. The object of the activities of these societies was mainly the poor, who were incapable of supporting their children on their own and had hitherto relied on community support. The new trend was also facilitated by the new type of enlightened school, which accepted the idea of vocational preparation for the child, in contradistinction to the old type of education, which concerned itself only with introducing the child into the world of Jewish values. Finally, the new pulpit of the preaching rabbi contributed its share. It became the acknowledged duty of the modern rabbi to encourage parents to prepare their children for a useful occupation and to admonish children and adults alike to avoid reprehensible business practices.

From time to time the results that had been achieved were evaluated. Those who opposed any enlargement of the rights of Jews, beyond what had already been granted them, pointed to the example of those states where freedom of occupational choice had indeed been granted. The Jews of Prussia and Alsace, they claimed, had not used their new opportunities to any significant extent. On the other hand, Jewish spokesmen and their Christian supporters retorted that Jews had indeed turned to new fields of activity. One speaker in the Landtag of Baden in 1833, a non-Jewish professor by the name of Zell, gave on the basis of official sources the following details:

In our own country we have 570 master craftsmen, 341 trainees [*Gesellen*], 155 apprentices. . . . 206 Israelites occupy themselves as farmers on their own land, 22 are lessees and serfs, 26 belong to the learned class.

But all these together did not amount to more than twelve percent of the total Jewish population, and everyone agreed that the bulk of Jewry still adhered to trade of one kind or another. As a justification for that state of affairs, however, good arguments could be mustered. There were difficulties inherent in the situation, and there was resistance on the part of the non-Jewish population to the integration of Jews in the ranks of the respective crafts. About this many stories were told, running from physical resistance on the part of peasants to prevent Jews from occupying legally acquired land to more refined exclusions like refusing cooperation, rejecting Jewish apprentices, and so on. Some of the Jewish spokesmen also had an explanation for this resistance. Until Jews achieved full political emancipation, people would not regard them as equals. Once full political rights were granted, occupational distribution would follow. Still another reason put forward to explain the small number of Jews in the new occupations was the shortness of time allowed for the change to take place. Since these discussions had taken place in the 1830s and 1840s, only about one generation of Jews had enjoyed the changed circumstances. All these answers implied that equality before the law and sufficient time would entirely remove the Jewish concentration in a particular occupational field. The same expectation was implied in the accusations of the opponents who reproached the Jews for the slowness of the process. They certainly expected the Jews to adjust radically and sometimes said so explicitly. Karl Streckfuss, a high official in the Prussian government, discussed the problem in 1833 and arrived at the following conclusion:

There is only one expedient to remove this nuisance, namely not to give permission from now on to any Jew to trade, until out of the total number of their coreligionists the number of individuals in other crafts, services, and labors will be in the same proportion to those Jews still in trade as exists among other groups in the nation in which they wish to be accepted.

Although not too many would have agreed to the implementation of such a step, the underlying utopian expectation was shared by many, Jews and non-Jews alike.

I have found virtually no one among the Jews who dared to question the possibility, not to say the desirability, of such an occupational dispersion. The historian Jost, who also wrote on contemporary problems, observed once that setting Jewish peasants among non-Jews would involve such difficulties as impediments to Jewish education and the preservation of religious institutions and religious identity. The remark was made in a controversy with Streckfuss. Ten years later, a Christian observer, I.G. Hoffmann—an economist and statistician—analyzed the problem thoroughly. Hoffmann dismissed the old jibes about the Jewish incapacity for hard work. Interestingly enough, he did not resort to the newly available examples of Jewish craftsmen and peasants to prove his contention, but pointed rather to the physical endurance of Jewish peddlers. Such men, he observed, carried a load on their shoulders six days a week, eating only the very meager kosher food that they were able to carry with them. Why, then, did Jews persist in their traditional occupations even when the legal opportunity to change had been presented to them? But legal possibility is not the same as sociological probability. Hoffmann developed the thesis that, as long as Jews stayed together as a religious group, they would also be conspicuously concentrated in certain areas of economic activity. This theory was not the same as the old contention that such Jewish observances as the Sabbath and dietary law prevented Jews from entering other occupations; rather, Hoffmann maintained that the Jewish religion kept Jews together as a social group. Hence, neither were they themselves willing to take up occupations that would connect them too intimately with non-Jews, nor in many cases were they accepted if indeed they were so willing. Even the non-eligibility of the Jew for intermarriage would exclude him as an equal competitor for jobs connected with private households, where business contact was the accepted channel for creating family bonds. There was, too, the additional obstacle that, because of his religious observances, the Jew's free time for companionship with others was necessarily restricted.

Thus, according to Hoffmann, religious coherence led to social exclusion and self-separation, which in turn led to a comparative concentration in one economic sector. In his analysis, Hoffmann came very close to a modern sociological analysis and recognized that a radical dispersion throughout the social and economic spheres was an unattainable utopian desire. Hoffmann's detached analysis, however, did not destroy the idea of such a utopia in the public mind; and Jews and non-Jews continued to measure Jewish economic existence by that idea. Jewish occupational concentration remained a source of self-reproach for Jews, and for non-Jews a source of resentment.

IV

The difficulties in economic dispersion were interconnected with the difficulties in social integration. But here too the difficulties were disregarded by commitment to a utopian ideal that envisioned the full social absorption of Jews into non-Jewish society. Once again, Mendelssohn was the source of this utopian ideal, and he contributed to it both by his personal example and his philosophy.

The free contact which Mendelssohn enjoyed with members of enlightened non-Jewish society became the example to be followed. In point of fact, Mendelssohn's integration into Berlin society was not as complete as his biographers would have us believe. His meetings with non-Jewish friends took place either in his own home or in those of some of his intimate friends. But much of the social life in Berlin was being carried on at that time in formal circles, and Mendelssohn was not a member in most of these, either because he did not wish to belong to them or because he realized he would be incongruous in their midst. Not all enlightened persons found it possible to come into contact with him either. Spalding, for instance, declined to do so, saying that Mendelssohn ought to be baptized. But Spalding was an exception; most people in Berlin, and especially visitors from abroad, regarded it as a point of honor to see the famous philosopher. They were well received, and Mendelssohn's home became a meeting place of the enlightened.

At any rate, the positive features in Mendelssohn's relations with non-Jews were far more impressive than any mutual reservations. The free social intercourse, therefore, was remembered much more clearly than the hesitations. Mendelssohn's connections with his friends—a personal achievement under the very specific conditions of Berlin at that time—was taken as a breach in the walls of social segregation through which anyone else could follow. Mendelssohn himself sometimes endowed his personal experience with a general significance, stating that common humanity binds more than Jewish-Christian differences separate. This was no doubt the feeling of those like him who shared a friendship or spiritual companionship with non-Jews in any of the newly formed social settings. The most famous of these settings were the salons of Berlin and Vienna, which are too well known to be described here. But one remark is called for in a general evaluation of this phenomenon. The salons were attended by persons of every status: intellectuals, aristocrats, officials, and diplomats. But they functioned exclusively in Jewish houses; this seems to indicate a greater achievement in social emancipation than was in fact the case. For those who attended, these meetings might well have done so only as a sort of deviation from their regular social path. The salons did not necessarily establish lifelong connections or a reciprocity between units of the two societies. Mutual visiting between families of the two communities would have been a less conspicuous, but socially far more significant gesture.

The meetings of Jews and non-Jews under these special circumstances certainly did not mean a removal of social barriers between the two societies. They were, however, responsible for stimulating the idea of social integration in the minds of many. And as these social openings were followed by changes in the field of legislation, it seemed that times and conditions were indeed radically changing. The idea arose that integration would have no limits; the belief was similar to the one of a limitless occupational dispersion. On the occasion of the so-called first emancipation of Prussia in 1812, David Friedländer, who was instrumental in bringing about this political achievement, enjoined upon his fellow Jews the duty of adapting themselves to the demands of the new situation. First and foremost, schools and synagogues would have to be reformed and made appropriate to serve the newly-born free citizen of the state. And Friedländer's program also included the social aspect; here is what he puts in the mouth of a Jewish householder who has become conscious of his new obligations:

> I am a Prussian citizen. I have sworn solemnly to promote and support the weal of my Fatherland. Both duty and gratitude demand that I achieve this with all my might. First of all, I must endeavor to join with my fellow citizens, to approach them in custom and habit, to enter with them into social and personal connections; for the bonds of sociability and love bind more closely and strongly than the law itself. And only through these bonds can I achieve the aim of living with my fellow citizens in harmony, peace, and friendship.

That was the program for the new-born Jewish citizen of Prussia, and it assumed as self-understood that the endeavor by the Jews would be fully requited.

Friedländer seems to have regarded Jewish exclusiveness, as evidenced by Jewish ritual, dietary laws, and the like, to be the main obstacle in the way of fraternization between Jews and non-Jews. The wish to be accepted in non-Jewish society became a mighty social reason for abandoning Jewish observances. In some cases, as in that of Friedländer, it was done in full consciousness of the connection between means and ends. And as the aim was conceived of not only as a fulfillment of personal aspiration but also as a desirable objective for the benefit of society as a whole, the relinquishing of Jewish ways of life was given an ideological justification too.

We are capable of following the channels through which acceptance in non-Jewish society was sought. The least binding association was to be found in attending public performances of drama and opera. This was not an entirely new practice in Germany, and certainly not in Italy or England. From the middle of the eighteenth century we hear rabbis preaching against such goings-on (though the occasions may have been exceptional). But from the 1770s on, such attendance became the order of the day in Berlin and later in Königsberg, Breslau, and so forth. Some young Jews also attended church in a clandestine fashion to hear famous Protestant preachers of the time.

Now such attendance presupposes a certain capacity for mentally participating in the performances. We must regard it as an indication of a partial identification with non-Jewish society. On the part of non-Jewish society, it must be seen as a sign of comparative tolerance.

A greater intimacy was to be seen in the case of Jews frequenting coffee houses, beer-halls, and the like, which they did not always do unmolested. We know from the life story of Solomon Maimon that he was abused when attending such a place in Berlin. In 1797, the owner of a coffee house in Hamburg announced, under public pressure, that his establishment would henceforth be closed to Jews.

With the approach of legal emancipation, aspirations began to run even higher. Social life in Germany was very much concentrated in various societies, open or semiclandestine. These societies now became the channels for social climbing and, for Jews, the coveted aim of social aspiration. In some, indeed, they were accepted; but the rule seems to have been rejection, either through the secret ballot of the members or by a specific bylaw of the society. We hear about this state of affairs once again from Streckfuss in 1833. He used the fact as a proof that Jews were not acceptable in society and therefore that granting them full political equality would run against general opinion. His Jewish opponents, among them Jost and Creizenach, rejected this conclusion but did not repudiate the fact. We have reason to assume that the explicit exclusion of Jews from such formal societies began in the period of the first emancipation, in the first decade of the nineteenth century, precisely when Jews thought they had good reason for being generally accepted.

Two special cases must be mentioned where Jewish eligibility was openly discussed and decided upon. These were the *Burschenschaften* and the Freemasons. The first was a typical German creation from the period of national resurgence. Its purpose was to give German university students a framework for self-education and self-expression. As in the whole German national movement, liberal and nationalist tendencies were here blended together too. No wonder the admittance of Jews was resented by those who regarded the *Burschenschaft* as a means of fostering specifically German historical values. The liberals were in a minority, and when the central organ of the society decided in 1818 on the question of admitting Jews, the most it could achieve was a compromise. It was left to the local chapters of the society to decide for or against the move. But the constitution of the same year went further; it excluded Jews entirely. This decision was not repealed until the 1830s, when the original freedom of each local chapter to decide for itself was restored.

The case of the Freemasons was more complicated. The Freemasons was a creation of the eighteenth century. Coming from England, the association played its greatest role in France and Germany during the transition from the society of estates to one of voluntary associations between free individuals. Naturally, the Freemasons also became a possible channel for Jews to aspire to Gentile society. In England, France, and Holland, some Jews had been accepted, by the second half of the eighteenth century. In Germany, though not too many could have applied, Jews were in fact excluded, either by a clause in the constitution which explicitly posited Christianity as a prerequisite for admittance, or by the ritual and wording of the oath with its Christian content. Nevertheless, some adventurous Jews did find their way into these societies, either as full-fledged Jews or by being baptized. At that time, the societies were particularly receptive to all sorts of exotic and esoteric teachings and the doubtful personalities who espoused them. One of the branches of the Freemasons, the Asiatic

Brethren, was cofounded in 1782 by a Jew, as has been detected with great ingenuity by Gershom Scholem. I am convinced that the Jew, Dobruschka by name, established the chapter with the clear intention of presenting the opportunity for Jews and non-Jews to meet socially.

The general tendency of the more respectable branches of the Freemasons was not to accept Jews. The cases of admission that did happen were exceptions. A change came about only during the French occupation, in Kassel for instance, where mixed lodges were established with 60 percent Germans, 30 percent French, and 10 percent Jews. In Frankfurt in 1809, also under French occupation, a lodge was founded which was generally regarded as a Jewish lodge, with the name *Aurore Naissante*, though some Christians had also joined it. The establishment of a Jewish lodge, we may assume, was only a makeshift, as Jews found that access to other lodges was barred. This was the time of the rush out of the ghetto; the Jews misunderstood the signs of the times and chose to believe in an unrestrained access to non-Jewish society. Their aspiration was certainly not to have separate societies, but to be accepted into the others. But the onrush to the lodges had the reverse effect, and one branch of the Freemasons, the so-called "eclectic lodges," now deliberately introduced a Christian ritual in order to keep Jews out. About the same time, in Berlin, the *Nationale Mutterloge zu den drei Kugeln* changed its hitherto indirect exclusion of Jews into an outright one. This might have been the result of an attempt by Jews to get into Christian lodges by complying with the Christian-oriented rituals. Indeed we find Jews in Frankfurt some years later being accused of doing so.

Ineligible for Christian lodges, Jews tried to form their own. This was only partly dictated by the need to have a social meeting place, if not with Christians, then at least in a parallel fashion. Indirectly, it could also open the doors of the Christian lodges. For it was an old rule of the Freemasons that a member of a duly accredited lodge had access to the activities of any other, as a visitor. The Jewish issue was therefore discussed in this double aspect: first, ought Jews be accepted at all, and then, if not, could they be admitted as visitors if they were members of another lodge?

The whole problem assumed a new facet in the nineteenth century. For the time of the adventurers had passed, the lodges had become the depository of respectable burghers, and membership carried with it a certain prestige value. The lodges were now locally oriented, and Jews now tried to get into the local respectable society of non-Jews. The decision on admittance, however, could not be made locally, for every lodge was affiliated with some central authority from which it received its legitimacy. We know of a case in which a local lodge in Cologne accepted a Jew in the 1840s; and since this was against the rules of the parent lodge, the chapter was duly disenfranchised.

The question of admitting Jews to lodges became a very complicated issue. The whole tendency of the Freemasons was to eschew religious differences. The Freemasons partly owed their existence to the loss of the church's influence and the need to find a suitable substitute. But on the other hand, the attachment to Christian ethics was stressed, and some symbols of Christian origin were retained, as mentioned above. Thus, the exclusion of Jews was almost automatic, unless some changes were to be made in the formulation of aims and the practice of ritual. Most of the lodges were reluctant to make these changes.

On the Jewish side, the desirability of being accepted as a Freemason was especially great. As I have said, an air of respectability accrued along with membership, which was semiclandestine. The Jew who was accepted had the best of both worlds: he did not have to sever any of his Jewish ties, and at the same time he was accepted by the outside world. It was difficult for the lodges to justify the policy of rejecting Jews, as this was admittedly against their basic principles, humanity and morality being the only criteria for acceptance.

The controversy over this issue went on for the better part of the nineteenth century; and in the era of liberalism, more and more lodges decided to open their doors to Jews. In 1838, the Frankfurt lodge, which had decided to exclude Jews during the Napoleonic time, appointed Philip Jacob Cretzschmar, one of its high officials, to inquire into the matter and present a recommendation. Cretzschmar came to the conclusion that the exclusion had been dictated at that time by special circumstances and should now be repealed. The Bayreuth lodge decided to admit Jews in 1847, and at an earlier date to receive them as visitors. The *Mutterloge* of Berlin, which commanded the loyalty of a great number of lodges, kept strictly to the exclusion policy, but the question of admitting Jewish visitors was repeatedly discussed. Local lodges were asked to vote on the question, and it is to be observed that objections gradually declined until the 1880s, when a new anti-Semitic wave radically turned the tide once again.

I offer this data by way of example only; the field has not yet received its share of historical attention. But these examples seem to me quite representative. We may say that from the 1830s on, a gradual integration process took place. However, from the standpoint of Jewish aspirations, the achievements were certainly not satisfactory. For the long resistance showed that the desired social equality was far from being taken for granted. It was bad enough that Jews were excluded from clubs and private meetings. But that their right of admittance was doubted where the idea of common humanity ruled supreme, demonstrated that they were indeed still considered a special case. As a contemporary remarked upon the appearance of Cretzschmar's recommendations:

> The barbarity in the world of the Freemasons is much more sinful than that of the profane societies in casinos and the like, where people begrudge even the most educated Jew the happiness of one sociable hour which he wishes

to spend with his neighbors. . . . It is apt to impose upon this whole noble institution the stamp of intolerance, whereas its very being is imbued with love and tolerance.

Indeed, the case of the Freemasons is compelling proof that the idea of total emancipation was only an unattainable utopia.

Emancipation and Jewish Studies

I

6

Modern Jewish experience, to be fully understood, must be viewed under the aspect of emancipation, that process, starting in the late eighteenth century, whereby the Jews of Western and Central Europe achieved civic and social rights, thus paving the way for their entry into the larger society. The ramifications of emancipation are, of course, exceedingly widespread, not to say complex. In order to keep the present discussion within manageable limits, I shall restrict myself to some historical observations, with ultimate reference to the relationship between emancipation and the evolution of scholarly Jewish research. In this I take my cue from Leopold (Yom Tov Lippmann) Zunz, the founder of *Wissenschaft des Judentums*—the scientific inquiry into Jewish history, literature, and religion that developed in Europe in the nineteenth century—who remarked that the political emancipation of the Jews would be attained only when the study of Judaism was similarly emancipated, that is, established within the academy.

Zunz, in turn, might very well have taken his cue from two intellectual events whose occurence, a scant two decades apart, cannot have been altogether a coincidence. I refer to the publication, in 1663 and 1689, respectively, of Spinoza's *Tractatus theologico-politicus*, which ushers in the beginning of modern biblical criticism (and hence of modern Jewish scholarly investigation) and John Locke's *First Letter Concerning Toleration*, which, for the first time ever, talks of a secular state that would include Jews as citizens. Although Jewish emancipation had to wait one hundred years before it was transformed from a glimmer of thought into a political program, and although *Wissenschaft des Judentums* did not emerge until the second decade of the nineteenth century, certainly what had been initiated by the two seventeenth-century philosophers can be seen as an anticipation of future developments.

The inclusion of Jews as citizens of their respective lands could be contemplated, as Locke suggested, only in accordance with the notion of a secular state. As long as the state was conceived as subordinate to the Christian church, or to a Christian system of values, there could be no thought of granting Jews citizenship. Prior to the secularization of the European polity, Jews were accepted as residents, tolerated (with varying degrees of benignity), and even, in some instances (Holland for example), treated with generosity. Their fundamental status, however, remained that of aliens; according to the definition of a mid-eighteenth-century German scholar of law, Jews were to be considered as being *in civitate*, resident in the state, but not *de civitate*, of it. Similar formulations persisted until well into the nineteenth century, when they were taken up by opponents of Jewish emancipation in the British Parliament. In some instances—the majority of the Swiss cantons, England up to the time of Cromwell, certain districts in otherwise beneficent Holland—Jews were excluded altogether. But even in places where Jews were permitted to reside, they lived under the constant threat of expulsion. Thus, for example, Jews were driven from Vienna in 1670, and from Prague in 1745.

It can be said that homelessness—and of a unique kind—was the basic condition of Jewish existence prior to emancipation. For unlike the Gypsies, say, whose vagrant life was accepted by the host societies as a sociological fact, Jewish homelessness was considered by Christians and Jews alike as having a theological dimension. The Jews, as their prayers testified, ascribed their plight to divine punishment for past sins; their exile would last until God willed otherwise. Christians, on the other hand, regarded the exile of the Jews as the result of the latter's rejection of Jesus; only through conversion to Christianity could that guilt be expiated and Jewish homelessness brought to an end. Emancipation changed all this and brought an unexpected turn in the fate of the Jews: they had not converted to Christianity, nor, from their own point of view, had they become worthy of deliverance, and yet they were redeemed from homelessness. Henceforth, following the promulgation of the various edicts of state designated by the term "emancipation," Jewish residency was recognized as lawful, no longer subject to expulsion at the whim of the sovereign power.

The first association that the term "emancipation" usually evokes is that of equal rights. In actuality, however, the granting of political and social equality belongs to a later phase of the process. In its initial stage, emancipation concerned itself merely with recognizing the right of Jewish residency. Such recognition was first accorded the Jews of the Austrian Empire, in 1781–82, by Emperor Joseph II, within the framework of reforms known as the *Toleranzpatent*. The Emperor's decrees fell short of granting Jews equal rights with the rest of the population, and indeed grave professional and personal restrictions remained in force; for example, Jews were not free to change residence or to marry without permission. Nevertheless, the imperial edict was hailed by Jewish notables of the day, by Moses Mendelssohn in Berlin as well as by the renowned Chief Rabbi of Prague, Yehezkel Landau, who in a sermon declared, "The Emperor has removed the stigma of serfdom from us." The fact that the Emperor had remembered the Jews in his general legislation was interpreted as an implicit recognition of their legal incorporation into the Austrian state; the Jews were on the way to becoming *de civitate*, so to speak. This alone was sufficient cause for Jewish celebration.

II

The Hapsburg edict, as seen in retrospect, marks an important turning point in the history of European Jewry. Similar legislation soon followed in other countries, not so much in consequence of the Austrian example but rather as an effect of the same political and social developments that prompted the Emperor's action. These can be subsumed under the rubric of enlightened absolutism, and as represented by Joseph II and the rulers of the petty German states, the particular system, while it did not bring about the complete detachment of state from church, was still greatly instrumental in advancing the progress of secularization. Political decisions, under the enlightened monarchs, were largely motivated by utilitarian principles—which worked to the advantage of Jewish emancipation, for the Jews were regarded as a useful element in society. Altogether the state, in such instances, considered itself as a kind of educational institution whose task it was, through wise legislation, to bring benefits to the various national groups under its jurisdiction and make possible their contribution to the common weal. Thus it was that Jews living in the enlightened German states at the end of the eighteenth and the beginning of the nineteenth centuries, although they had not become citizens enjoying full rights, had at least acquired the right to a home and a secure residence.

The changes were of a more radical nature in those countries where Jews were accorded their new status not as a result of special reforms but in the course of civil revolutions. When the French Revolution proclaimed liberty, equality, and fraternity for all Frenchmen, the Jews, who did not count as such, were not included in the bounty. On the other hand, they could not be left in their old condition as non-citizens. The question therefore arose as to whether to expel the Jews from the country or to grant them citizenship. The latter solution was ultimately adopted by a decision of the National Assembly (1790–91) and this legislation set an example for all the regions that subsequently came under French sway during the Revolution and the later Napoleonic conquests—the Rhineland, Holland, Westphalia, northern Italy, etc.—where the Jews achieved not merely citizenship, but also equal civil rights. Prussia, which had wrestled with the Jewish problem ever since the death of Frederick II in 1786, remained an exception: only in the course of the Hardenberg Reform (1812), which aimed at a complete reorganization of the internal structure of the state, did Jews become full citizens, and then with the reservation that they could not occupy government positions.

These gains, it should be noted, were not achieved without opposition. The issue of granting citizenship to the Jewish population was a matter of vigorous dispute, in legislative bodies as well as in organs of public opinion; but at this stage of the developments, the contrary voices, if not entirely muted, were at least neutralized by the impetus of events. However, with the defeat of Napoleon the particular momentum was brought to a halt and attempts were made to undo the advances, an effort that was partly successful, especially in Germany, where Jewish citizenship was hardly ever revoked but the attendant privileges were often severely restricted. This is the situation that prevailed between the years 1815 and 1830, a period of stagnation and regression. Not until the emergence of liberalism did the struggle for Jewish rights resume, and only then, under the impulse of the new movement, did the term "emancipation" come to be applied to the Jewish cause. This happened in England, where the struggle of the Catholics for political equality, fought under the name of Catholic emancipation, had just come to an end. The term was now transferred to the equivalent Jewish struggle, then only beginning in England. The term "emancipation," if one is to retain strict historical accuracy, is thus to be limited to the struggle for equal *political* rights for Jews. In popular usage, of course, "emancipation" has come to include the whole process of Jewish assimilation into the larger society. This expansion of the concept is the product of a later generation.

At any rate, "emancipation" became the slogan of the liberal fighters for the Jewish cause, who argued that Jewish emancipation meant righting the political disabilities that had been imposed on a religious minority made to suffer because of its nonconformism. Their efforts witnessed steady results. Thus, in 1858, Lionel de Rothschild became the first Jew to hold a seat in the British Parliament. In Switzerland, emancipation was practically effected in 1866. The constitutions of the new national states in Italy and Germany contained paragraphs concerning the equality of all citizens. The same principle was accepted in Austro-Hungary in the course of the political reorganizations after the war against Prussia in 1866. By 1870, all the Jews in Western and Central Europe had become full-fledged citizens of their respective countries.

III

In order to comprehend the historical significance of this process, we must first try to understand what the conferring of citizenship meant to the Jews themselves as well as to the conferers. What happened can be summed up briefly as follows: the European states, in making citizens of the Jews, now incorporated into their societies a group of people who were strangers to them in religion, history, and culture, and who had been allowed to exist up to then only on the fringes of the polity. This was itself made possible by a prior "declaration" of the states to the effect that they were to be considered secular establishments, independent of religious institutions and value-systems. At the same time, the theological obstacles that had formerly substantiated the exclusion of the Jews were set aside.

Yet revolutionary as all this certainly was, formal acknowledgment of the changed Jewish status did not signify commensurate changes in actual attitudes toward the Jewish minority. Jews now had citizenship, but this fact (as also the theological revisions on which it was based) did not immediately serve to accomplish the incorporation of the Jews into the general society. When the states in question proclaimed their secularity, they did not thereby sever their connection with the church and the Christian faith. For a brief period, to be sure, during the heady first days of the French Revolution, church and state were declared separate, but by the time of Napoleon the breach had been healed and a *modus vivendi* worked out in the form of the concordat with Rome. This agreement defined the respective spheres of influence of both church and state and spelled out the roles each was to play, separately and together, in securing the loyalty of the citizenry to the state. Indeed, the modern states continued to employ religious symbols and terminology in their patriotic appeals. As the religious tradition upon which the states drew was invariably Christian, the Jews continued to remain outside the pale of the dominant civic ideology. Formal emancipation did not prove sufficient to alter the outsider status of the Jews or effect their social integration. A few organizations that had been closed to Jews before emancipation (such as some Masonic lodges) now opened their doors to them, but this was not generally the case and the Jewish situation for the most part remained as problematic as ever.

One does not have to search far for the reasons. The much-acclaimed secularization of the state, a development that was to have paved the way for Jewish entry into the general society, proved to be a highly ambiguous process. As already noted, secularization did not mark the elimination of Christian elements from European culture; on the contrary, Christian concepts and symbols often retained their original force and character even after having been appropriated for the secular purposes of art, literature, and political or social ideology. Thus the state, even though now nominally secular, continued to evince a Christian character, rendering the Jewish situation as precarious as before. Those who had hoped that, following the naturalization of the Jews, the gap between Jews and non-Jews would be completely bridged, had reason for anxiety. There seemed every danger of a permanent estrangement from the state and the society that the Jews had formally joined.

For many Christians this danger could be averted only by viewing the emancipation of the Jews not as the final phase of the process but rather as a first step toward their baptism, an act which would signal their full assimilation into the broader society. This was the case even at the time of Emperor Joseph II's *Toleranzpatent*, when Moses Mendelssohn was publicly admonished to draw the logical conclusion of his own teaching and convert to Christianity. It was also true in France, where Henri Grégoire, an Alsatian priest who was one of the most enthusiastic spokesmen for the Jewish cause in the National Assembly, derived his partiality toward Jewish emancipation from a chiliastic belief in the necessity of Jewish conversion as a prelude to the millennium. The most significant example in this regard was afforded by Wilhelm von Humboldt who, during the negotiations that led to the Prussian *Judenedikt* of 1812, headed the department for religious affairs of the Prussian administration and played an important role in the formulation of the new legislation.

Humboldt, who was rather well-versed in Jewish matters, did not share the general view of his contemporaries regarding the function of the state. According to him, the task of the state was not to provide for the good of the citizenry by the passage of suitable laws and edicts, but rather to create a framework within which the free play of forces would make possible the spontaneous evolution of humane attributes. With respect to the Jews, this meant that they be taken into the society without reservation and given full citizenship. Any failings on their part—such as their stubborn clinging to archaic customs, which Humboldt regarded as the chief Jewish shortcoming—would disappear in an atmosphere of political and social freedom. Humboldt believed that the Jews themselves would gradually come to recognize the superficiality of their ceremonial laws and would ultimately, and of their own accord, turn to the higher faith of Christianity. Humboldt did not have actual conversion in mind; but as a humanist whose philosophy was rooted in the Christian ethos, he believed that the Jews, too, could be led to humanism via the Christian path.

To be sure, not all Christians who took part in the cause of Jewish emancipation hoped for such a radical adaptation to the Christian environment, but even the moderate spokesmen had some expectations in this direction. They looked to emancipation to bring about a broadening of Jewish occupational patterns, as well as changes in what they regarded as questionable Jewish business ethics. Many were of the opinion that the anomalous status of the Jews could be reversed only by their total assimilation into the general life of the country. It was taken for granted that future Jewish generations would adopt the prevailing manners and culture, including language, of the countries they inhabited. The governments themselves had insured this by obliging Jews either to attend public schools or to establish their own modern educational institutions. Finally, there were hints, and in some cases even official measures, pressing Jews to reform their religion. At the same time, hand in hand with the endeavors designed to effect the Jews' cultural and social integration, there were indications that the Jews would be expected to loosen their ties with fellow

Jews abroad. The philosopher Johann Fichte, no great friend of the Jews, spoke of "a mighty [Jewish] state spread over all European countries," a kind of international union linked by a series of business associations, family ties, and mutual demonstrations of solidarity. The states embarking on emancipation were prepared to absorb those Jews living within their own borders; they were not prepared to acknowledge the existence of a trans-national Jewry with a commonality of interests other than religion. It was expected of the Jews that henceforth their highest loyalty would be to the states that had granted them citizenship.

IV

And what of the Jews? Were they willing to pay the price demanded of them by emancipation? Franz Rosenzweig once noted that the tacit expectation of emancipators like Humboldt, who regarded a Jewish movement to Christian humanism as inevitable, was opposed by the equally tacit steadfastness of men like Moses Mendelssohn, Abraham Geiger, Gabriel Riesser, and Leopold Zunz, who, in spite of their eagerness for emancipation, never for one moment considered surrendering their Judaism. On the other hand, Jews readily accepted the other conditions posed by emancipation. They did so without fully realizing the consequences of their side of the bargain and without knowing whether they would be able to carry out the obligations they had taken upon themselves. Mendelssohn, the most prominent of the Jewish advocates of emancipation, strongly opposed the popular rationalist notion that Judaism and Christianity would eventually become one. However, beyond this Mendelssohn had no compunctions in urging enthusiastic Jewish entry into the life of society. He nurtured utopian ideals of a separation between church and state, even between society and religion. He expected that Jews and Christians would meet on the neutral ground of a secularist society where the differences in their religions need not constitute an obstacle. In this Mendelssohn was typical of his generation of Jews, recent escapees from the ghetto who believed, with an optimism made possible only by lack of experience, that they could comply with all the demands imposed on them and yet keep their Judaism intact.

If the final results of emancipation fell short of expectations, and Jews even many generations later continued to retain a strong sense of group consciousness and coherence transcending the national borders of their respective European states, this cannot be attributed to any lack of eagerness on their part for emancipation. Nor was it due to the strong opposition, in government and without, that emancipation continued to encounter at every turn. Nor did the cement of religion, as asserted by the official leadership, form the chief ingredient of Jewish cohesion and solidarity. More compelling than all these elements was the fact—the existential fact, as it were—of Jewish community, which, out of its own inner necessities and traditions, resisted the higher blandishments of emancipation. Quite simply, the fact of Jewishness derived from one's being born a Jew. This elementary circumstance sufficed to make one part of the Jewish group and to share in its fate. And so long as Jews wished to remain Jews—a tendency reinforced by the endurance of endogamous marriage—the future of the group was assured and the existence of the Jewish community, in social isolation from its neighbors, remained a fact.

Therein lay the problem. Jewish existence was a fact, a stubborn fact defying regnant ideology and philosophy. In an age of rationalist ascendancy, the old world of faith was collapsing and it was expected that Judaism, too, would share in the general disintegration. Indeed, the theme of the bankruptcy of Judaism found repeated echo among liberals of the Humboldt stripe, the advocates of complete Jewish assimilation. Humboldt's thesis calling for the conversion of the Jews to Christianity, not as an act of faith but as an earnest of their allegiance to the shared culture, was taken up by Theodor Mommsen in his polemics against Heinrich von Treitschke. Mommsen, while roundly condemning Treitschke's anti-Semitism, at the same time felt called upon to admonish culturally assimilated Jews for their failure to convert to Christianity. He reminded them that, in the process of merging with German culture, they had absorbed many essential Christian elements and that their formal conversion therefore would only confirm what they had already accepted in fact. But Mommsen was mistaken on this point. For while it was certainly true that emancipated Jews very often accepted Christian assumptions, even the most assimilated among them felt some vestigial attachment to Judaism. Hence their conversion, if not altogether an intellectual violation, would have constituted an emotional betrayal.

Indeed, on the question of Christianity there was a profound disparity between what assimilated Jews thought and what they actually felt. Assimilated Jews, as they moved more and more into the cultural mainstream, acquired a familiarity with the Christian tradition and may even have acknowledged its primacy, but they could never internalize Christian attitudes and values to the extent of those who were born into that tradition. On the other hand, their ties to Judaism lacked cognitive content, since the secular culture had not absorbed the Jewish tradition as it had the Christian. As a consequence, the Jewish minority neglected its own culture in favor of that of the Christian majority. Abetting the process was the fact of the historical rivalry between Christianity and Judaism. Christian doctrine had traditionally looked upon Judaism as an outmoded, inferior creed, and this theologically inspired prejudice, like so many others, lost no force in the age of growing secularization. Caught up in the rush of assimilation, the Jews themselves ran the risk of accepting the Christian evaluation of their own tradition.

That Judaism did not succumb entirely to the danger is due to the fact that not all Jews were affected in this fashion. For a great many, the disparagement of Jewish validity evoked an upsurge of Jewish self-assertion. Thus the emancipation of the Jews led not only to entry into general social and political life but also to spiritual reflection. The various new movements that sprang from this development, from Reform Judaism to neo-Orthodoxy, considered themselves to be movements of Jewish regeneration. In formulating their ideologies and programs, they harked back to past phases in the evolution of Judaism; their hope was to shape the future in accordance with the image of an idealized past. Thus it was that the study of the Jewish past, *Wissenschaft des Judentums*, became not only a scientific end in itself but a religious pursuit. The theologians enlisted scholarship for the purpose of reviving the Jewish spirit.

But this was to come later. In its original impulse, *Wissenschaft des Judentums* professed no connection with any national-religious purpose. The science of Judaism was formally defined as the historical-philological exploration of the Jewish heritage, from the Bible and the Talmud to medieval poetry, philosophy, Kabbalah, and including Jewish history. The methods of study were to be the same as those employed in all historical scholarship; appropriate aspects of Judaism would be made subject to the same rigorous investigation. However, the exploration of the past is never conducted in a vacuum; for all peoples, Jews and non-Jews alike, it is an exercise inevitably tied to contemporary social and spiritual trends and needs, and can be carried out as such without necessarily impairing its scientific character. Thus Zunz and his associates, the founders of the science of Judaism, could uphold the postulates of scientific methodology and yet assume that their exploration of Jewish traditional sources was no mere scholastic exercise. Scientific preoccupation with the whole of Jewish tradition, they believed, would serve to foster greater spiritual identification with the totality of Jewish culture, thought, and experience.

V

In aim and method, the science of Judaism resembled its general models. *Wissenschaft des Judentums* held that Jewish institutions and ideas evolved from the same laws as those of other societies and could therefore be approached through the standard disciplines. But while the full apparatus of great universities stood at the disposal of scholars probing the cultures of Europe, nothing similar was available for the exploration of Judaism. Equivalent Jewish studies were conducted either by scholars working in privacy or under the auspices of certain rabbinical seminaries, a fact that placed grave limitations on both the quality and the quantity of the research. Zunz and his associates sought to secure the legitimation of the new Jewish science by having it accepted in the academy, but their efforts met with little or no understanding and their attempt to establish a chair of Judaica at one of the German universities came to nought. Zunz could not fail to recognize the significance of the dismissal: as long as the study of Judaism was not yet on a par with general studies, Jewish emancipation would remain incomplete.

Zunz's conclusion has to a large extent been borne out by subsequent historical experience. The Jewish bid for political equality was to find its most daring expression in Zionism, pointedly defined as *auto*-emancipation by Leon (Yehuda Leib) Pinsker, one of the founding fathers of the Jewish nationalist movement. Characteristically enough, the return to Zion was accompanied by a Jewish cultural renaissance, which found expression not only in the revival of the Hebrew language and in an upsurge of creative activity, but also in the intensive cultivation of Jewish studies. The establishment of the Hebrew University, already contemplated in the initial stages of the national movement, was strongly motivated by the desire for a free academic institution that might engage in the exploration of the Jewish past without let or hindrance. The founders of the university no doubt also hoped that scholarly inquiry into the nature of Judaism, in addition to being a desirable end in itself, would yield a further benefit. As the heirs of Zunz, they too were of the notion that the proper presentation of Jewish history and culture might serve as a basis for greater national identification.

This is not the place to detail the accomplishments of the Hebrew University with respect to Jewish studies, but it would hardly be far-fetched to say that in this instance national emancipation proceeded hand in hand with academic emancipation. A similar flourishing, moreover, has taken place in the Diaspora. Departments of Jewish studies are now an established part of many universities around the world, especially in the United States, where there are several hundred chairs in Jewish history and philosophy alone. Most of the scholars working in the field of Judaica, Jews and non-Jews alike, belong to the World Union of Jewish Studies.

This quantitative expansion raises the question of the quality of the achievement. In other words, is the work being done by Jewish historians, for example, on a level with that of general historians? It is a question that has a social as well as a scholastic dimension, for the emancipation implied in the acceptance by the academy of Jewish studies is genuine and meaningful only insofar as it is grounded in authentic scholarship. In cases where departments and courses in Jewish studies have come into being for non-academic reasons—for instance, to accommodate the sensibilities of local Jewish communities—that acceptance, and the larger, social acceptance it implies, may well be fictitious, and this in the long run can be worse than not being accepted at all.

Although there are many Jewish scholars of international reputation who can hold their own in any company, the average practitioner of Jewish studies still has special hurdles to overcome, especially as one approaches higher historical analysis and presentation. Here the inhibitions of traditionalism, on the one hand, and a tendency toward apologetics, on the other, can function as deterrents to scholarly objectivity. The minority status that for so long was the lot of Jews has left its mark. It shows itself most notably in the defensiveness that continues to haunt so much of contemporary Jewish activity, including scholarship. The emancipation of the Jews in modern times, even Jewish auto-emancipation in the independent state of Israel, has not liberated them from their minority complex. No matter what its causes and the multiform external factors that have contributed to it, this complex can be fully overcome only by self-analysis, by scholarship of the most exacting kind. It is one of the blessings of emancipation that such self-analysis can now proceed, although the paradoxical and ambiguous fact, essentially unchanged over two centuries of secularization and enlightenment, remains as it was in the beginning: emancipation does not grant automatic freedom, only the opportunity to become free.

PART
II

SELF-EMANCIPATION

The Jewish National Movement

A SOCIOLOGICAL ANALYSIS

I

It is safe to say that all the modern national movements emerged from the existence of a "Nation," that is to say a group that had inhabited a certain territory exclusively, even while other groups of the same ethnic origin might have existed dispersed among other nations. This ethnic group could be recognized by its language and by the attachment to certain traditional ways of life. Moreover, the keeping up of a tradition— even if only in the field of folklore—presupposes a certain degree of historical consciousness. Indeed, every ethnic group usually has an image of its historical past even if only expressed in some semimythological saga or popular heroic poem.[1]

This experience was common to all the generations that preceded nationalism proper. What did not happen in those prior stages and what can be considered the real turning point in the development of nationalism is that the attributes of any ethnic group, its association with its homeland, practice of certain customs and use of native language, became incumbent on its members, obliging them to uphold and further these national peculiarities without regard for their usefulness or even at the cost of great losses in other fields. This consideration is apt to provide us with the best definition of modern nationalism: it is the transforming of ethnical facts into ultimate values. While national attributes, such as attachment to one's birthplace, clinging to the mother tongue, and a certain preference for one's ethnic group members are universal phenomena, it is the elevation of these traits to supreme, perhaps even sole, values that

7

89

may be regarded as the distinctive characteristic of modern nationalism.

The origin and nature of the historical factors that brought about this turning point in human history cannot be fully discussed here. It certainly has something to do with the eclipse of other sets of values, primarily religious, and with the enervation of political forces in the age of the dynasties and the disintegration of the old estates.[2] Our aim here is to give an account of one of these national movements which seems to be at variance with the normal pattern of nationalism but which nevertheless any comprehensive sociological theory of nationalism must take into account.

II

The deviation of Jewish nationalism from the normal is apparent in its prenationalistic foundations.[3] Jewish society lacked two of the traits that characterized the prenationalistic phase of ethnic groups. Scattered across four continents, Jews had no territory of their own, nor did they possess a common language. Indeed while many nationalist movements strove and succeeded in raising a particular dialect to the level of a literary language and from this dominant position it exercised a unifying function, eighteenth-century Jewry was a Babel of tongues. Half spoke Yiddish, others Ladino, and yet others the language of their native countries.

In spite of these deficiencies, nobody would have doubted at the end of the eighteenth century that the Jews were an ethnic unit, separate from the local inhabitants in any place where they may have built a community. Similarly, the unity of these communities all over the world was also taken for granted. This state of affairs is explainable to a great extent by the religious distinctiveness of the Jews, for the adherence of the Jews to their ancient faith was the apparent reason for their political and social disabilities. Individuals who accepted the religion of their non-Jewish society changed by implication their political and social status. Nonetheless, the description of Jewish society as a purely religious unit is not complete. Belonging to the Jewish community was indeed dependent on the acceptance of the Jewish faith. But once an adherence to this faith was established, it entailed much more than mere religious affiliation. The tenets of the Jewish faith are embodied and enmeshed in an old and complicated tradition, which abounds in historical reminiscences as well as national aspirations with regard to the future. The destruction of the Temple in Jerusalem by Titus was referred to in the daily prayers and especially remembered at one season of the year that was dedicated to mourning for their lost glory, this mourning culminating in the day of fasting on the ninth of Av, the date of the actual destruction of the Temple. But even more frequent than the sad remembrances of things past were the prayers for the future redemption. The popular version of the messianic belief had it that the redemption would come about in a miraculous way; some even believed that it would possess spiritual or eschatological features, such as the renewal of prophecy or the resurrection of the dead. But even so, the political aspects of the deliverance were not lacking either. The expectation of redemption in Jewish thought has always been bound up with national fate.[4] Acceptance of or adherence to the Jewish faith entailed, therefore, at the same time, the consciousness of being a son of a nation, ill-fated in the present, divinely endowed in the past, and with splendid prospects for the future. While with respect to the first two factors of prenationalistic conditions in national movements, territory and language, the Jews were at a disadvantage in comparison with other ethnic groups, with regard to their historical consciousness they were indubitably in advance of them. Their historical awareness served, moreover, not only to compensate for their territorial deficiency, but even to correct it. For their memory of the land of their past served in a sense as a symbolic substitute for it.

As far as national consciousness is concerned, we may reasonably maintain that on the threshold of modern times the Jews were better prepared for a national movement than any other ethnic group in Europe. It is true that before the historical consciousness could become an ingredient of modern nationalism it first had to undergo certain transformations. The miraculous and eschatological elements had to be replaced by realistic concepts. But by the same token all nations had to undergo equally important changes in their mental attitude before they could be caught up by a national movement. Jewish society itself achieved this transformation with the appearance of modern Zionism. In it Jewish messianic belief was, so to speak, purged of its miraculous elements and retained only its political, social, and some of its spiritual objectives. But even in this phase of development, modern nationalism leaned heavily on the old messianism and derived from it much of its ideological and even more of its emotional appeal. Yet all this was accomplished, as is well known, only at the end of the nineteenth and the beginning of the twentieth century. Thus, in spite of having preceded other nations in possessing the potentialities of modern nationalism, the Jewish national movement lagged behind most of the European nations in its actual development.

The retardation of Jewish nationalism is easily explained by the fact that the Jewish nation, as we have noted, possessed the prenationalistic characteristics in a symbolic or token form only. In reality Jewish society was embodied into the structure of non-Jewish societies. Economically and politically it represented one section of non-Jewish society, albeit one of very special character and unusual standing. As mentioned above, the nationalism of other European peoples arose as a by-product of the disintegration of the estates on which the prenationalistic society of Europe was built. Disintegration meant a loosening of the bonds by which the individual was tied to his estate, his corporation and his church. But no such change had occurred in his belonging to an ethnic group. On the contrary, the displaced individuals continued to be kept together by their common attachment to their birthplace, their language, and their cultural tradition. The disintegration of the old social structure provided these national elements with the chance to become an important factor in the reintegration of the uprooted individuals.

But here the case of the Jews was quite different. The same factors that led to the disintegration of the other estates affected equally the position of the Jews. They, like all other individuals, were suddenly or gradually freed from bondage to legally defined estates. Instead they were to be regarded as independent citizens of their respective countries. The so-called emancipation of the Jews is only a special case of the rejection of the idea of the estates on which the old European society was founded.[5] But from the standpoint of the old Jewish society this had more far-reaching consequences than for any other estate. In the case of the Jews no chance of reintegration on the basis of the ethnic elements was to appear. Although we observed that national consciousness was conspicuously developed, the lack of concrete elements of national unity could not be easily made up for. The tokens and symbols that in the old days replaced these elements lost their power over the individuals who by the disintegration of Jewish society came into contact with the individuals of other estates. The second phase of the development that followed, the reintegration, did not bring the Jews back to their own national tradition but on the contrary led them into the society of those nations in the midst of which they dwelt. The process of assimilation, which affected the first generations who enjoyed civil emancipation, was strongly supported by the idea of nationalism. Overnight, Jews became French, German or Hungarian patriots. This assumption of nationalism was in the case of the Jews perhaps not so natural as with other parts of the population. But very often it was experienced even more consciously and was backed by a greater ideological assurance. The Jew who lacked the elements of autochthonous patriotism acquired his attachment to the new national movement more through the acceptance of its ideas than by the possession of its ethnic ingredients. And this led in turn to the discarding of his own national consciousness.[6] Thus the impact of modern nationalism on Jewish society, instead of producing a Jewish variation of the national movements, led to the integration of Jewish individuals into the movements of other nationalities.

Put differently, it is a commonplace that the nationalist movement is inconceivable without the Age of Enlightenment that preceded it. It was the corrosive power of rationalism that had undermined the ideological base of the old society as it pointed out the patent absurdity of founding and organizing a society along the principle of the segregation of estates of one and the same nation.[7] But as man cannot live by reason alone and logic seldom serves as communal cement, the societies that arose on the ruins of the old sought new symbols of reintegration, and found them in the elevation of ethnic elements into ultimate values. In the instance of

Jewish society this dialectical process was stopped halfway. The old, indeed, dissolved under rational scrutiny, but this left Jews not atomized among themselves but scattered in different Gentile societies, bereft of distinctive symbols, and at one with their neighbors in place of birth. Thus no corresponding reformation of Jewish society took place.

III

The old messianic idea did not disappear entirely under the impact of rationalism. The idea was alive in the Jewish masses. As late as 1840 there was a widespread rumor in the Balkans and in Eastern Europe that the messianic year had arrived which was destined to bring about the great turning point in Jewish history.[8] Many held this belief genuinely and were waiting in a state of mental agitation. For one of these believers, Rabbi Yehuda Alkalay (1798–1878), the messianic expectation of this year became a starting point for the transition from the traditional miraculous messianism to a realistic one. This change of conception was caused by the coincidence of the messianic expectation with the rescue of the Jewish community in Damascus, charged with ritual murder, by the two leading figures of French and English Jewry, Adolphe Crémieux and Moses Montefiore. As the miraculous events of the redemption failed to appear, Alkalay inferred that the rescue of this one community is a model for the messianic procedure. The further stages of redemption were supposed to be achieved through similar activities of outstanding Jews.

Alkalay was an undistinguished preacher of a little Sephardic community in Semlin near Belgrade.[9] Until the year of his newly found conviction he was hardly known nor did he wish to be known outside his limited circle. But after having convinced himself of the truth that the era of the Messiah had arrived and that the redemption would have to be achieved by human action, he felt himself compelled to convey this message to his fellow nationalists. Not only did Alkalay in the remaining thirty-seven years of his life publish numerous pamphlets and articles to spread his ideas, but also he traveled on two occasions to Western Europe and later settled in Palestine in order to convince Jews and non-Jews of the truth of his mission. He tried to induce people to implement the practical conclusion of his belief. This amounted indeed to an organized resettlement of Jewry, or some part of it, in their homeland, and their equipment with the attributes of a united modern nation. For although Alkalay started as a preacher imbued with the traditional and especially kabbalistic sources, he gradually acquired the elements of a fully-fledged national *Weltanschauung*. He propagated the idea of national unity. The instrument of unification was supposed to be an overall organization that should have included the whole of world Jewry. Alkalay conceived national unity to be based on a common language, which should be Hebrew after undergoing modernization. Religion, it was understood, would play its part in the new national life in Palestine. But as at that time the controversy between Orthodox and Reform Jews appeared likely to lead to a schism, Alkalay characteristically sought in the idea of national unity the remedy for this. Therein we may recognize the sign that nationalism was becoming with him the leading and all-embracing idea. If the designation *prophets* should indeed be found adequate to describe the men who strove to awaken the national consciousness in modern nations (as indicated in the title of the well-known book of Hans Kohn), Alkalay, who wrote in the language of the ancient prophets and often let himself be carried away by their pathos, should certainly have a place among them.

Alkalay does not stand alone as the originator of nationalism by linking it up with the old messianic belief. Z. H. Kalisher (1795–1874), a German rabbinic scholar of Polish origin, who refused to accept any position in communal life,[10] developed his ideas on similar lines. Imbued with Jewish tradition but keeping himself free from any communal engagement, he was free to contemplate the events that had befallen Jewish existence in his lifetime. The great experience of his youth was the emancipation of the Jews in France and in the German countries at the time of Napoleon. He explained these events not as a part of the general political and social processes in their respective countries, but exclusively in terms derived from Jewish tradition. The emancipation and even more the ascendance of Jewish individuals like, for instance, the Rothschilds, to unheard of economic and political influence appeared to him to be the fulfillment of the old prophecy of liberation, which according to Jewish tradition was to terminate the exile. It is true, this was not the whole fulfillment. For such a fulfillment entailed the ingathering of the Jews in their homeland. But neither could the social and political freedom that the Jews achieved in their respective countries be without significance. By interpreting events of emancipation in terms of messianism, Kalisher at the same time transformed these very terms. From the first stage of deliverance, which was brought about by human activity, he inferred the nature of the next stages. These next steps were also to be achieved by human agency. Out of this interpretation of the emancipation arose the demand for the ingathering of at least some part of Jewry in Palestine.

In order to appreciate these nationalist theories and place them in the correct historical perspective, one has to keep in mind the underlying motives of their promoters. These theories were derived from the reinterpretation of the old messianic tradition in the light of the new historic experiences. In view of later developments it is well to remember that modern anti-Semitism was not amongst these experiences. The activities of Alkalay and Kalisher took place during the flourishing period of Middle European liberalism, i.e., between 1840–1875, when optimism as to the possible integration of Jews into the life of European nations was almost universal. Certain obstacles that were sometimes put in the way of achieving full civil rights as well as certain signs of reservation in social rapprochement were interpreted as residues of waning prejudices. Alkalay and Kalisher were among the optimists. Until the seventies they never used the argument that Jews needed a country for securing their physical existence, which was to become one of the main planks of Zionism proper. To explain, therefore, early Jewish nationalism as a mental expression of material needs would mean only the transference of a preconceived theory to a special case. The data of the case itself do not bear out the truth of this theory.

The same can be stated about the motives of the third representative of early Jewish nationalism, the socialist Moses Hess (1812–1875). The nationalism of Hess is different from that of the two others in its terms of reference and the basic beliefs on which it was founded.

Hess was not an Orthodox Jew but a social revolutionist and philosopher with a Hegelian tinge.[11] His switching over to Jewish nationalism in the sixties can be understood as the result of both personal disillusionment and despair of the social revolution which was expected at an earlier date but which failed to materialize. But the psychological promptings of any social theory are of little concern in their historical evaluation. The relevant question to be asked is what reasons and arguments were put forward in support of the theory. Hess bases his Jewish nationalism on the concept of a "national spirit", which, in the ancient Jewish state, permeated the entire life of the Jewish people. Since the dispersion, the spirit was supposed to be embodied in the Jewish religious institutions. As these institutions were at that time rapidly disintegrating, the gradual disappearance of the Jewish national spirit was the most probable, and from the standpoint of a Jewish patriot the most lamentable, prospect. In order to rescue this spirit and give it the chance of revival, the only solution was the reconstruction of a fully-fledged national life in the ancient homeland. The argument of Hess is phrased in terms of social philosophy, while the resentment against the non-Jewish contemporary society, which had not fulfilled the expectation of treating the Jews as equals, provided the emotional climate. But any criticism of the political standing of Jewry that could have led to a diagnosis excluding emancipation as a possible solution to the Jewish problem is absent from the theory of Hess as it is absent from those of Alkalay and Kalisher. More obvious than in the case of Alkalay and Kalisher is the dependence of Hess's theory on the general trend of nationalism in Europe. The use of such terms as nationality, national renaissance, creative genius of the nation indicate the source of influence, i.e., Romanticism, which provided all the national movements with their respective ideological tools. Hess's book, *Rome and Jerusalem*, as its title also indicates, was written under the impact of the events that had led to the unification of Italy in 1859. Hess refers expressly to this fact, giving the Jewish cause the name "The Last National Problem," after Italy had solved its own.

But on this point there is no basic difference between Hess and his two nationalist contemporaries, Alkalay and Kalisher. It can easily be proved that they all received impulses of thought and promptings of feelings from non-Jewish sources. All three use one characteristic argument in their appeal to those who are nationally indifferent. Jews, who are the descendants of a holy and ancient nation, should not be behind the newly created nations of the Balkans.

The real difference between Alkalay and Kalisher on the one hand and Hess on the other is the spiritual background from which their respective nationalist drive stemmed. While the first two were originally steeped in the sources of Jewish tradition, including the Bible, Talmud, and Kabbalah, Hess had only a faint idea of all this. He acquired some knowledge of Jewish institutions and concepts from his contact with religious life in his childhood. But for precise information he had to rely on secondhand sources. In his knowledge of Jewish history and its evaluation he was strongly influenced by the historian Heinrich Graetz (1817–1891). Graetz can be fairly characterized as being intentionally liberal minded, but in actual presentation of facts he displayed a very strong national bias.[12] With Hess it was this last feature of Graetz's history that asserted its influence. The fabric of Hess's philosophical outlook was woven out of strands that were of modern European, primarily Hegelian, origin. He was far from being a religious Jew in any traditional sense, and, judged by his activities and writings until his national phase, he must be counted as one of those of Jewish race who were absorbed by European movements and systems of thought. That such a Jew should have rediscovered his own Jewish past and been able to erect upon Jewish tradition a new prospect for the future was a strange phenomenon.

Hess is the first figure of Jewish nationalism who did not grow directly out of Jewish tradition. His Jewishness came back to him after a period of estrangement.[13] Thus Hess and his two contemporaries Alkalay and Kalisher prefigure the two main types of Jewish nationalism: the one that had to overcome the unrealistic elements of traditional messianism; the other that, after having forsaken the tradition altogether, had to recover its cultural and political implications.

IV

That a change of heart such as Hess's was possible is related to the process of secularization that Jewish tradition had to undergo before it could be channeled toward nationalism. Even after having achieved, to a great extent, integration into the respective nations of their birth places, the Jews, as long as they were recognized as a distinct group, could not have denied their past. Except in the case of joining the alien religious community, the neglect of Jewish tradition was not tantamount to total negation of nor to complete indifference to one's Jewish origin and background. And insofar as they had any intention of reintegrating themselves as a religious minority in separate communities, it was incumbent upon them to take cognizance of the main ideas that clung to the name of a Jew. Messianism, a common concept of Jewish and Christian religion, was one of the ideas that Jews had to give an account of. For the interpretation of this concept was one of the dividing points between Judaism and Christianity. Christianity maintained that the Messiah had arrived in the person of Jesus. The Jews expected the advent of the Messiah in the future.

Indeed even the conception of Jewish liberalism did not forsake the old traditional messianic belief, but had only reinterpreted it.[14] First of all, it severed messianism from the idea of returning to the ancient homeland. Second, it detached it from the expectation of a personal redeemer. Instead, the liberal thinkers identified messianic belief with hope for a better future for mankind. Liberalism had conceived an era of political and religious freedom, and Jews had actually experienced a turn for the better in their destinies. The prevalence of tolerance and freedom on a worldwide scale was visualized for the future and this was equated with the Messianic Age. The similarity of this conception with that of Kalisher is striking. The liberals as well as the nationalist Kalisher started from the fact of the political and social liberation of the Jews in the Western European countries. Where they do differ fundamentally is in the following up of the consequences. Kalisher retained in his nationalist conception the idea of regathering the Jews in their homeland as the ultimate stage of messanism. But this could be achieved only by transcending the given political and social status of the Jews in the present. The liberals on the other hand used the messianic idea only to justify the political achievement which Jewry had reached or was to reach in the near future, i.e. the integration of the Jews into the life of their respective countries. These two contradictory conceptions growing out of the same tradition represent a striking example of the way differing intellectual matrices condition the adaptation of an identical idea. In modern sociological terms we may call the conception of liberalism an ideology and that of the nationalists an utopia in the sense defined by Karl Mannheim.[15] The messianic idea of liberalism had no other social function but to further the aims of the individuals in the community to which they wished to belong. Contrary to this, the nationalist conception could succeed only by the renouncing of prospects on the part of individuals who were in the sphere of possible achievement. It was a utopia, i.e., an image of the future, that people were called upon to strive for not for the satisfaction of their immediate needs but out of a belief that by doing so they would fulfill a preordained course of historical development.

Through the above statement about the utopian character of Jewish nationalism we seem to have arrived at the main feature that gives it a unique place among the national movements. Every national idea that served a national movement envisaged a prospective change in the political structure of the country concerned. Sometimes it aimed at the elimination of foreign rule and in any case at the taking over of government by other groups than those which were in power at the time when the movement started. The national movements were also tied up with social changes. Certain strata of the society that were connected with national movements hoped for better positions and brighter prospects. National movements found their supporters mainly in the strata that were on the move, so to speak, those who hoped to find satisfaction in a new order of things. Thus the national idea seems explainable in terms of class ideology, and indeed attempts at just such an interpretation have been often made. Even if future research should vindicate this theory, it has no right, yet, to be offered as a total explanation of nationalism, for the case of Jewish nationalism shows its inadequacy. Here the idea of nationalism emerged not as an ideology covering the interest of any distinct class but rather as a national utopia to be followed because of its being prefigured by traditional messianism.

By attributing the emergence of Jewish nationalism to the re-vitalization of the messianic utopia, we do not mean to say that the mere suggestion of regathering of the Jews in their homeland was instrumental in initiating the national movement. The idea was, indeed, repeatedly aired and propagated also in the pre-nationalistic era. The historical connection between the Jews and their ancient homeland being a conspicuous feature in Jewish as well as Christian tradition, the inference that Jews should return to it did not need much ingenuity. The idea of the restoration of the Jews gained currency especially in England, where the awakened interest in the Old Testament in the wake of the Puritan revolution strongly stimulated a concern with the concrete history of the Jewish nation.[16] Most of the adherents of Jewish restoration, it is true, connected the return of the Jews to Palestine with hopes for their conversion to Christianity. Some of them, however, separated the two ideas and presented the plan of the Jews' return to their fatherland as the realization of the Jewish national aspiration—the novel by George Eliot *Daniel Deronda* written 1874 being the best example of such an anticipation of modern Zionism grown out of the English restorational tradition.[17]

Among Jews too, imaginative writers and social projectors came forward again with the idea of establishing a Jewish commonwealth, either in Palestine or elsewhere, with the view of solving the Jewish problem. A case in point was the effort of Mordecai Manuel Noah, one-time consul of the United States in Tunis, who in 1825 issued an appeal to European Jewry to establish a Jewish state named "Ararat" on the Grand Island of the Niagara River.[18] Later Noah fostered the idea of the restoration in Palestine.

Historians of Zionism were very zealous to collect such early expressions of nationalism, conceiving them to be forerunners of Zionism.[19] In the original historical setting these utterances of a new approach to messianism were of no consequence. The propagators of these ideas had never succeeded in realizing any of their plans. No organizations or societies were set up for the propagation and advancement of their ideas. The general Jewish public took almost no cognizance of these ideas and their promoters, and if it did so, its attitude was expressed in mockery and derision. The suggestions and their originators were indeed very soon forgotten. They left no mark behind them and scarcely ever influenced the course of coming events. Their historical significance is in something else. In the case of the Christian promoters, it shows how deeply the name of the Jews and the land of Israel were associated also in the mind of Christians. Without this association the comparative success of Zionism, dependent as it was on the support or at least the understanding of the Gentile world, would have been inconceivable. In the case of the Jews the recurrent revival of the idea is a proof of the potency of modern nationalism, which was inherent in the messianic tradition.

Only the three figures mentioned above together with several contemporaries of theirs who were active from the sixties of the nineteenth century can be called forerunners of modern Zionism, meaning those who initiated and influenced the movement in a real historical sense. Alkalay, who began his activities twenty years earlier, did not succeed until the sixties in finding any substantial and lasting support. From this time on one can see a connection between the activities of the various nationalists. The three great figures whom we have described not only knew of each other but also supported each other mutually. They succeeded in founding a more or less interconnected society among themselves together with some other less conspicuous personalities who were influenced by them or who had reached the same conclusions independently. Moreover, from the sixties onward there is an uninterrupted development, and we may speak clearly of historical causation as we witness the ideas and activities of these early nationalists leading the way to the full-fledged national movement, which was founded in the 1880s under the impact of the Russian pogroms and the rise of modern anti-Semitism in Germany.

The difference between earlier times, when nationalist ideas were kindled only to be soon extinguished, and the sixties of the nineteenth century, when they were caught up in a strain of historical development, is not difficult to explain. The sixties represent the completion of emancipation in most Western European countries. Where it was not yet wholly accomplished, it was thought to be just around the corner. As long as the struggle for political equality was going on, the idea of a Jewish nationalism could not be tolerated. For the argument that the Jews are a national entity in itself was one of the main weapons of the enemies of emancipation. The Jewish answer to this was the declaration and indeed the manifestation of willingness to integrate themselves into the ranks of the other nations. The acceptance of an idea of nationalism on a new basis was apt to belie the validity of the Jewish answer. Small wonder that wherever the idea was suggested it met with an adverse response and it was disregarded or suppressed. From the sixties on, when the emancipation was as good as completed, the idea of nationalism could be propagated as the next phase. Sometimes, as in the case of Kalisher, this was suggested to be the natural continuation of the emancipation itself. The successes of the sixties brought about in this way the first success in the development of Jewish nationalism.

But what was the nature of this success? The colonization of Palestine started only in the eighties after the upheavals in Rumania and the bloody pogroms in Russia. There was an abortive attempt at colonization in 1879 by local Jews in Jerusalem who were strongly influenced by these fore-runners, especially Kalisher. The first agricultural school, Mikveh Yisrael near Jaffa, had been founded by 1870. But this was done by the Franco-Jewish organization Alliance Israélite, which was not prompted by any national ideology, although some of the forerunners tried to influence it in this direction. By and large one cannot say that the forerunners had succeeded in realizing much of their chief aim, i.e., the ingathering of Jews in their homeland.

The forerunners could have boasted of a success of a different kind, the uniting of the adherents of their idea through mutual contact. These first nationalists were widely scattered, but they succeeded in keeping some communication between themselves. The common idea became a basis of social unity.

From the standpoint of a relation between social needs and ideas the connection is apparently this: the need did not create the idea but the idea created the social unit. We were unable to detect a social need correspond-ing to the emergence of the messianic-nationalist ideologies. There was no problem of Jewish disability or social discrimination to be solved. These nationalists believed in the possibility of integration of Jews into the society of their respective countries. They certainly did not see any need for a place to emigrate to. Until the seventies, when the troubles in Rumania started, there had been no Jewish exodus from any country in Europe. The first nationalists, instead of producing an idea in order to satisfy a need, were looking for a need that would correspond to their ideas. Kalisher seized upon any rumors that reached him of Jews wishing to emigrate as a godsent opportunity to prove that people could be found who were ready to go to Palestine. In this way he tried to refute the argument that his idea had no hold on reality. He never descended to the level of pragmatism to prove the truth of his idea from its necessity and usefulness. If anywhere there was an idea that preceded its social utility, it was here.

V

As our case in point demonstrates that ideas at times do appear in advance of their need, it conversely shows the limited power of any idea as long as it is not linked up with a social necessity. We have noted above the failure of the first nationalists to achieve even a fraction of their ultimate aim, namely, the gathering of the Jews in their homeland. The reasons for this are quite obvious. The reestablishment of a Jewish commonwealth or even only the resettlement of the homeland demanded more than the creation of a movement similar to the movements that were flourishing among other nations. The achievement of the real aims entailed, in this case, uprooting people out of their surroundings and replanting them in another country under new conditions. The history of the Jewish national movement bears out the statement that this was beyond the strength of the national idea in itself. It could accomplish its task only when other forces were linked up with it. The first real objectives were realized only in the eighties when political and economic factors—persecutions and defamation in Rumania and bloody pogroms and civil disqualifications in Russia—set in motion a good many European Jews. The uprooting was now brought about by other factors and the idea of nationalism had only a secondary task, that of reintegration and resettlement in the right place. In this it succeeded, though not on a very large scale. Out of the two-and-a-half million people who emigrated from Rumania and Russia between the years 1880 and 1914 only some 70,000 settled in Palestine. In this relation between the possible and actual number of emigrants to Palestine we find a quantitative expression of the power of the national idea. It demonstrates its strength as well as its limitations. The emigrants who went to other countries instead of Palestine followed the line of economic and political pressure, though admittedly a few may have been drawn by the idea of a land of liberty where Jewish suffering would finally be ended. They settled wherever entry was granted and where conditions offered a chance of making a livelihood. No idea of collective purpose was attached to the emigration. With some notable exceptions at its initial stage, the whole process of emigration was accomplished by private initiative. Public agencies such as Jewish and non-Jewish philanthropic societies looked after emigrants only on a humanitarian basis or on that of Jewish solidarity. Those who went to Palestine, on the other hand, followed an ideal and were conscious both of their self-sacrifice for the common goal and of the historic role they were playing.

The historical task conceived by the pioneers was, it is true, no more the mere fulfillment of the messianic promise nor even its nationalistic derivation. During the last but decisive phase of the emigration before World War I, between 1904 and 1914, the so-called Second Aliyah arrived. This consisted mainly of former students, graduates of the Talmud academies (*yeshivot*), "externs," who privately prepared themselves for entrance examinations to the universities but rarely succeeded, in short intellectually minded young people imbued with a variety of social and socialistic ideologies. Most of these pioneers had been at odds with their traditional Jewish background and maintained some contact with the modern social and philosophical trends prevalent in society at large, which had penetrated at least the periphery of Jewish society. Despairing of the realization of their personal as well as social aims they set out to create a new society. They brought with them a spectrum of ideologies ranging from orthodox Marxism to near anarchism, and a kind of Tolstoyan quest for the natural, pristine state of Man. Some of the pioneers evaluated these ideologies as being of primary importance and in theory even outweighing the national considerations, which however were never discarded. Much intellectual effort went into the attempt to harmonize these respective ideologies with Jewish nationalism, which seemed to be unrelated to or even inconsistent with them.[20] In whatever fashion the conflict was intellectually resolved, the fact is undeniable that both emotionally and practically nationalism prevailed. For attachment to the national objectives alone could motivate all these to prefer Palestine to other countries of possible emigration. Those in whom the Jewish national renaissance was not a component of their ideology went elsewhere, or, if their attachment to this ideal was not strong enough, they left the country after having encountered the usual hardships of pioneering. Those who remained drew strength to endure the hardship out of their conviction that it was done in the service of their cause. Individually, devotion to the special non-national objectives might have been as strong as the affection for the national ideal or perhaps even greater. But with regard to other objectives the pioneers were divided, while in the adherence to the national revival they were united. Attachment to the national cause united the pioneers also with their precursors, the settlers of the early eighties, from whom socially and religiously they were divided as widely as possible. The commitment to the ideal of national renaissance appeared to be a stronger force than all the social or ideological differences.

The idea of nationalism proved itself incapable of a mass uprooting of people from a well balanced social setting. But it proved strong enough to reintegrate those who were uprooted. And this was a formidable task in the case of Jews. For as we have seen above, the elements of nationalism were here almost entirely lacking. The settlers had to create not only the material conditions for their existence but also the very means of their national reintegration. The idea of national unity preceded the means of unification. The first settlers had scarcely a common language, in any case no language they could consider a medium of social cohesion. Neither was there a real attachment to the landscape of their new country. The concept of the Holy Land and the belief in the greatness of the ancient fatherland were no more than ideas. The actual confrontation with the new country demanded an adaptation to new conditions with regard to climate and a new and strange physical environment. Only through a special effort did they succeed in finding poetic expression for the attachment to the scenery and surroundings of the country.

All this had been accomplished in its fundamental stages by the first decade preceding World War I. This period, the time of the Second *aliyah*, was politically an unsuccessful time. Nevertheless, during this time the foundations were laid for the new nation to develop. The utopia began to become a reality. That the idea of Zionism was conceptually nothing more than an utopia was recognized by none other than its greatest exponent,

Theodor Herzl. In the preface to his *Judenstaat*,[21] in which he outlined the scheme of action for implementing his idea, he anticipated the criticism that he was expounding a mere utopia. His answer was that it was indeed a utopia, with a qualification. Other utopists set forth the design of a machine, but their plans failed to provide for the driving force that would set the machine in motion. He, on the other hand, had only to suggest the scheme, because the driving energy, namely, Jewish distress, had been there before. *Judennot* would set the machine in motion once it had been constructed. Therein Herzl proved himself a prophet with a limitation, for he foresaw the future but not the course of events that would lead to it.

For the feat was not accomplished, as Herzl had claimed, through the pressure of Jewish suffering. Jewish suffering as Herzl experienced it, namely, defamation in the West and pogroms in the East, had other immediate effects. In the West it prompted some individuals like Herzl himself to a soul-searching that resulted, in some cases, in people's actively joining the national movement. But on the whole it brought about only apologetics and the organization for self-protection. In the Eastern countries it brought about a flight and started a stream of emigrants to overseas countries. It did not produce, as Herzl imagined it would do, a voluntary exodus from any country. At the crucial point of development, when the nucleus of the nation was created, it did not contribute to the solution of the Jewish problem. Palestine of that time was not considered a possible country for emigration by those who sought only peace and livelihood. The sixty or seventy thousand people who were absorbed in Palestine in the formative years of the new nation represent a negligible percentage of the emigrants of those years. They could easily have found their way to some other country where the bulk of the Jewish emigration was absorbed.

The driving force, which indeed was there when Herzl appeared on the scene, was modern Jewish nationalism, drawing its strength from the old but transformed messianism. Of this Herzl, while conceiving his plan, had not the slightest knowledge. Brought up in the atmosphere of assimilated Jewry of Budapest and Vienna, Herzl was unaware of the existence of the national movement when in the wake of the Dreyfus affair in 1896 he arrived at the idea of solving the Jewish problem by the creation of a Jewish state.[22] The idea would have indeed fallen into the dustbin of unredeemed utopias were it not for the enthusiasm of the nationalists who hailed Herzl as the godsent leader, arriving as it were from another planet. By the force of nationalism deriving its strength from the deeper sources of messianism, Herzl's utopia became ultimately a reality.

The Forerunners of Zionism

8

A study of the history of Zionism reveals similarities to other modern movements, such as socialism and Jewish socialism. Once Zionism came of age and emerged into the full light of history, historians discovered that its acknowledged leaders were in fact the standard bearers who had brought the ideas of others to fruition. Thus concepts such as "forerunners of Zionism" and "prehistory" (*Vorgeschichte*) of Zionism were created by writers to describe phenomena that seemed to them to constitute the practical or theoretical prologue to the birth of the movement itself.

EARLY INTERPRETATIONS

The concept "forerunners of Zionism" was never defined by the historians who used it, and it is only in context that we can guess its meaning. In Nahum Sokolow's book, *History of Zionism* (1919), the term is applied so broadly that its meaning becomes vague. In his introduction Sokolow writes: "I had to go back to the beginning of this idea and extend the meaning of 'Zionism' to all aspirations and efforts tending in the same direction" (p. vii). By applying the term "Zionist" to any Jew or Gentile who had ever expressed ideas reminiscent of those of the Zionist movement, Sokolow made it practically impossible to distinguish between the later Zionists and their predecessors.

Real content is given to the concept by Adolf Böhm in his book *Die Zionistische Bewegung* (1920). Böhm distinguishes between the Zionists and their forerunners on the one hand, and the aspirations and movements from which Zionism inherited its consciousness of the historical link between the Jewish people and *Eretz Israel* on the other. He sees the essence of these movements and aspirations in their "*Eretz-Israelness*", "*Palestinismus*"—a term he applies to all those manifestations, both material (the recurrent Jewish immigrations to *Eretz Israel*) and spiritual (the belief in a miraculous redemption in Zion), which testified to the actual and emotional ties between the Jews of the Diaspora and the land of Israel which existed from the destruction of the Second Temple to the modern era of assimilation. Böhm distinguishes between the protagonists of the Zionist idea from the beginning of the *Hibbath Zion* (Lovers of Zion) movement on, and those who anticipated them in advocating this idea at a time when among the masses of the people and their leaders the tendency to assimilation still prevailed. It is the latter group, who espoused and propagated the Zionist idea during the period of assimilation, that Böhm labels "forerunners of Zionism."

In his theoretical discussion, Böhm attempts to establish a well-defined terminology describing the forerunners; however, in the actual presentation of the facts he follows Sokolow's example and includes all those who had expressed their approval of the return of the Jews to their homeland. In this category he included Jews—ranging from the American Jewish journalist Mordecai Manuel Noah (1785–1851, on whom more later) to the Hebrew writer of the Enlightenment Peretz Smolenskin (1842–1885)—and non-Jews, ranging from the novelist George Eliot, who had shown herself highly sympathetic to the idea of a Jewish national revival in her novel *Daniel Deronda* (1876), to the British lawyer, journalist, and adventurer Laurence Oliphant (1829–1888), who had actively encouraged the return of the Jews to *Eretz Israel*.

Sokolow and Böhm used the historical approach typical in the current Zionist historiography, whose literature was not solely scientific in its aims, but also proselytizing. It is clear that their vagueness about the concept "forerunners of Zionism" (and the concept of Zionism itself) was due not only to the usual difficulties encountered by historians in defining the limits of any historical period. Proof of the early origins of Zionism gave it credence in the eyes of a generation whose political and even moral judgments were based on historical considerations—the influence of historicism, a doctrine whose impact on modern thought cannot be overestimated.

This approach was criticized by Zionists living in *Eretz Israel*, who claimed that Zionism no longer needed to justify its existence and called rather for its sociological analysis. In this light, Zionism was the answer to the problem of Diaspora Jewry, who were secularized and no longer thought in terms of a miraculous redemption. Thus neither the messianic movements among the Jews, nor the various programs proposed by Christians for a return of the Jews to Zion came under the heading of Zionist history, since those projects were not usually motivated by a wish to solve the problems of the Jewish communities or to satisfy their needs.

But if motivation is what defines a "forerunner," then those with the right motives are Zionists even if they preceded the Zionist movement, and those with the wrong motives are not Zionists even if they actually contributed to its formation. According to this criterion it was possible for the proponents of this definition to find "Zionists" among the German Jews of the Enlightenment, and to call Mordecai Manuel Noah "the first Zionist." Rabbi Kalisher (1795–1874) and his followers, who initiated a movement for the return of the Jews to *Eretz Israel* in anticipation of the coming of the Messiah, on the other hand, cannot be considered Zionists at all—unless the Rabbi's real motive was to find practical solutions to practical problems, couched in traditional-messianic terms in order to avoid the disfavor of his Orthodox religious peers.

A different approach is developed in Ben-Zion Dinur's (Dinaburg) book *Mevasrei ha-Zionuth* [The Forerunners of Zionism], (1939), a collection of sources prefaced by the author for the period "from the failure of the Shabbetaian movement to the beginnings of *Hibbath Zion*." Dinur was the first historian of Zionism to combine a professional mastery of his material with a willingness to define his terms, and the selection and analysis of the source material in this collection proceeds in strict accordance with the conceptual framework established by the author.

According to Dinur, the emergence of the forerunners period is to be determined on the basis of the relationship between secularization and the movement of national revival. He sees the decline of the Shabbetaian movement as marking the beginning of the modern period in Jewish history, and the most striking characteristic of this new period he sees as the positive attitude toward life ("the sanctification of life instead of the sanctification of God" or martyrdom). But the national movement, which Dinur regards as the supreme affirmation of life, did not appear right at the beginning of this turning point. Rather it brought the Enlightenment, which is usually regarded as the antithesis of the national movement. But Dinur's main thesis, substantiated by a wealth of newly revealed historical documentation, discerns alongside the dominant trend of Enlightenment and assimilation the first glimmer of the dawning nationalism, from the revival of the Hebrew language to a secular conception of the Jewish national entity and its political and cultural potentialities.

The question is whether Dinur's exposition and analysis (which have been accepted by Israeli historians) justify his conclusion that these early expressions of nationalism were in fact the harbingers of the Zionist movement. In order to answer this question we must first clarify the meaning of the concept "forerunners."

SOCIALLY UNIFYING FORCE

Zionist history deals with the process leading to the realization of the Zionist goal. In accordance with this limitation we are bound to begin the history of the "forerunners of Zionism" at the point at which the ideas advocated by the forerunners were translated into action, and not when these ideas were in formation.

This restriction could oblige us to discard the term "forerunners of Zionism" altogether. Zionist history is universally agreed to begin with the outset of settlement in *Eretz Israel* in the early 1800s; before this time both Zionism and its forerunners exist only as ideas and their proponents. Should the distinction then be based on the difference between thought and action?

Our answer to this question is based on sociological considerations. Let us disregard for a moment the goals of Zionism, and examine its potency as a social force. To what degree did Zionism unite a group of like thinkers behind a common aim? A partisan periodical unites its readers behind a belief; at the other extreme we find actual social cohesion through the commitment to a belief such as in monastic communities. Between the two lies a whole range of social behavior with varying degrees of cohesiveness. Zionism produced the entire range of social expression, from readers' circles and political groups to the close communal life of the *kvutza*. The *kvutza*-form of settlement was an expression of the idea of a socialist utopia, which went hand in hand with Zionism, but its staying power derived strictly from its national-Zionist sense of mission.

This social strength distinguishes Zionism from other contemporary Jewish trends and movements and encourages the study of it as a sociological phenomenon. The birth of modern Zionism coincided with a movement of emigration among the Jews of Eastern Europe. Emigration was a solution to economic problems, but as a socially unifying force it proved almost completely barren. The few societies formed for the purpose of joint emigration—some combining the goal of emigration with definite social programs—soon disintegrated, and emigration was largely based on individual initiative, with support from relatives or immigrant aid societies. This emigration was a "natural" movement, a population transfer from one country to another as a result of political and economic pressures. And the adjustment of the emigrants to their new life depended on social and economic conditions. Emigration was not the fulfillment of an ideal, as it was with Zionism.

The Zionist movement grew out of economic, political, and social pressures, but in the course of its development, in the definition of its goals, and even in the choice of its means, it was guided by an idea that was not simply the product of such pressures. The adherence to a specific land set it apart from the immigration movement in general. To this were added social, religious, and cultural utopias,[1] images of a society in which social or religious principles would be realized, or in which unique cultural values would be created. A fundamentally irrational belief, whether related to adherence to a religious tradition or to historical links in a purely secular-national sense—connected these utopian aspirations to *Eretz Israel*, the only possible location for their realization.

Among the emigrants to other countries, family ties usually predominated, but the Zionists were bound together on the basis of shared ideological aspirations of the various *aliyoth*. The more strongly the *aliyah* was influenced by an ideological trend, the more pronounced was its supra-familial structure: the BILU pioneers of the early 1880s were more supra-familial than the Rumanian immigration of the same period, and the Second (1905–14) and Third (1919–23) *aliyoth* than the later waves of immigration, which were motivated more by necessity than by ideology. At certain stages the hold that Zionism had on its adherents was almost as strong as that exerted by religious movements in their initial stages, when they tend to disrupt accepted social forms and draw individuals into their own frame-works.

PREMATURE SCHEMES AND EARLY "PROJECT-MAKERS"

The Zionist idea that the Jews should return to their ancient homeland through colonization and political activity has been expressed many times since the seventeenth century by Jews and non-Jews alike. But it remained quiescent both as a socially unifying force and in terms of realizing its goals. Ideas that emerge but become influential only at a later stage are common enough in history, and the usual sociological explanation is that their influence does not depend on the degree of their "rightness" or "justice" but on their coinciding with political and social conditions that lend them urgency. But this explanation does not account for the way the idea actually infiltrates into a society, a process that must take place grad-ually, accompanied by temporary setbacks and involving a hard social struggle. Furthermore, the idea is at first important only to a limited number of individuals, who because of their special social position and/or particu-lar personal characteristics become its disseminators when their society is largely indifferent to it. To most of their contemporaries they appear to be eccentrics, but the historian appreciates their role as forerunners when he can show that the personal and objective factors motivating them are similar to those which were decisive in the eventual emergence of the movement on a socially significant scale. The identification of such "forerunners" cannot be made on the basis of analogies in the content of the idea alone. It is only in analyzing the historical process as a whole that we can decide whether we are indeed dealing with a "forerunner" or simply with a chance similarity in thought. Such coincidental similarities are common enough, and there is no modern idea for which analogies have not been discovered, even in totally alien cultural and intellectual contexts.

This is especially true of the Zionist idea. The general conception of the return of the Jews to their homeland or the establishment of a Jewish state in some other place was in the air wherever Jews constituted a separate and distinct social body. The historical link between the Jews and *Eretz Israel* is in the Christian and the Jewish traditions, and it did not take much imagination or original thought to propose the establishment of a Jewish state. Not surprisingly, projects and project-makers (*Projectenmacher*) drawing on these traditions abounded especially during the first two centuries of the modern period.

The intellectual caliber of these schemes can be measured in part by the type of person who produced them. Their chief similarity is their impractical and sometimes absurd detachment from reality. The material means that the "project-makers" could mobilize for the realization of their schemes were far short of their grandiose requirements, and they were soon reduced to ridicule and oblivion.

The "project-makers" of the seventeenth, eighteenth, and nineteenth centuries were solitary figures isolated from the mainstream of socio-historical development. A seventeenth century example is the Danish writer Holger Paulli and other Christians like him, who preached the return of the Jews to Zion from motives of Christian millennialism. In the nineteenth century, there is Mordecai Manuel Noah, author of the famous Ararat scheme, who proclaims the foundation of the Jewish state on an island in America over which he presides, appoints unsuspecting rabbis and scholars in Europe as his representatives, and decrees the abolition of laws and customs in his first proclamation. Noah includes the education of the Indians in his program, declaring them the descendants of the Ten Lost Tribes. Having laid the foundation stone of the new state, conducting the consecration ceremony in a church for lack of an available synagogue, Noah sits back and waits for the immigrants to start streaming in from the four corners of the earth. This is a prime example of a crank who has abandoned the world of reality, although he was previously the American consul in Tunis.

This type differs radically from the messianic visionary of earlier generations who was involved in his society and sustained by the great faith of his contemporaries. This occurred in a transitional period when the faith in a miraculous redemption was rapidly waning, while the practical possibility of a return to *Eretz Israel* was still nascent. In this transition period the idea of national redemption was the domain of isolated eccentrics whose efforts were sporadic and premature.

EMANCIPATION OVERSHADOWS NATIONAL REVIVAL

The "project-makers" of the period between active messianism and the beginning of the Zionist movement proper can by no means be described as the "forerunners of Zionism." Even Dinur, who sees this whole interim period as the period of the "forerunners," does so not because of these projects but because of the emergence of certain historical trends—for example, the revival of the Hebrew language and the desire to engage in productive work—which were later to become part of Zionist involvement and, second, because it was during this period that a type of Jew emerged who was capable of engaging in effective political activity as a result of a new approach to the secular world. A realistic view of the Jewish people is evident in the writings of such thinkers as Spinoza and Mendelssohn, and even of Christian statesmen whose involvement with Jewish questions was a real one due to their participation in the debate on the improvement of Jewish living conditions and the struggle for equal rights for the Jews. These polemicists (as Dinur has successfully shown) frequently represent the Jewish people as a living nation whose return to their historical homeland can be considered and debated as a real political possibility.

If we define forerunners in terms of the idea alone, then Dinur's approach is certainly valid. The Jewish people is perceived as a real entity, and the possibility of a national revival is suggested. But the question remains: Is the idea at this stage a potential socially unifying force, which we found above to be the chief test of its vitality in all the stages of its development? The idea in this period is expressed in the opinions of individuals, which never become a rallying point for action. Such an idea is incapable of exerting any real influence on the historical process at this time.

The national idea was still overshadowed by the idea of social and political emancipation, which burst into the confines of Jewish life at that time. These goals became paramount, breaking down the old structure of Jewish society. It is to this idea that subsidiary trends, such as the desire to engage in productive labor, the revival of the Hebrew language (the literature of the Enlightenment), and even the new scientific approach to Judaism, now increasingly attached themselves. Most important of all, it is to this idea that the younger generation, its eyes fixed on the goal of *emancipation* (which seemed within reach), attached itself. The idea of the return to *Eretz Israel* receded into the past, rather than heralding a future movement.

FROM EQUAL RIGHTS TO NATIONAL RIGHTS

At what point then do the forerunners appear, signaling the renewed vitality of the Zionist idea as an active force? In terms of our previous definition, the forerunners of Zionism are the first advocates of the Zionist idea who inspired any of the forms of social *cohesiveness* described above. This places the forerunners in the late 1850s–early 1860s, when the first advocates of Zion—Rabbi Kalisher, Rabbi Guttmacher, Luria, and finally Moses Hess attracted a following, however limited and scattered, united by personal and organizational bonds in the common belief in the future of the nation in its historical homeland. The very fact that these men, so different not only in their backgrounds but also in the basis of their common belief, could come together at all—with Rabbi Kalisher, the most practical member, acting as the central axis of the group—this fact alone proves that the idea of the return of the Jews to their land had now become a socially unifying force.

It is not difficult to understand why this generation was ready to receive the ideas that previous generations had rejected or ignored. During this period, the struggle for equal rights in the West was coming to an end, and the idea of equality and emancipation was losing its impetus as an ideal to be transformed into reality. At this point a split took place in social and intellectual trends. The mainstream continued on its course from the achievement of equal rights to full absorption into Gentile society. On the intellectual plane, the demand for equality led to an ideology that sought to consolidate and justify what had already been achieved. At this stage, however, an opening appeared for an apparently contradictory aspiration, one that had existed before but had been pushed aside by the opposing trend. At the beginning of the struggle for equal rights it had seemed to Jews and non-Jews alike that national aspiration on the part of the Jews was contrary to the struggle for full citizenship and should therefore be abandoned. Now that the movement for emancipation had attained its goal, however, the national movement could appear not as its antithesis but as its complement. In contrast to later Zionism, the forerunners did not base their ideas on the castigation of Jewish life in the Diaspora. Consequently, the forerunners did not prepare to transfer the Jews from the West but to create a kind of model nation in *Eretz Israel*, both by educating the Jews already living there and by bringing there Jews from countries that had not granted them equal rights. What would happen after this was either not discussed (by Rabbi Alkalay or Moses Hess, for example), or was left to Divine Providence (by Rabbi Kalisher, for example, for whom making *Eretz Israel* into a "settled land" was merely a preparatory step toward miraculous events whose scope and nature were beyond human speculation).

In any case, the character of the message—immanent in the national aspirations that were voiced at the exact moment of time when the conflicting trend of historical development, namely emancipation, reached its full development and an opening for a turning point presented itself—became clear by the ties that now began to be formed between individuals on a basis of a renewal of the belief in a national future in the pristine homeland. Here begins a typical dialectical process, developing according to the pattern of thesis, antithesis, and synthesis. The forerunners emerge at the beginning of the transition from the antithesis—the rejection of the belief in a miraculous return of the Jews to Zion—to the synthesis, which is modern Zionism.

THE TRUE FORERUNNERS

Rabbi Kalisher

This merging of the renewal of the belief in national rebirth and the conclusion of the struggle for equal rights can also be discerned in the lives and intellectual development of the three forerunners, Rabbi Kalisher, Rabbi Alkalay and Moses Hess. Rabbi Kalisher was still thinking in terms of a genuine messianic movement in 1836, when he approached Asher Anschel Rothschild and urged him to purchase the whole of *Eretz Israel* from the Ottoman ruler Mohammed Ali—or at least Jerusalem or the Temple Mount, in order to provide an opening for a miraculous redemption by an "awakening from below": the transformation of *Eretz Israel* into a "settled land" or the reinstatement of sacrificial offerings—two activities which, according to the interpretation of Jewish tradition by Rabbi Kalisher, were prerequisites for the coming of the Messiah. At about the same time the Rabbi approached Sir Moses Montefiore with a similar request. After this, however, he abandoned all such activities and devoted himself to talmudic study and to the practical problems that had arisen among the religious life of Western Jewry as a result of the radical changes brought about by the emancipation movement. It was only in 1860, with the founding of the Society for the Settlement of *Eretz Israel*, that Rabbi Kalisher—by then 65 years old—resumed his earlier activities, with the aim of making *Eretz Israel* a "settled land" now taking first place and the offering up of sacrifices thrust into the background. Rabbi Kalisher's renewed vigor and successful pursuit of practical aims through messianic motivation attest to the fact that the time was now ripe for the national movement to reassert itself.

Moses Hess

A similar pattern was followed by Moses Hess. He traced his first stirrings of Jewish national aspirations to the shame and rage aroused by the blood libel against the Jews of Damascus in the year 1840. At the time, however, Hess's writings gave no indication of these national aspirations. Even in his intimate correspondence with his Jewish friend Auerbach he gives no expression to the feelings of outrage he was to recall twenty years later. Hess's own explanation for this delayed reaction was that the Jewish pain was overshadowed at the time by "the greater pain aroused in me by the European proletariat." The truth of the matter is that Hess's rage did not turn him to specifically Jewish aspirations, and his concern for the proletariat included a belief in the solution of the Jewish problem. It was only after the experience of the next twenty years, which did not see the solution to the problems of the proletariat but did see a measure of emancipation for the Jews, that Hess's sentiments could turn to a specifically Jewish aspiration. In developing his new theory Hess drew on the material provided by the historical school of Graetz and his associates (which was also a synthesis produced by the dialectic of the times), and with its help he arrived at a definition of Judaism as an ethnic-spiritual entity that should be preserved and strengthened because it contained forces of the future. The linking of this future to *Eretz Israel*, where the spiritual revival was destined to be fully realized, was exclusive to Hess (among "secularists") at the time: it was not, however, intended as a rejection of equal rights but as a complement to it, and it could be accepted as such only in the 1860s when the struggle for equal rights seemed to be over.

Rabbi Alkalay

The importance of the sixties as a turning point is equally apparent in the activities of the third forerunner, Rabbi Alkalay. While his initial awakening was not connected with developments in Western Jewry (about which he knew only by hearsay), their reactions to his ideas, which he began to publish in the forties, are an indication of the mood at that time. In so far as any attention at all was paid to the Rabbi's views at this stage, it was derisive, stemming partly from a Western feeling of superiority to the Sephardi preacher and his homiletical style, and partly from a process of disillusionment with the dreams of redemption, which Rabbi Alkalay was trying to revive without making any clear distinction between their messianic and realistic elements. Equally typical was the Rabbi's failure in England in 1852, where he received more support from Christians than from Jews—a fact that should not surprise us in the light of the literal belief in the biblical prophecies of the return of the Jews to Zion among English Christian fundamentalists on the one hand, and on the other— the fact that these were the years of the struggle for equal rights among British Jewry, to whom any mention of *Eretz Israel* as the land of their future seemed incompatible with their present aspirations. All Rabbi Alkalay's efforts were, in fact, fruitless until the sixties, when his work as a propagandist became a link in the chain of activities conducted by Rabbi Kalisher and his circle. Until this time too his publications were only intermittent: between his first and second books in Hebrew (his first two books were written in Ladino and thus only for a limited circle of readers), five years elapsed, and in the next eight years (1848–1856) he produced only three pamphlets. From then on, however, he is more prolific (in the form of books, pamphlets, and newspaper articles), and the contents themselves become increasingly clear as the gap between the homiletical background and the realistic intentions widens, and the confidence of the writer grows with his observation of events and his extraordinary receptiveness toward the first sign of national crystallization, such as the emergence of a Hebrew press, the foundation of the Alliance Israélite Universelle, etc.—a receptiveness unmatched even by his fellow forerunners Rabbi Kalisher and Moses Hess. The fact that Rabbi Alkalay, like Rabbi Kalisher, was approaching his sixtieth year when his most fruitful and important period commenced, is testimony in itself to the suprapersonal causes of this turning point.

UNITED BY MARGINAL POSITION IN SOCIETY

Finally, we shall attempt to answer the question: what distinguished the forerunners from their contemporaries and made it possible for them to influence the future? The historian may attribute these powers to individual personality. But objective factors and social forces may have contributed to making these individuals into the bearers of ideas or players of historical roles. The factor common to all the forerunners is their marginal position in Western Jewry, their ambivalent feelings during the events that signaled the process of abandonment of the hopes of national redemption. This was primarily the result of their geographical origins: Rabbi Kalisher on the border between East and West, and Rabbi Alkalay on the very edge of the "West" in the Balkans (Hungary, especially during the period of reform, followed the lead of the West). But their geographical situation also had cultural implications. Rabbi Kalisher and Rabbi Alkalay belonged to the West insofar as they were capable of reacting to its historical developments, but at the same time they were independent of it, inasmuch as their foundations had not yet been shaken by developments in the West.

In a slightly different sense the term "marginal" can also be applied to Moses Hess's position vis-à-vis Western Jewry. Hess ascribed his ability to relate to the problem of Jewish nationality to his experiences in France, then the major power in Europe. But his emigration from Germany has additional significance. Having uprooted himself from his native soil and broken off relations with his family, he abandoned his position in society and isolated himself from Jewish public life; all these factors combined to place him outside the equal rights movement. Hess was a harbinger of the future because he gave expression to trends that were only reaching maturity in his day. Hess's withdrawal from the mainstream of society—unlike Graetz, for example, who was involved in Jewish public life in Germany— drove him to the far-reaching conclusion that the future of the Jewish people lay in *Eretz Israel*. This points to the interesting paradox that the men closest to Hess intellectually—the members of the historical school in Germany—did not go along with his main ideas and the enthusiasm with which they greeted his book was due to its premises rather than its conclusion; whereas the men who shared Hess's aspirations, Kalisher and his circle, based these aspirations on intellectual premises that were completely different from Hess's. What unites the forerunners as a limited historical phenomenon is therefore not the similarity in their way of thinking, but their common marginal position in society and the common aspirations this position inspired.

Situating Zionism in Contemporary Jewish History

9

A methodological comment is in order as regards the word "contemporary" in our title. From its inception, one of the goals of Zionism was to detach itself completely from the previous generations, the span of time the Jewish People spent in exile. They sought instead to substitute an attachment to pre-exilic times when the nation still lived on its native soil. Granted that the actual deeds of Zionism occurred wholly within the modern era and that it is this era that informs every expression and manifestation of the movement, still, reality is one thing and consciousness quite another. According to the perceptions of the standard-bearers of Zionism it was axiomatic that the generations of exile were to be skipped over and to start anew at the same place where national existence had been interrupted before the exile. To this day there are traces left of this perception in such expressions as "national rebirth." It was as though the nation were in hibernation or embalmed and they set out to awaken, to revitalize, and to reestablish it.

This Zionist self-perception obliges a historian who would assess its character to avoid comparing it with contemporary movements. It is only proper that an examination of the Zionist essence be conducted against the background of Jewish history in its entirety. Against such a perspective the first question to be addressed concerns the correctness of the Zionist diagnosis with regard to the nature of the Jewish People in exile. For if the nation ceased to exist from the moment it was exiled, it follows that the task of Zionism was not so much to resuscitate it as to create it *ex nihilo*. But when Zionism's historic hour arrived, it did find foundations on which it could build. What then, is the nature of those foundations?

As is well known, such expressions as *Uma, Goy, Le'om* and *Am* (nation, people, gentile, folk—the translations are only approximations and equivalences, ed.), which originated in the Biblical Age and in the Second Commonwealth Period, were extant throughout subsequent periods down to the Middle Ages and were applied both by Jews and non-Jews. And this was so even though the Jews lacked nationally identifying characteristics, the conventional attributes of other people. They neither lived on their own land nor spoke a uniform language, and they certainly were not ruled by their own government. The conclusion to be drawn from this is that the usually acceptable conditions testifying to the existence of a people are not adequate here. Such conditions are only circumstantial signs and as such do not replace the sense of belonging to one another shared by members of a people. As long as this feeling persists—and it is of no importance where it originates—there can be no doubt as to the existence of that people.

Undeniably, that kind of kindred feeling and a mutual attachment was a hallmark of the Jewish People in its dispersion. Their consciousness of a common origin anchored in the Biblical stories is a factor of the greatest significance. As early a scholar as Johan Gottfried Herder (1744–1803) noted that the Israelites are unique in that they are the only people who possess a historic story out of the depths of the ancient period. While this story holds an admixture of mythical and legendary strata, on the whole it reflects an actual historical reality; it is also *witness* to a special religious consciousness separating out this people from all the peoples in its surroundings.

No less real was the trait borne by the Jewish congregation from the times of the Second Commonwealth (530 B.C.E.–70 C.E.). Here one is no longer dealing with legendary deeds but with the commemoration of social and cultural institutions, such as the Sanhedrin, the *Batei Din*, the Temple, the synagogues, and the houses of study. Some of these survived thanks to more than a mere multi-generational memory through the mediating effect of the literature of the times, the Mishnah and the two versions of the Talmud (Babylonian and Jerusalemite). They actively escorted later generations. Though the Temple was destroyed, the Sanhedrin disestablished, *Batei Din* still conducted their cases of law according to the same juridical principles that were in force when they were first promulgated. The synagogues and the houses of study, even when they were not exact duplicates of the archetypes, were basically of the same nature. Furthermore, the partial shrinkage in the scope of the Law occasioned by the destruction of the Temple and the disbanding of the Sanhedrin was not considered to be final. It held only for "these times," which in *halakhic* terms applied to the period between the destruction of the Temple and its rebuilding. This would come about with the advent of the Redeemer, who, no matter how long he tarried would certainly arrive. Consequently, the belief in Redemption was not merely a tenet of popular folk-religion. It is rooted in the cognitive mode of the *Halakhah*, which has served as the legal basis both for public and individual life in traditional society.

But the Western world's leap into modernity shook the foundations of traditional society and along with them weakened and almost destroyed the pillars that until then had held up an overarching Jewish national unity.

The tremors did not effect all segments of Jewry equally. As a result of the upheaval, conditions of Jewish existence in the West came to be based on a new juridical principle, on their status as citizens of the state. Simultaneously, Jews there formed cultural attachments to their environment resulting in a dilution of internal Jewish cohesion. In tandem, and not unrelatedly, tradition itself became the target of historical and rationalistic critique, thus losing its power to shore up national unity.

At first these tremors shook Western Jewry alone, while in Eastern Europe there were only the hesitant beginnings of such changes, viewed expectantly or fearfully according to the perspective of the viewers. Even in Islamic lands, including *Eretz Israel*, where the conventional conditions of Jewish existence persisted, the first shock waves of modernization (to use a modern word) were felt.

This was the situation in world Jewry when the Zionist idea was first launched. The main tenet of the idea, which unites all the ideological trends that developed in the movement or coalesced around it, was the demand to ensure Jewish continuity by accelerating the realization of a vision for the future. That vision, central to the national tradition, postulated the return of the People to its historic homeland. The strength and vitality of this idea as a real factor in determining the shape of history can be assessed by studying its struggle with the three opposing views in the Jewish public arena: with Orthodoxy, with liberalism, and with socialism.

Of course, people who belonged to these three camps also joined the Zionist movement—some individuals among them even became its standard-bearers—and yet they remained, as before, Orthodox, liberals, or socialists. Nonetheless, the opponents of Zionism in all three camps could regard themselves as sole authentic spokesmen for their movements. Most of the members of all three camps staunchly held to their opposition to Zionism; each camp for its own reasons.

ORTHODOXY

The explicit and central reason for the opposition of the Orthodox stemmed from the contradiction between Zionist aspirations to bring the Jewish People back to its homeland through human endeavor and the popular religious belief in the coming redemption through supernatural wonders. In vain did Orthodox Zionists cite ostensibly authoritative sources that the belief in a miraculous redemption is not a necessary principle of the religion. Nor did it avail them to show that some of the greatest Jewish sages in the past thought that redemption, or at least its beginning stages, was conceivable or even conditional on human initiative. Apparently the reliance on belief in miraculous redemption was nothing other than the crystallization into dogma of a deeply basic psychological position. This in turn was the heritage of the historic experience of long generations of exilic life. During that time Jews survived because of the relative tolerance that, for reasons of their own, the non-Jewish authorities displayed toward them. Jews in exile could of course dream about the fall of all the kingdoms, about the changed circumstances of the world once the Jewish People returned to its home to rule over other peoples; but they utterly lacked the real means to bring about this goal. Instead of forging practical implements they dealt in spiritual preparation, and in place of a vision of an achievable future there were recurrent hallucinatory delusions and outbursts of ecstatic messianism. The Jews of those times lacked neither initiative nor the ability to act incisively, but the energies and the initiatives were devoted to the solution of short-range problems. The very thought of a basic transformation of the situation was unthinkable.

Consequently, this state of mind, which was at base a reaction to a specific historic situation, was so crystallized as to become an articulated, well-defined mentality. This mentality was transmitted as an integral part of the collective culture from generation to generation. Orthodox Jewry retained this mentality even when the external situation did not warrant it, and even in periods when the situation called for initiative and public enterprise. Indeed, Orthodox Jewry not only failed to respond to the Zionist plan of action but also did not even take a real part in the struggle for emancipation and stood on the sidelines in the face of the awakening of the Jewish masses who sought a way out of their situation in overseas immigration. In sum, Orthodoxy had strong reservations about anything like what the late Jacob Kellner called "social planning as opposed to piecemeal efforts to succor needy victims of circumstance." The position of the Orthodox can best be summed up in the two talmudic aphorisms: "sit by quiescently and do nothing is preferable . . ." and "the heavens will forfend . . ." Admittedly, apart from this mentality there was another factor, i.e., Orthodoxy's fear that the traditional way of life would not be maintained by the masses in the face of changed external circumstances. This motif also played an important part in Orthodox Jewry's opposition to Zionism and reinforced the avowed ideology about loyalty to the belief in a supernatural redemption.

LIBERALISM

Opposition to Zionism also came from the other side of the public arena, from the liberals. It was liberalism, in the broadest construction of the term, that secured citizenship and equality—in principle—for the Jews of the West. Although the struggle to achieve this goal was conducted according to the local conditions obtaining in every country, in the eyes of its ideologues it was meant to serve as an instrument in the all-European and worldwide solution to the Jewish problem. At the end of the eighteenth century, Jewry, scattered throughout many lands, appeared to be a unified polity, or according to the hostile view of the philosopher Fichte . . . "extending over almost all the countries of Europe there is an enormous state . . . engaged in an eternal war with all the others . . . it is of course, Jewry." The aim of those who granted emancipation to the Jews was to dismember that society on the assumption that each country would absorb and assimilate all the Jews living within its confines. This underlying and unspoken assumption was indicated occasionally in the steps taken by the emancipating countries to prevent the infiltration of "foreign" Jews into their borders. The Jewish recipients of emancipation were resigned to this unwritten condition and the more alert among them fully understood both the practical significance and the principles behind it. This was so in the case of Rumanian Jewry in 1872.

Rumania was the first weak link in the hopeful chain liberals had forged as regards the absorption of all the Jews in their countries of domicile. The plight of Rumanian Jewry impelled Jewish dignitaries in the U.S. to influence President Grant to appoint the Sephardic-American Jew Benjamin Peixotto as American Consul to Bucharest. Peixotto quickly concluded that Rumanian Jewry in its entirety could not possibly be absorbed there and that the solution was to help them to emigrate to the U.S. To implement the plan he tried to mobilize the support of European Jewry, and he invited the representatives of important European Jewish communities to a conference in Brussels. En route to the meeting he stopped off in Berlin and met with the "Rumania Committee," which had been organized in response to his initiative. Among the invitees was the world-famous German-Jewish author Berthold Auerbach. The American Consul spoke about the issue at hand and said that according to the information he had there were about 18,000 Jews ready to emigrate immediately and that according to his estimate the number would eventually reach 100,000. Berthold Auerbach strongly protested against the very idea of putting mass immigration on the Jewish public agenda. According to him this was a most dangerous proposal, for what if tomorrow the Jews of Galicia were to be endangered—would another conference be called to deal with their immigration? But overriding his skepticism as to the practical aspects, he gave vent to his anxiety about the status of Jews in general and not only those who were presently in trouble. "With the idea of mass immigration we introduce the blemish of 'Gypsification' into the status of the Jews," which might cast suspicion even on the status of those Jews who achieved citizenship years ago. He ended the speech with his characteristic pathos: "We are rooted in the country where our parents and parents' parents are resting in their graves." An almost identical position was held by the *Allgemeine Zeitung des Judenthums*, the semiofficial organ of German Jewry. It was also the stand adopted by the conference in Brussels, where the representative of other European Jewish communities joined the chairman, Adolphe Crémieux, who was president of the Alliance Israélite Universelle, in rejecting immigration. The resolution they adopted was worded to read that Rumanian Jewry considered immigration to be a solution bordering on the criminal. Indeed this is an accurate picture of the conviction of all those who thought that the problem in every land ought to be solved through the absorption of Jews by and in the midst of the local populations. The idea of immigration was simply thrown out. There were two aspects to the rejection, local and global. Severally, the French feared an immigration of German Jews, the Germans feared an influx of Russians, the Hungarians were anxious about the Jews of Galicia. Collectivly, they all shrank from the emigration of Rumanian Jewry headed for the United States. For this would have adverse implications for the model they had embraced for their own countries.

Given this background, is there any wonder that those who held these views opposed Zionism? Immigration to *Eretz Israel* raised additional apprehensions to the ones perceived about immigration to any other country. To concentrate a Jewish population in the land of the Patriarchs, even more so, to reestablish a Jewish state there would only serve to remind people of the alien nature of Jews in every land of domicile. It would fuel the distrust that they had not severed their loyalty to the Jewish People as a whole, as they were required to do in keeping with the classic principle of citizenship. From the start this trepidation played no small part in the opposition of liberals to Zionism. Testimony to this antagonism can be seen in Berthold Auerbach's reaction to the idea of Jewish national rebirth as it was proposed in Moses Hess's *Rome and Jerusalem.* The two had been friends since their youth when Judaism was dear to them both. But their paths parted when the socialist Hess settled in France whereas Auerbach's brilliant literary career opened a channel for his rapid social advancement. When Hess's interest in the Jewish question was rekindled, and when he had completed the manuscript of *Rome and Jerusalem,* he approached his former friend to take advantage of his contacts to find a German publisher. Auerbach, after reading only half the manuscript, reacted most violently. He equated the raising up of the idea of Jewish national rebirth with an incendiary act and accused Hess of returning to the German-Jewish arena he had abandoned so as to destroy what others had built up through decades of patient labor. He applied the Biblical verse, "Who made you a ruler and Judge over us?" to Hess, citing it in its original Hebrew. The process of Jewish integration into a liberalized Germany of the sixties had made impressive gains, and a person like Auerbach, who had a highly developed public consciousness, understood the price Jewry had to pay for that integration. Auerbach is merely paradigmatic of all those whose faith in the liberal model perforce meant they objected vehemently to the Zionist plan. Indeed this repudiation was a constant escort of Zionism, beginning with the apoplexy with which Rabbi Moritz Goodman reacted to Herzl's "invention" of Zionism down to Edwin Montagu's intrigues to frustrate the Balfour Declaration in Lloyd George's cabinet.

SOCIALISM

Whereas the first two opponents of Zionism, Orthodoxy and liberalism, gave battle in defense of their old well-fortified positions, the third rival, socialism, entered the public arena contemporaneously with Zionism. The major part of socialism's conception about the solution of the Jewish question was enunciated by Karl Marx himself quite early in his career and it is a moral drawn directly from his general historic concepts. Jewry's existence is deeply rooted in the capitalist regime where it fills the role of commercial and financial intermediary. As for Judaism's belief and its value systems, they are merely ideological projections of the economic systems' data. It follows that with the disappearance of the system, Judaism too would disappear. Jews qua Jews would become liberated from their Judaism to take up their place as human beings in the socialist society of the future, which would have no religious, national or class differences.

In the course of presenting his 1844 thesis about the *"Judenfrage,"* Marx sounded some hostile and insulting anti-Jewish notes, but that is not why the thesis did not make much headway among the Jews of the time. It could have been acceptable to anyone who accepted socialist theory as a whole, but at the time there were but few Jewish intellectuals—Moses Hess is a notable exception—who were attracted to it. Meanwhile there were few Jews among the proletariat, and it was primarily to them that Marx had held out the promise of liberation from oppression through the socialist revolution. This changed in the last third of the nineteenth century with the rise of a Jewish industrial proletariat in the Russian Empire, particularly in Poland and in Lithuania. Henceforward socialist theory gained much wider acceptance in Jewish public opinion. This was paralleled by the awakening of Jewish national sentiment, so that the two ideologies, socialism and Zionism, became competitors for the soul of the Jews, and quite frequently the arena in which the struggle waged was in the consciousness of the very same person.

Zionism's struggle with socialism differed from, and was also more difficult than, its battle with Orthodoxy and liberalism. The argumentation of the former could be dismissed by claiming that they clutched at old truisms and overlooked the signs of the times, which demanded foresight and vision. But socialism also held aloft a vision to counter the Zionist one, a vision with a broader scope, for it promised not only the redemption of the Jews but of all the world's oppressed. Furthermore, socialists claimed that their forecast about the passing of capitalism, which would be displaced by the socialist system, was based upon a scientific analysis of the economic and social processes, thus placing its validity beyond doubt. Zionism on the other hand, was allegedly hopelessly deluded by romantic imagination, captivated by historic memories of a distant past, straining to reconstruct a nation at the time that even existing nations were doomed to disintegrate, a time when humanity as a whole would unite in a redeemed socialist society.

How did Zionism cope with its opponents? It did not succeed in over-coming them; and it certainly did not destroy them utterly; but it did effect some breaks in their defensive walls. Or rather, historical processes and events made the cracks through which Zionism could infiltrate and attract some adherents of the "enemy" camps. It even gained strength from the ideological luggage that the new supporters brought out with them. Or-thodoxy's wall of absolute opposition was the first to crack and this through the efforts of such harbingers of Zionism as Rabbi Yehuda Alkalay, Rabbi Zvi Hirsch Kalisher, Elijah Guttmacher, Natan Friedland, and others. They all demanded a broad based public activity to bring about the resettlement of *Eretz Israel* so as to prepare the way for the miraculous redemption that was sure to follow in its footsteps. All these early Orthodox supporters stressed that the widespread notion that the entire redemptive process from beginning to end was predicated on supernatural miracles and not on natural events was erroneous and must be cast off.

ORTHODOX RADICALS

Why did these pious Jews turn away from the conventions of the Orthodox path? They observed what had befallen Jewish polity since the emancipation of ghettos in Western countries and interpreted the events according to tradition's concepts, reading into them signs that attested to the advent of the long awaited redemption. Two things of enormous sig-nificance now occurred. The first was that edicts were pronounced and broadcast by scholars considered to be eminently vested with *halakhic* and religious authority to the effect that belief in an absolutely supernatural redemption was not acceptable dogma. Secondly, work for the resettlement of *Eretz Israel* was granted actual messianic status because it was now perceived as being a necessary precondition for the advancement of re-demption. From a study of the lives of Alkalay, Kalisher and Friedland it is evident that we are dealing here with a traditional interpretation of messianism in the fullest sense. They did not stop with noble speeches but spent all their efforts to convince people of the justice of their views. This is always the way of messianically imbued people, utterly convinced that they do nothing that is not ordained from on high, a task allotted to them long ago, as if by an ancient decree. This messianic determinism is a quality that informs the actions of the Zionist movement in its entirety, as we shall see further on in our discussion.

In granting these early heralds of Zionism such a crucial role in the annals of the movement I take issue with some of my colleagues who tend to underrate the importance of their contribution, some of them even writ-ing them off as altogether marginal. In my view these historians fail to understand the mental processes and the spiritual dedication of those who regard themselves as subject to religious tradition; particularly to the *Ha-lakhah*. Let us but imagine that the prohibition against "scaling the walls"

("Ve'shelo-yaalu-behoma min hagolah") i.e., to initiate a return of the Jewish People to its homeland and to reinstitute political independence there (*Midrash Rabbah, Shir Hashirim* B) had assumed the character not merely of an order *nisi* but of absolute and definitive *halakhic* restraining order such as the banning of all Jews from visiting the Temple Mount—which is still in effect today. Had this been the case then there would have been a very real taboo to all Zionist activity, and this taboo would have been insurmountable except through rejecting religion. In that eventuality Zionists would have been reduced to dependence on the extreme wing of the movement only and it is doubtful whether Zionism could have found support among the wide masses. Granted that a taboo of the type described was not invoked, there was certainly some recoil due to the belief in a messianic redemption. It is to the credit of orthodox harbingers of Zionism that by presenting the redemptive process in a new light they removed the hurdle in the way of human endeavor to return the people to its home. Furthermore, they affixed the label of messianism to the process, thereby granting the force of a legitimate inspirational source to the enterprise.

EMERGENT NATIONAL CONSCIOUSNESS

The historical events that breached the liberal barricade are clear. The rise of anti-Semitism in the West and the outbreak of pogroms in Russia raised serious doubts as to the feasibility of solving the Jewish question everywhere by adherence to the liberal model. Less than a decade had elapsed since Peixotto's plan had been rejected by representatives of Jewish communities of the West. The flight of thousands of victims of the pogroms to Galician cities forced them to look to emigration to find safe refuge. Yet even after the pogroms the rejection of the idea of emigration by the official leadership of Russian Jewry continued. But this was a tactical step to avoid giving the Russian authorities a pretext to undercut the status of Jews. In the minds of the Jewish public, emigration now enjoyed a growing acceptability as a rescue operation and a significant minority adopted it over the years.

There arose within this minority the well-known polemic between those who preferred America and those who opted for immigration to *Eretz Israel*. The rationale of the latter was predicated on their conviction that national rebirth was unthinkable anywhere other than in the historic land of the Jewish People. The idea of a renaissance was not a reaction to the pogroms. The historic record shows—and not only in the case of the Jews— that public misfortunes do not generally give birth to new ideas, but indeed do give impetus and vigor to ideas that had lain passive in the mind even before the outbreak of the misfortunes. It is also well known that a national consciousness had begun to find a voice in the writings of such authors and publicists as Peretz, Smolenskin, David Gordon, and others, a full decade before the outbreak of anti-Semitic riots in Russia. These expressions of national consciousness were variously spurred by the words of the visionaries cited above and by the example of the nationalist movements of other peoples. They disregarded the homiletic elements in the words of the visionaries and took from the foreign sources whatever they found relevant to the conditions of Jewish existence. Thus an entire national ideology came into being. It assigned a crucial value to anything that stressed the singularity of the Jews, their being, their consciousness, anything that made them different from other peoples, their affinity to their homeland, their original language, their cultural heritage, their religion, and even the scholarly study of history. There was only one ideologue who drew a positive conclusion from this ideology, i.e., *aliyah* to *Eretz Israel*. He was Eliezer Ben Yehuda, who was the most consistent and positive practitioner of nationalist ideology. But there were others who drew at least negative conclusions from the assumption of Jewish uniqueness—rejection of the liberal model. Acceptance of the liberal solution was predicated on their jettisoning all signs testifying to singularity.

But such developments did not manifest themselves in the life of Eastern European Jewry. That segment found itself slowly pushed out of its traditional life forms, but the vacuum thereby created was not refilled, as it was in the West, by foreign cultural components but by an indigenous cultural creativity. Some of the more notable among these were the cultivation of two national languages, Yiddish and Hebrew, and the growth of a considerable body of literature in each of them. An impressive circulation of Hebrew newspapers and periodicals, renewal of the educational system so as to bring it into line with modern educational trends, in short, everything which the *Haskalah* (Jewish Enlightenment) in its Eastern European version was capable of providing also went in to fill the void. It was only on the fringes of Eastern European society, only among Jews who no longer lived in the Pale of Settlement, that an "open" life style similar to the one developed by Western Jews emerged. That life style was marked by an almost complete accommodation to the culture of its environment. Yet since these Jews on the margin did not seem to offer a viable model to the community as a whole, when the partisans of nationalist ideologies claimed that the Jewish People were a tangible fact they had something of substance on which to support their case. The bloody pogroms provided the catalyst to turn nationalist theories into a decisive factor in the decision of potential emigrants to come to *Eretz Israel*. This very factor was operative at an even earlier date in Rumania albeit under less dramatic circumstances.

HOW JEWISH NATIONAL CONSCIOUSNESS DIFFERS

The impact of historical events and developments on the new national ideal has been frequently described and adduced by a variety of Zionist historians. The question that is difficult to answer is how this ideal ever drew near to realization when it lacked all the requisite elements therefor.

The Jewish national movement differed from all other national movements in that the task of the latter was to awaken in peoples resident in their homeland a cultivation of their unique values, a determination to unite under self rule, and in some instances a battle to liberate themselves from foreign domination. But the Jewish national movement undertook to assemble the dispersed elements of the people from the ends of the earth to a land in which they held almost no beach-head, a land that was considered desolate, neglected, and underdeveloped in comparison with the lands where the dispersed were living. Those who refused to believe in the feasibility of achieving the goal were not necessarily cynics and skeptics. Indeed the ultimate success of the movement is not easily explainable.

UNREQUITED LOVE VS. TANGIBLE FOUNDATIONS

Maybe some explanation can be found in the study of Zionism's confrontation with its third rival, revolutionary socialism. This movement operated in tandem with Zionism in Jewish society and competed with it for the loyalties of the best of idealistic youth. This youth could no longer tolerate life in the *stedtl*, which they found both ugly and inadequate. The erosion of its religious elements had undercut the metaphysical justification of life in exile, thus making it unbearable. Two possible escape routes from this situation appeared simultaneously on the horizon, Zionism and radical socialism. Both of them demanded an unflagging commitment of their supporters and both of them presented a challenge to young people who were actuated by moral sensitivity. Despite the ostensibly rational plane on which the debate between the two camps was conducted, the decision about which of them to join as often as not was determined by one's latent psychological motivation. One of socialism's arguments against Zionism was based on the latter's declared aspiration "to return the pristine splendor" of the Jewish People, that is, to resume Jewish history where it had been forcibly terminated when the Jews were exiled from their home. To socialist eyes this was a mere daydream, tantamount to inventing a people through sheer exercise of imaginative will. As against the illusory People

126

of the Zionist vision, socialists pointed to an existent reality, the international proletariat of which they considered themselves a part. Therefore they were sure that their stuggle for liberating the working class was intertwined with their Jewish vision.

And now, when we assess this debate in retrospect, we can state with absolute impartiality that those who advanced the "realistic" thesis were bereft of reality whereas the "visionaries" found tangible foundations albeit not strictly according to their scenario. Insofar as the concept of an international proletariat on which the revolutionaries based their hopes goes, its end reveals what it was from its very beginning; it was no more than the stillborn child of an abstract ideological concept. What Jewish socialists really found were divisions of the Polish and Russian proletariat, and to the extent that the infatuation of Jewish radicals was directed toward them, it remained an unrequited love.

SYMBOLS DO NOT MAKE A PEOPLE

We are dealing with the history of the socialist movement as such, only in order to give facts intended to serve as a background against which we can better understand what transpired in the Zionist movement. Such a comparison yields the following: whereas the clarion call of the Jewish socialists disintegrated on the solid wall of events, Zionism's call found a responsive sounding board in the public and the call did not remain unanswered (whether positive or negative, there was a *response*). Those who disagreed took issue by trying to discredit a concept that was handed to them as a convenient handle by the Zionists themselves: the return to a long dead past. This arose through the confusion of the symbolic plane with the real one. Zionism did not resurrect the Maccabees or Bar Kokhba's warriors from their graves but converted them along with a wealth of other concepts derived from the nation's past and tradition into symbols that could be identified with the new national aspirations. But even the richest system of symbols cannot create a people; it can be effective only if there is a national organism that can react—that lives. Indeed this was the fateful issue that confronted the earliest Zionists. It was decided affirmatively almost by way of an historical experiment; the early results indicating which way the experiment would go were available from the results of the early efforts at settlement. Eastern European Jewry, amongst whom national feelings rode high, avidly kept abreast of developments in this field. The importance of this close interest transcends even the material support without which the enterprise could not have succeeded. It was crucial that those who were actively involved in the experiment of settling the Land were given a feeling that they were emissaries and that they were acting on behalf of those who looked on. This feeling was grounded in the belief that a sizable public even when it does not give the enterprise the material support that it deserves, nonetheless never stops taking a vital interest in how it develops. A complete acceptance, and a total identification with the network of symbols of the new nationalism were not a *sine qua non* for active personal participation in the national enterprise.

Among the first members of Hovevei Zion (the proto-Zionist "Lovers of Zion") movement in Russia there were some of the greatest of the ultra-Orthodox rabbis. They had strong reservations about nationalist ideology and explained their support for Hovevei Zion on *halakhic* grounds, i.e., the *mitzvah* of settling in *Eretz Israel*. Similarly, among Yemenite Jews as well as other Eastern Jewish communities there was an active belief in a messianism uncomplicated by the need for transfiguration into modern nationalism. Consequently the partnership was not based on a necessary unity of thought but on the fact of belonging to the national experience, a national experience, furthermore, out of which the exigencies of modern life had built a wide variety of expressions and thought patterns. Rudiments of an earlier epoch when national belonging was more manifest remained, even in places where a conscious affinity had almost completely receded. Jewish solidarity, which was seen among Jews of the West despite their integration into the foreign environment, was a vestige of the old idea of a nation. In view of the role that such solidarity played in material support for the early Zionist settlement efforts, and in the maintenance of other institutions in the *Yishuv* even afterwards, we must regard the people who responded out of a sense of solidarity as full partners in the national enterprise. The weakening of national consciousness among Jews of the West did not prevent the ultimate return to this consciousness of a number of unique people by means of a kind of dialectic shortcut. Perhaps it was precisely such a shortcut that created the scope and the broad national horizons which characterized the leadership of the movement that rose in the West with Theodor Herzl at its head.

It was not only in its confrontation with socialism that this broad public response discriminated in favor of Zionism. Rescue plans meant to alleviate the special phenomenon of Jewish suffering and oppression were circulated both before and after the advent of Zionism. All the schemes, beginning with Mordecai Manuel Noah's Ararat plan down to Israel Zangwill's territorialism failed to elicit meaningful public support and remained unlikely utopias. Indeed Zionism was called a utopia by Herzl himself, and had it remained in the realm of a search for a Jewish territory wherever one could be found, as it originally formulated itself in his mind, it too would have been another of the unrealized utopias. But not only did Herzl base his program on the motivating drive of Jewish suffering, he also realized the unifying power of symbols and thought it possible to invent an *ad hoc* symbol, to unfurl a flag that would attract loyal supporters of the Zionist idea around it. Yet Herzl was not in need of artificial symbols, and this saved his plan from the realm of utopia, in the negative construction of that term. He found a wealth of ready-made symbols available, not symbols bespeaking a rescue plan in the face of Jewish oppression but pointing instead precisely in the direction of an utopian national renaissance. This was utopia in a positive sense, a vision of a future worthy of support because of its inherent value.

THE TOPOGRAPHY OF UTOPIA

But there are differences between utopias just as there are between symbols. It is through this discrimination that one can define the essence of Zionism and locate its place and its significance in Jewish history of the last few generations. When Zionism appeared in the Jewish public arena, it did so as a utopia, and furthermore, as a utopia that splintered into several divergent ones; a messianic variant in the eyes of those who regarded Zionism as paving the way for the messiah, a religious or moral variant in the eyes of those with expectations for a rejuvenation of Jewish religion or Jewish morality, and a social or socialist utopia in accordance with the trends of thought of those items. Nor do these exhaust the list.

The question arises as to how the partisans of these disparate utopias could live together and, in practice, work together for a common goal. The answer is that all these utopias had as a common denominator the belief that it was only in *Eretz Israel* that their utopia could be realized. This was, of course, an irrational belief, and Zionism's opponents, particularly in the liberal and socialist camps, used every opportunity to ridicule Zionism on that score. They could not know that it was just this irrational aspect that gave Zionism its greatest strength.

Any utopia is the vision of a future *not yet realized* and is, by definition, irrational. It can be realized only when those who believe in it know that its future is assured, is inevitable, because it has been ordained. The paradox here is that precisely the belief in its inevitability makes the believers in a given utopia strive all the more for its realization. The early Zionists rebelled against the conditions of life in their lands and utterly rejected all other options that were ostensibly open, such as emigration to other lands. Slowly the ideal of national rebirth gained ground, and support of this ideal was enhanced by challenges and drives originating both outside Jewry and from within. It now appeared that Zionism was the only viable portrayal of the future, and it called for a total mobilization of all the strength and all the resources of those who identified with it. This identification, as all identifications with visions of a future utopia, expressed itself through the medium of symbols. Without doubt, these symbols were readily available in the history and traditions of the Jewish People. Still, the abundance of symbols exploited by the earliest Zionists, such as the names they gave to new settlements in *Eretz Israel* and to Zionist associations abroad, were merely ancillary, hinting and alluding to the messianic redemption of the tradition. The central role in this process was assigned to the fortunate choice of "Zion," which the movement adopted for its name. Zion came to connote the symbol of national renaissance and also the concrete *topos* for its realization. Henceforward both constructions of the word became inextricably bound up with each other so that subsequent attempts to separate them by choosing another site for the realization of Jewish national rebirth were doomed to failure. From this very nexus stems the irrational belief of the various utopian Zionists that their ideals could come to fruition only in *Eretz Israel*. This belief they held in common, brought them under one roof and created the minimal basis for cooperation between them.

The question as to whether Zionism should properly be regarded as a messianic movement has exercised some of the best minds. Those who have reservations about the term have some weighty reasons for their reluctance. They are apprehensive lest irrational tendencies should penetrate into affairs whose conduct should be predicated on wisdom and stability. But such a danger cannot be avoided by beclouding historical truth. Both the content and the direction that national life ought to assume were at issue even among the early visionaries holding diverse ideas of utopian Zionism. What was not at issue was their common determination to deflect the course of evolving Jewish history. Gone was the traditional conviction that the Jewish People could survive exilic life. It was replaced by their shared view that what future there was would unfold only in the land of their fathers. The decisiveness with which they held to this conviction typifies Zionism and determines its place in the annals of the Jewish People.

Zionism and Jewish Identity

10

Jewish identity is as problematic in the modern world as it was not in pre-modern times. In the Middle Ages and until the breaking up of the ghetto in the eighteenth century, whatever the burdens of Jewish life might have been, a self-questioning skepticism about individual identity was not one of them. Jewry and Judaism were defined quite simply in that period as contrasts to Christianity and Islam. The political and social position of the Jew lay in the space granted him by those two rivals—a space that was at times suffocatingly minimal, at times more generous.

Within those confines the Jewish community survived, retained and developed its religion, and cultivated an entire civilization: law, language, folklore, memories of a common past, and expectations of a common future. It was, indeed, through these elements of traditional culture that the Jew of pre-modern times achieved identification with his community. Not that there was no such thing as alienation, or even the defection of individuals and groups to rival religions (as society was divided along the lines of religious affiliation, the Jew who left his own community had no choice but to join another through religious conversion). But what was not known, up to the middle of the seventeenth century, was a case like that of Spinoza, the case of someone surviving as a Jewish heretic without converting to Christianity.

All this changed in the course of the political and social emancipation of the Jews in the eighteenth and nineteenth centuries and the concomitant secularization of both state and society throughout the West. It is noteworthy that the very term used to describe the struggle for a new status—"emancipation"—is a term of celebration, connoting breakthrough and liberation. I do not mean here to pass judgment in retrospect on the question of whether celebration was, or still is, warranted, but to spell out the price that had to be paid for this achievement in the loss of individual identity. For, as the history of the generations succeeding the emancipation testifies, freedom from the constrictions of the ghetto did not lead automatically to integration into society at large. Nor did the loss of contact with ghetto culture lead easily to the acquisition of another culture. Though there were cases of successful assimilation, with or without conversion, collectively speaking the adaptation of emancipated Jews to their environment, and the adaptation of their environment to them, turned out to be a more complicated and painful process than the early champions of emancipation had imagined.

The problematic aspects of emancipation became obvious early on, even before modern anti-Semitism, which is the reaction to Jewish emancipation, had set in. It is difficult now, especially from the viewpoint of America, to imagine the pressures to which German and French Jews were exposed in the nineteenth century. They were asked to adopt the pattern of conduct prevailing in the surrounding society, to merge into the national culture, and to wipe out or at least cover over any Jewish features that may have persisted in their mental or even physical makeup. Virtually nowhere in Europe did the idea of pluralism, or anything remotely like it, take hold. Indeed, not even the official spokesmen of Judaism felt the need for such a concept. Having newly defined Judaism as a religious creed and only a religious creed, they considered that in all other respects Jews belonged to the general category of citizens. In reality, however, Judaism even in its post-emancipation version continued to represent an entire minority culture, and the Jews a conspicuous subgroup. The problem was that no ideology had been developed to justify or account for this state of affairs. The resulting burden of a split and confused identity caused terrible suffering among many Jews, whose very personalities were disfigured by the dilemma.

Zionism appeared to offer a solution—one can almost say salvation—to Jews caught in this predicament. For if, as Zionism held, the Jews were to be defined as a nation, with a collective past *and* a collective future, then Jewish "peculiarity" not only became intelligible but was worth preserving and cultivating. The problem of identity was of course not the only problem to which Zionism was a response—we need only mention such factors as the homelessness of East European Jews who had been compelled to emigrate to the West, the emergence of political anti-Semitism, and not least the impact of the new semi-secular messianism among Jews envisaging a revival of the ancient Jewish homeland—but still, many who joined the Zionist movement were indeed motivated by the belief that they would gain thereby a defensible definition of their group identity.[1]

The published correspondence of Martin Buber shows the liberating effect his message of Jewish nationalism had on some of the outstanding Jewish intellectuals of his day. Active in the cultural environment of Vienna, Prague, and Berlin, they still felt themselves to be different, set apart, but lacking the intellectual tools to account for that sense of difference and the ambivalence that went along with it. Buber's conception of Jewish nationalism, with its claim to embody a unique set of spiritual values, was exactly the formula these intellectuals needed to come to terms with their situation.

Nor was Buber the only Zionist ideologue whose arguments appealed on the intellectual level. The Hebrew writer Ahad Ha'am proposed that Jewish intellectuals in the West were not free to speak their own minds because of an inner anxiety about being stamped as Jewish, and were thus inhibited from realizing their full creative potential. Zionism, he argued, with its promise of an all embracing Jewish cultural environment, offered the Jewish personality the opportunity of unhampered and harmonious development. Other Zionist writers argued along the same lines, and their arguments were gratefully received by the class of intellectuals to whom they were addressed.

Did Zionism live up to its promise? The answer one gives will depend upon one's notion of what constitutes a Jewish environment. Two extreme visions of such an environment were proposed in the early days of the Zionist movement, one religious vision and one secular vision.

Religious Zionists imagined that by a return to the Jewish homeland and the establishment there of an exclusive Jewish society, all the historic wounds inflicted on the Jewish psyche would automatically heal. In the occlusion of Palestine they hoped to rebuild a Jewish community untroubled by the forces of assimilation and religious reform. Thus, one prominent rabbi, Akiva Josef Schlesinger from Pressburg (Bratislava), despairing of the struggle against what he regarded as the absolute decline of Jewish life in Europe, left in 1870 for Palestine, where he aimed to establish a community that would be immune to the dangers of modernity. He conceived a kind of order self-supporting through physical labor, agriculture, and industry, but otherwise dedicated to the Orthodox way of life.

Schlesinger antagonized the leaders of the old religious community already resident in Palestine, whose ideal was the contemplative life, dedicated to prayer and the study of Torah, in return for which they expected to be supported (as indeed they were) by pious Jews around the world. This, however, did not deter Schlesinger or other religious Zionists from believing that the new movement, though apparently in conflict with some elements of the tradition, would lead ultimately to its rehabilitation. In the thought of Rabbi Abraham Isaac Kook this belief was founded upon a veritable messianism. A great talmudic scholar and a genuinely creative mystic, Kook conceived of the Jewish national revival as the first step toward the spiritualization anticipated by the Jewish tradition for the messianic age. Similarly, Rabbi Yehuda Fishman-Maimon proposed to reestablish the ancient judicial institution of the Sanhedrin, a proposal cautiously countenanced by Rabbi Kook as well. Though seemingly of practical purpose, this suggestion was also prompted by quasi-messianic expectations, as it was felt that the restoration of Jewish society in the ancient homeland would be incomplete without the institutions that had conducted the affairs of the community in ancient times.

Quite apart from messianic stirrings like these, religious Zionists based their hopes for a regeneration of Judaism on their analysis of the effect of emancipation on the traditional religious loyalties of Jews. The price of political emancipation was assimilation, and assimilation meant a defection from traditional Jewish life throughout the West. In place of emancipation, the Zionists offered *self*-emancipation, a process of inner liberation that, in addition to restoring political self-respect to the Jews, would restore religious self-respect as well. Had not Theodor Herzl himself declared that the return to the Jewish land would have to be preceded by a return to Judaism?

Unfortunately, the Judaism to which Herzl or any other modern Zionist was ready to return was not the Judaism of the pre-emancipatory period, the deterioration of which was so much deplored by traditionalists. In fact, the traditionalist analysis was overly simple. Simultaneously with political and social emancipation, the Jewish community had become confronted with all the forces of modernity itself, and there was no way it could have escaped the dissolution of old patterns of life, which was modernity's legacy everywhere. The most the traditionalists could have hoped for through their program for a culturally self-sufficient society was that Jews would no longer totally disavow their cultural heritage. This, however, would hardly be tantamount to a reinstitution of religion in the life of the community.

If the expectations of the religious, then, amounted to a romantic longing for a lost past, the other extreme of the ideological spectrum, the secular wing of the Zionist movement, harbored similarly illusory ideas about the harmonious identity to be engendered by the new society. Onetime Enlightenment intellectuals and socialists, strong critics of Jewish tradition, the secularists conceived of the return to the ancient homeland as an absolutely new beginning, which meant leaving behind all that had attached itself to Jewish life throughout the long sojourn in foreign countries, including what the Jews themselves had created in the constraining circumstances of exile. Into this category fell not only the Jewish mode of life in ghetto and *shtetl*, but the whole of Rabbinic Judaism. The only element of the past to be absorbed by the culture of the future was to be the Hebrew Bible, the creation of the national genius in its pristine state.

It goes without saying that the secular Zionists were no more able than the traditionalists to live up to the consequences of their ideas. They certainly did not abandon the cultural heritage of post-biblical times. Even the revival of the Hebrew language, no doubt the greatest cultural achievement of the national movement, and an indispensable precondition of its success, could never have been accomplished on the basis of biblical vocabulary alone, as some purists would have had it. Modern Hebrew absorbed elements from every historical stratum the language had passed through—biblical, talmudic, medieval, and pre-modern—and drew upon every literary form in which it had ever been employed. Nor did secular education in Palestine—and later in Israel—forgo the study of the classic talmudic literature, or the Hebrew poetry of the Middle Ages. Selected portions of these have become part and parcel of the school curriculum on all levels in present-day Israel.

A similar divergence is evident in the study and evaluation of Jewish history. Theoretically, a self-sufficient society and an independent state would have no use for the history of a Diaspora people. Nor could a record of passive suffering serve as inspiration to a free people. As the novelist Haim Hazaz put it in a fictional dialogue between two early pioneers, there was no such thing as Jewish "history"; history was something made by Gentiles, of which the Jews had been merely the passive victims. Practically, however, both in the pre-state period and thereafter, an immense interest has been expressed in almost every aspect of Jewish history, and on almost every level, both scholarly and popular. It is true that the first generation of *sabras* had its difficulties identifying with the history of Jewish martyrdom or sympathizing with the proverbial passivity of Diaspora Jews. To them, biblical times and the saga of Jewish independence during the period of the Second Commonwealth seemed more "relevant," and more real. But after the catastrophic destruction of European Jewry in World War II, the vanished world of the East European *shtetl* came to be idealized in the popular consciousness—a reversal so sudden and complete as to cast doubt on the depth of the previous estrangement.

The project of ignoring thousands of years of history and culture was utopian in any case. It had been the dream of the "Canaanites," a group of young intellectuals, to create a locally based civilization related to that of the autochthonous population of pre-biblical Palestine. Reflecting the deep attachment of the Palestinian-born generation to its physical environment, these intellectuals aimed to transform that attachment into a basis of collective identity, while at the same time excluding everything their parents had tried to transmit to them of their Jewish and even their Zionist heritage. As such, the Canaanite ideology may be seen as the extension of the secular Zionist idea to its extreme limit of consistency.

Certain of the early political thinkers of Zionism, starting with Herzl, imagined that once the Jewish state had gathered to itself all those Jews who would not or could not find a place in their respective countries of origin, all the remaining Jews would assimilate and be absorbed into their environment. Left to its own devices, the Jewish state would then develop a separate identity by resorting to an early phase of Jewish, or even pre-Judaic, culture. Some such idea was expressed by Jacob Klatzkin, a scholar and philosopher, in the 1920s, by Arthur Koestler in the late 1940s, and by Georges Friedmann, the French-Jewish sociologist, in the 1960s; it must be regarded as a fantasy. There was never a likelihood that the existence of a Jewish state would facilitate the assimilation of Jews in the Diaspora. What *could* happen was that the creation of a Jewish commonwealth in Palestine would make a point around which the communities of the Diaspora could rally, and from which they could receive cultural inspiration to keep them going and keep them Jewish.

To what extent the state of Israel actually performs this role will be discussed below. But it is certain that the opposite conception—of an ever-widening gap between the Jewish state and the Diaspora—is mistaken, just as the idea that Zionism could recapture a stage of development fifty or sixty generations old was and remains a figment of the imagination.

Given the illusions under which both religious and secular Zionists labored, and given too the extreme polarization between them, it may seem a wonder that they were able to cooperate at all on a common program. The fact that they did so suggests a basic acceptance of mutual identification as well as an understanding of the real historical forces that were at work.

Jewry in the last third of the nineteenth century, when Zionism emerged, was confronting two such historical forces, modernization and secularization. The traditional definition of Jews as the remnant of biblical Israel, loyal to the mission implied in its name, had been undermined, with everything that entailed by way of a loss of collective identity. The political program of emancipation seemed at first to offer a solution to this dilemma—albeit one that implied the ultimate disappearance of the Jews as a special entity—but as this process was resisted by internal as well as external forces (Jewish social cohesiveness on the one hand, anti-Semitism on the other), a redefinition of Judaism became intellectually imperative. This redefinition had to account for the continuing existence of the Jews as a collectivity without rescinding the insights and commitments that had newly imposed themselves upon Jewish consciousness. The term that offered itself was the Zionist one of the "nation."

There was nothing artificial about the use of this term, which in fact had long been present in the traditional conception of Jews and Judaism as well. Theologically, Judaism posited the existence of a Jewish nation, with a long and peculiar history related to the possession of its land of origin, a land to which Jewry was destined to return in an undefined but never doubted future. The elements of this nationalism are akin to those of European nationalism; and it is beyond doubt that the emergence of nationalist movements in the nineteenth century encouraged the full articulation of a Jewish parallel. The difference lay in the fact that other peoples already possessed the concrete elements of nationalism: they lived on their national ground, at least some of them spoke the national language, they were a compact (if politically oppressed) society.

In the case of the Jews the concrete elements of nationalism were still embryonic or dormant. The destitute communities of the Holy Land fulfilled a symbolic role as representatives of the Jewish claim to the country, but offered a limited foundation for a national movement. The rest of the prospective national body lived scattered among the nations of the earth, partly assimilated and thus shorn of obvious "national" qualities, partly still moored in the patterns of traditional life and thus unlikely to participate actively in the shaping of a national future. That in spite of these impediments the national movement succeeded in mustering the resources for a pioneering effort of resettlement, for the creation of a new society, and finally for the establishment of an independent state, will long remain a marvel—to anyone, at least, who believes that describing facts in chronological order is not tantamount to explaining them.

One of the forces propelling the Jewish national movement was the tradition of Jewish messianism. This force had erupted over and over again in earlier centuries with the appearance of so-called false messiahs, demonstrating the never-fading faith of the Jewish masses in the ultimate termination of the exile through miraculous redemption. The emphasis, however, was on the word "miraculous." According to tradition, redemption would take place through divine decree, the hastening of which, if possible at all, could be brought about by spiritual means alone. This traditional conception was transmuted in the modern period not only by secular thinkers, but also by some Orthodox rabbis, who, impressed by the events of political emancipation, concluded that the divine will demanded of the Jews that they take their destiny into their own hands.

The unwillingness to regard the present conditions of society as final— an attitude characterizing many Jewish reformers and revolutionaries in our time—has often been ascribed to the residues of a specific Jewish mentality, even in the case of individuals who have severed all conscious ties with their community. Though not easily demonstrated, the proposition deserves to be taken seriously. That the crumbling of the ghetto walls and the shedding of traditional restrictions released a tremendous amount of pent-up energy among Jews, an energy that astounded and at times frightened the surrounding world, is an observable though sometimes unwelcome fact. What the Jewish national movement accomplished was the channeling of a good part of this energy into the realization of the secularized messianic vision.

Secularization is often understood as the mere extraction of certain domains of life from the restrictive sphere of religion. Such extraction indeed occurs, but the most significant effects of secularization are to be seen when the emotion once directed at a religious term, image, or entire world-vision is transferred to its secular counterpart. The outstanding Jewish example of this phenomenon is the way in which Zionism retained the traditional and religiously sanctioned goal of a return to the ancestral homeland, attributing to it as well all the desirable features of a wholesome national existence: political independence, economic self-sufficiency, the return to nature and physical work, as well as the establishment of a society based on equality and justice. All these objectives were conceived by Zionism as inherent in the old Jewish idea of redemption, prevented from realization on account of the conditions of exile. True redemption—the establishment of a society free from the shackles of the *Galut*—would liberate the forces latent in the Jewish mentality and produce the miracle of the regeneration of Jewish life.

Utopian as this vision may have appeared to anyone who did not share it, whatever has been accomplished in its name—and this has been considerable—is due, paradoxically, to this utopian quality. The more tangible factors—pogroms, anti-Semitism in the West, and the resultant economic and political insecurities—were responsible in an immediate sense for the desire on the part of Jews to seek out new prospects and new vistas. Yet these pressures by themselves elicited only the accustomed response of escape through emigration. The majority of those uprooted by the anti-Jewish measures of the late nineteenth and early twentieth centuries went to countries where they hoped to find a better situation, leaving the problem of their identity to the exigencies of chance. It was just this abandoning of the fortunes of Jewry and Judaism to the hazards of chance that the Jewish national movement attempted to combat. In adopting its vision of national reconstruction, it wished to erect a secure framework for the inevitable process of modernization, without incurring the loss of Jewish identity.

Modernization, of course, involves change, which is why the dream of a new society constructed according to some ideal religious or secular image turned out to be utopian. The society of the early pioneers and of the Mandate period, no less than the society of present-day Israel, took on all the features of modernity, including the modern tension between tradition and innovation. This tension was and still is evident in many walks of life, especially in areas connected with religion. The utopians who, if they were religious, hoped to restore national unity by reinstating the primacy of religion, or, if they were secular, hoped to eliminate it altogether, would both have reason to be disappointed.

Religion does loom large on the Israeli public scene, not only insofar as the state takes cognizance of religious values, but also in that one section of Jewish religious law—the section dealing with matters of personal status, especially marriage and divorce—is included as part of the Israeli legal system. But it would be hasty and incorrect to conclude from the quasi-official status of the Jewish religion that Israel is a theocratic society. The retention of rabbinical jurisdiction over one facet of life is not only an anomaly by the standards of Western secularized countries, it contradicts the basic rule of Israeli society as well—the rule that the individual is free to choose whether and to what extent he will subscribe to religious practice and accept religious teaching.

But if the contradiction between religion and modern life remains, in some domains, in full force in Israel, in other respects tradition has been transformed into viable modern patterns. The recurring festivals of the religious calendar, for example, are celebrated at least by a minority in strict accordance with ritual law, and this fact alone lends them an air of antiquity and authority. In the initial stages of national reconstruction, attempts were made to divest the ancient festivals of their religious character and to turn them into mere national commemorations; this tendency has now receded, and public celebrations, as in the army, are for the most part traditional in character. Though the arrangement leads at times to conflict between religious zealots and the nonobservant—with the former trying to impose strict observance on the latter—on the whole, the traditional celebration of festivals fulfills a unifying function. By assimilating them into the national consciousness, Israelis also demonstrate their ties to Jewry and Judaism—just as, conversely, the celebration of Israeli national holidays (Independence Day, Memorial Day) has become a regular part of the calendar for most Jewish communities abroad.

Finally, where it was once predicted that the divergence between Jewish and Israeli identity would increase over time, it has actually diminished. This is the result of an internal Israeli development, but one which has had a parallel in the Diaspora. Outside Israel there was the expectation, or rather the apprehension, that the overwhelming focus on helping Israel and the preoccupation with Israel's military crises would divert energy and attention from the needs and potentialities of the Diaspora communities. Tension and competition between Israel and the Diaspora have indeed arisen on both the material and on the spiritual levels, but in the final reckoning the ascendancy of Israel has elicited in the Diaspora forces and energies of an unexpected magnitude, and a great deal of the resulting benefit has redounded to Diaspora life.

At the same time, the utopian expectations associated with the emergence of Zionism and the creation of Israel have failed to materialize. What has evolved is a kind of collective Jewish destiny, beyond the decision of individuals and groups. To become or not to become a Zionist was at one time a matter of free choice for Jews, and many declined the Zionist option. Thus, Hermann Cohen, the distinguished German-Jewish philosopher, when asked why he, though a committed Jew, was not a Zionist, answered: "Those people wish to be happy." For Cohen, the Zionist desire to extricate the Jews from the duality of life in the Diaspora would have entailed the elimination of precisely the most intriguing element of Jewish existence. This little anecdote took place before the Balfour Declaration of 1917, before the Holocaust, before the struggle for the survival of Jewry and Judaism in an independent Jewish state. Today the situation is reversed: it is those Jews who declare themselves non-Zionists or anti-Zionists who display the longing for happiness. Were it not for Israelis and Zionists, they seem to be saying, we could live in happiness and peace. Yet happiness of that sort, alas, seems not to be the lot of the Jew. His real choice, which is moral choice, is whether to ignore his situation or confront it with a full sense of the responsibilities it entails.

Zionism Versus Anti-Semitism

11

Ever since its emergence as a national movement, Zionism has had its ideological and political opponents. Within Jewry itself, opposition arose in the early days both from the Left—the socialists and Communists—and from the Right—the Orthodox. It is perhaps a sign of the times that when one speaks of anti-Zionism today, one is inclined rather to think of resistance and animosity from without. What internal resentment and criticism exist are directed more against particular features of Zionist activity and aspiration than against the phenomenon as a whole, and even such criticism falls silent when confronted with the expressions of absolute denial coming from outside. Thus, in 1975, when the out-and-out assault of the United Nations General Assembly against Zionism occurred, identifying it with racism, Jewry found itself discriminated against at its very core, and reacted by rallying as one around the beleaguered camp of the Zionists.

Recent events have turned the notions of anti-Zionist and anti-Semite into veritable synonyms. At the same time, they have raised the question of the possible historical relation between the national movement of the Jewish people and modern anti-Semitism, a relation that is more complex than a superficial acquaintance with either phenomenon would suggest.

It is a truism, and one which the founders of Zionism were themselves quick to acknowledge, that the Zionist political program was connected in some way with the prevalence of anti-Semitism in Europe in the late nineteenth century. Did not Theodor Herzl evolve his Zionist program under the impact of the Dreyfus affair, the drama he observed as an eyewitness in Paris in the mid-1890s? Did not Leon (Yehuda Leib) Pinsker write his Zionist pamphlet, *Auto-Emancipation,* in reaction to the bloody pogroms of Russia in 1881? Indeed, two staple arguments of early Zionists in favor of their ideological and political programs were the reluctance of Western societies to accept even emancipated Jews as equals and, in the East, the forestalling of emancipation by the Russian pogroms. And if, on the one hand, the founders of Zionism acknowledged the link between their political program and European anti-Semitism, external opponents of Zionism, on the other hand, often used this same connection as an ideological weapon to discredit the movement. Zionism was represented by its detractors as a mere reflection of anti-Semitism, and, as such, devoid of any deeper historical or spiritual significance.

But how important *was* the factor of anti-Semitism in the development of Zionism, and how important does it remain today? What *is* the precise relation between these two phenomena? At times, indeed, the conceptual framework of the two trends has seemed so intimately connected as to be almost identical. Thus, if there is one notion central to anti-Semitism in most of its ideological variants, it is the notion of race or its synonym, blood, employed as a means both of designating and of deprecating the Jews. Now, many Zionist thinkers, from Moses Hess to Martin Buber, used these same terms in delineating the boundaries of Jewish national existence. Did they then adopt the terminology of their enemies? In the case of Martin Buber, who began his Zionist activities toward the close of the nineteenth century, it is theoretically possible that such a process could have taken place. Moses Hess, however, wrote his *Rome and Jerusalem* in 1862, almost two decades before either Zionism or modern anti-Semitism appeared on the scene. This suggests that, whatever the parallels between the two phenomena, each had its own independent roots in the past.

Such, indeed, was the case. Hess himself, in Zionist historiography, is designated a "forerunner" of Zionism. The term indicates that although Zionism did not achieve the characteristics of a full-blown movement until the 1880s or perhaps even the 1890s it had a preparatory stage, a kind of subterranean preexistence, that preceded the movement proper by decades. And the same is true of modern anti-Semitism. The very term anti-Semitism—which was a creation of Wilhelm Marr—emerged only in the fall of 1879, coinciding with the eruption of the movement connected with the names of Adolf Stocker and Henrich von Treitschke. Yet the movement did not drop from the sky: it too had its forerunners, in Bruno Bauer and Richard Wagner in Germany; Adolph Toussenell in France; and Sebastian Brunner in Austria—to mention only a few. These figures were celebrated by later anti-Semites as early recognizers of the anti-Semitic "truth"—much in the same way as the Zionists of later days identified Hess and others as ideological anticipators.

To zero in on the actual source of the obvious parallelism between anti-Semitic and Zionist ideas we have to operate from the broader historical perspective. Both anti-Semitism and Zionism appeared against a background of ideological confusion into which Jewish existence had been thrown by the abandonment of the old theological definition of Judaism and the Jewish people. Both the Jewish and the Christian traditions had once accounted for the Jewish Diaspora by seeing it as divinely sanctioned. To

Christians, the Diaspora would be terminated by the absorption of the Jews into Gentile society upon their conversion at the end of the days; to Jews, it would be terminated through the ingathering of the Jews into their homeland with the coming of the Messiah. Once divested of these shielding interpretations by the growth of rationalism and historical criticism, Jewish existence turned into an enigma.

Jews at the end of the eighteenth century, and in most places even much later, retained the physical as well as the mental marks of a special collectivity, whose members, though dispersed over the whole of the Christian and Muslim world, were nonetheless linked together through apparent signs of affinity and solidarity. What they lacked was a plausible ideological justification for this state of affairs. Nor did this embarrassing situation contain any hint of the destiny yet awaiting the remnants of this ancient nation—unless one believed in the idea of emancipation.

Emancipation in its limited political or legal sense meant the granting of citizenship to the Jewish inhabitants of a country—a concession that the secular modern state, contrary to its Christian predecessor, was indeed capable of bestowing. Yet in a broader and deeper sense the idea of emancipation meant the attempt to put an end to the anomaly of Jewish existence, offering Jews of every country the chance to be absorbed into the local population.

Whether such a solution of the Jewish problem ever stood a chance of being implemented will always remain a matter of speculation. Had the Almighty inspired the rulers of all the countries where Jews lived to emancipate them exactly at the same time, they might indeed have been absorbed by the majority. Yet inasmuch as the granting of emancipation depended upon the phase of economic, political, and intellectual development a country had reached, the idea that it could have occurred simultaneously even in the European states alone is fantasy. It took some three generations from the time of the emancipation of the Jews of France, after the revolution, to the corresponding enfranchisement of German and Austro-Hungarian Jewry. And even before the emancipation of Russian Jewry was seriously contemplated, the reaction to emancipation had already made itself felt in Gemany, France, and Austria-Hungary. With the rise of the anti-Semitic movement, the concept of emancipation as the ultimate solution of the Jewish problem was repudiated.

That such a solution was illusory anyway is apparent, at least in historical retrospect, from what was transpiring in the life of the Jewish community before anti-Semitism appeared on the scene. Even where the idea of emancipation had been hailed as the redeeming message of the day, internal as well as external forces were at work to block the absorption of Jews into non-Jewish society. The cohesion of Jews among themselves, supported as it was by their being concentrated in certain economic fields, by their religious nonconformity, as well as by some cultural factors, made them a conspicuous and puzzling phenomenon. Citizenship, whether actually achieved or merely ardently desired, seemed to create a new reality, giving the lie to the old idea of the Jews as a community in temporary exile or subject to divine degradation. Yet if the old patterns of thought were of no avail, new ones had to be invented to do justice to the prevailing conditions. Indeed, a good deal of thinking about Jews and Judaism in the course of the last two centuries, on the part of Jews, their friends, and their foes alike, has been motivated or controlled by the need to take account of this post-theological and post-emancipatory reality. And that is why the most bitter adversaries of Jews and Judaism seem at times to speak the same language as Jews deeply attached to their community and its cultural heritage, though the two have had absolutely conflicting intentions. It is the common object of their reflections which is mirrored in the thought processes of each.

Some strange parallelisms can be adduced to substantiate this thesis. One of the most severe critics of the Jewish aspiration to civic equality in the early nineteenth century was the Heidelberg theologian Heinrich Eberhard Gottlob Paulus. Paulus followed closely the Jews' attempts to achieve their political objectives. He paid special attention to the struggle of Frankfurt Jewry to retain the civil rights acquired during the French occupation of the city in the last decade of Napoleon's rule. He commented profusely on this matter as well as on the palpable political and cultural mutation which had taken place in German Jewry during his generation. A latitudinarian theologian, who reduced his own religion of Protestantism to some basic moral principles and a minimum of symbolically interpreted rituals, Paulus hailed the attempts of the early Jewish reformers to do the same within their own religion by transferring the Sabbath to Sunday and abolishing the dietary laws and circumcision—in short, by removing the signs of Jewish singularity, which were thought to constitute an obstacle to civil equality and social acceptance.

Such tokens of Jewish flexibility notwithstanding, however, Paulus was angered by the obvious reluctance of the bulk of the Jewish community to go along with the suggested adaptations. In the wake of the revolution of 1830, when the Jewish question was on the agenda of the Baden parliament and the Jewish cause had found an articulate advocate in the person of Gabriel Riesser, Paulus joined the fray with his pamphlet "The Jewish National Separation: Its Origin, Consequences, and the Means of its Correction." The thesis of the book, as indicated in the title, was that Jews were a nation apart, and would remain so as long as they were committed to their religion, whose basic intent and purpose were to preserve them in that condition. In a country that was not their own, therefore, Jews could not claim more than the bare protection of their lives and possessions. They might certainly not claim political equality.

The charge that the Jews were an unassimilable nation was a favorite of opponents of emancipation in France, Holland, Germany, and elsewhere. Yet Paulus gave it a particular slant. In contrast to others, he did not concentrate on such external expressions of Jewishness as social cohesion, professional one-sidedness, and the like. His basic argument was that the Jewish *religion*, by nature of its legal foundation and its claim to the allegiance of all those born of a Jewish mother, turned the Jews into a national body even when individuals failed to live up to all of its principles and demands. This, of course, is exactly what Jewish theologians had been saying since the Middle Ages, and so did modern Jewish nationalists who were religiously oriented. Reading Paulus, one thinks of Isaac Breuer, the leader of Agudat Israel, who, though a militant opponent of political Zionism, defined Judaism in legalistic terms as a nation bound to the constitution spelled out in Jewish law and transmitted through the channels of *halakhic* tradition.

Nationalism legalistically defined may have been an idiosyncracy of Paulus and Breuer, but a conception of the Jews as a nation on some other, possibly more secular, ground—the very core of Zionist ideology—seems to have been anticipated by all the opponents of Jewish emancipation. Arthur Schopenhauer, for instance, is to be counted among these, and indeed for that reason he has recently been styled a forerunner of Theodor Herzl. Another and most surprising instance centers on a hitherto unknown intellectual encounter that took place between Moses Hess and Bruno Bauer.

Bauer initiated his anti-Jewish career with his *Judenfrage* ("The Jewish Question," 1842). At the time he was a militant young Hegelian; he pursued his anti-Semitic course unabatedly, even after having turned staunchly conservative in the 1850s. Bauer thus served as a virtual bridge between the early anti-Semitism of the first half of the nineteenth century and the outbreak of the anti-Semitic movement proper in the 1880s. The encounter I am referring to occurred in the middle, with the appearance of Moses Hess's *Rome and Jerusalem*. This book is now recognized as an early Zionist classic. Theodor Herzl himself, who became acquainted with it after having developed his own Zionist project, called it a full-fledged anticipation of his ideas. At the time of its appearance, however, the book was a failure. It sold in the course of the first year no more than 160 copies. In Jewish quarters the book created quite a stir, but outside the Jewish pale it received only slight public attention. Hess's modern biographer, Edmund Silberner, collected some twenty references to it in the Jewish and non-Jewish press, most of the latter being short notices of little significance. But the most interesting review escaped his vigilance. It appeared in an unlikely place, the *Berliner Revue*, the organ of the extreme Prussian conservatives. The lengthy article, printed in two issues of the weekly, appeared anonymously, but the author was beyond all doubt Bruno Bauer, one of the major contributors to the *Revue*.

The gist of the review was this: the author of *Rome and Jerusalem* thinks he has made a great discovery in stating that the Jewish race represents a full-fledged nation with a particular spirit and destiny. Yet very soon he will have the opportunity to read the reviewer's *Das Judentum in der Fremde* ("Jewry Abroad") and realize that others before him have been aware of this state of affairs. Obviously, Bauer glossed over the fact that his own presentation of Jews as a race and a nation carried with it overtones of animosity and contempt, while that of Moses Hess was geared to a positive reevaluation of Jewish national abilities and the prospect of their revitalization. For Hess this meant the reestablishment of a Jewish commonwealth in Palestine. Bauer, on the other hand, denied the Jews' ability to maintain their own state. They were a nation, but one doomed to live in everlasting exile at the expense of other nations. Still, despite their conflicting visions of the future, the fact remains that Bauer, the anti-Semite, regarded his conception of Judaism as identical with that of Moses Hess, the Zionist.

Like Bruno Bauer, Richard Wagner too evolved his anti-Jewish theory decades before the outbreak of anti-Semitism proper. Wagner's *Judentum in der Musik* ("Jews in Music"), published anonymously after the 1848–49 revolution, and republished under his full name in 1869, rightly ranks as an anti-Semitic classic, and has been used as effective propaganda by all subsequent generations of anti-Semites. Though specifically aimed at discrediting Wagner's contemporaries and competitors Felix Mendelssohn-Bartholdy and Giacomo Meyerbeer, the book is sustained by vituperate generalizations on the alleged deficiencies of the Jewish character and spirit. Yet beneath the vitriol is a layer of astute observation on the process of Jewish cultural assimilation. According to Wagner, Jewish artists, by severing themselves from their own popular cultural tradition, have relinquished the source of inspiration for creative activity. Since Jews are incapable of merging with the deeper layers of their surrounding society, and since their efforts at assimilation are directed exclusively toward the culturally barren middle class, Jewish artists find themselves in a vacuum. To anybody acquainted with the teachings of Ahad Ha'am, these arguments must have a familiar ring; for that leading exponent of cultural Zionism expressed in almost identical terms his reservations about the attempts of the Jews to assimilate.

Finally, the very idea of a possible transplanting of the Jewish community to Palestine also turned up from time to time in the writings of the early anti-Semites. Usually the idea was brought up in a perfunctory fashion, but there is one example of a detailed proposal for founding a Jewish state in Palestine, presented by the central figure of Hungarian anti-Semitism, Gyozo Istoczy, to the Hungarian parliament in 1878. It was the time of the Berlin Congress, where the future of the Near East was among the subjects to be discussed. Istoczy formally requested that the Hungarian parliament resolve to support the establishment of a Jewish state in Palestine, should such a plan be recommended by the Berlin Congress. In enlarging upon the subject to show that such a plan would be appropriate as well as feasible, he pointed to the immense potentialities of a newly awakened Jewish nation, for whom the founding of its own state would be a highly desirable and expedient objective. Reading these passages in praise of the Jewish nation and the blessings of the future state, one would imagine oneself in the company not of one of the radical anti-Semites of the nineteenth century but of one of the great advocates of political Zionism.

But Istoczy's speech had only the façade of a Zionist oration. Very quickly he divulged his real intention in conjuring up the vision of a Jewish state in Palestine. Istoczy's speech made his listeners laugh—the idea of a Jewish state sounded to contemporaries like the figment of an excitable imagination. He then explained that what he meant to demonstrate was that although the Jews could have their own state if they really wanted one, so committed were they to the fancy of world domination that they preferred to invest their immense energy and power in conquering the commonwealths of others.

As with Istoczy, so with Wagner and Paulus. Wagner's analysis of the assimilationist state of mind did not evolve, as did that of Ahad Ha'am, in the service of a Jewish national renaissance, but rather had a purely negative intention, to substantiate the alleged artistic impotence of his Jewish competitors. Similarly with the application of the term "nation" by ideologues like Paulus or Schopenhauer; it was employed to obstruct the Jewish claim to be emancipated, and not, as in its Zionist counterpart, to stimulate the will of self-emancipation.

In spite of these qualifications, however, there remains a historical connection between early anti-Semitic tendencies and the subsequent emergence of Jewish nationalism. Yet the connection is not to be sought on the level of ideological congruency, but on the level of historical reality. To elaborate, let me quote a passage from Schopenhauer, which occurs in the second part of his *Parerga and Paralipomena*, written in the late 1840s. The philosopher describes the Jewish race as one that has been "driven from its native land some two thousand years ago, and has ever since existed and wandered homeless," while other great nations of antiquity "entirely disappeared":

> And so even today . . . this John Lackland among the nations is to be found all over the globe, nowhere at home and nowhere a stranger. Moreover it asserts its nationality with unprecedented obstinacy and . . . it would also like to set foot somewhere and take root in order to arrive once more in a country, without which of course a people is like a ball floating in air. Till then it lives parasitically on other nations and their soil, but yet it is inspired with the liveliest patriotism for its own nation . . . The rest of the Jews are the fatherland of the Jew . . . and no community on earth sticks so firmly together as does this.

On the basis of this characterization, Schopenhauer then protests the use of the term "confession" for Judaism, a term borrowed from the Christian church: "Jewish nation is the correct expression." And as the Jews are a nation, it would be absurd to concede them a share in the government or administration of any country, that is, to grant them full emancipation.

Here, the term "nation" is clearly applied in the service of politics: the denial of the Jews' claim to full emancipation. But does this mean that the premises on which the conclusion rests were unfounded, or that the description of Jewish characteristics had been pulled out of thin air? Schopenhauer's statement contains a description of Jewish collective behavior, an evaluation of the Jewish presence among the nations, and a hypothetical prognosis of future development. As to the designation of Jewish activity as parasitic, this is one of the most widely spread anti-Jewish stereotypes. It was probably introduced by J.G. Herder in the late eighteenth century, and was based upon the one-sidedness of Jewish occupational distribution and the widespread contempt among European intellectuals for the professions of trade, finance, and the like. Therein Schopenhauer simply followed the current trend of anti-Jewish opinion. The extraordinary degree of social cohesiveness and mutual solidarity of Jews, too, was often observed and commented upon, for the preservation of Jewish separateness ran counter to the expectation that with access to at least some social avenues the Jews would disperse and lose the character of a sub-society, a state within a state (as the slogan had it). It is a keen insight on the part of Schopenhauer into the nature of Jewish reality that in the long run this social cohesiveness would translate itself into a drive for political independence.

Most observers of Jewish cohesion stopped at the stage of criticism. They decried the manifestations of Jewish public life, the establishment of special Jewish institutions, Jewish scholarship, or a Jewish press, anything that went beyond the satisfaction of purely religious needs. All other symptoms of Jewishness, especially of Jewish cooperation on a larger than local level, were regarded as a virtual breach of the unwritten contract of assimilation-in-return-for-emancipation. Sometimes, indeed, the payment of the Jewish debt, in the currency of assimilation, was demanded even where formal emancipation was far from being complete.

An outstanding case in point is the suspicion that fell on the establishment of the Alliance Israélite Universelle in France in 1860. Admittedly, the founding of an organization with the declared purpose of furthering common Jewish interests on an international level was at variance with the expectation that world Jewry would dissolve itself into so many locally based religious communities. The founders of the Alliance themselves had to overcome their own misgivings on this score. Adversaries of Jewish public activity took the Alliance as proof positive of their contention that Jews were determined to maintain their international ties and to strive for their age-old sinister objectives. Scarcely another Jewish activity or phenomenon played such a conspicuous role in the thinking and imagination of anti-Semites all over Europe, among them prominently Gougenot des Mousseaux in France and Gyozo Istoczy in Hungary. The Alliance served to conjure up the phantom of the Jewish world conspiracy conducted from a secret center—later to become the focal theme of the *Protocols of the Elders of Zion.*

Being of an imaginary, and at times even of a clinical, character, such fantasies nevertheless did not lack a point of reference in historical reality. The point of reference consisted of the token remnants of pre-emancipatory Jewish life and the visible expressions of collective Jewish activity. Both of these phenomena appeared redundant or supererogatory in the light of the officially accepted designation of Jewry as a religious confession, and it was this redundancy that caused Schopenhauer and others to opt for the expression, Jewish "nation." Whether this was justifiable according to some preconceived idea of what constituted a nation is of little importance. Most Jews, especially in the West, lacked at that time any consciousness of Jewish nationality, though a small minority, the forerunners of Zionism, were already at work cultivating and formulating it—a fact of which Schopenhauer could not possibly have been aware. Had he been acquainted with the Eastern European Jewry of Russia, Poland, and Rumania, he could have observed there the elements of a full-fledged Jewish nationalism emerging through the process of secularization that affected Jewish society without the experience of emancipation and assimilation. There the Jewish masses, living in close physical proximity, speaking their own language, and immersed in their popular culture, represented a veritable national minority. The crystallization of Jewish nationlism at times reached the level of literary and ideological expression, and was clearly in evidence decades before the anti-Semitic reaction set in in the shape of the bloody pogroms of the 1880s. Of all of this Schopenhauer was of course ignorant. To his unfriendly but perceptive eye, it was sufficient to observe Jewish cohesion and solidarity in the West to speak of a Jewish nation and a Jewish nationality.

This leads us to an important point concerning the relationship between anti-Semitism and the Jewish national movement. It was not the emergence of the former that provoked the emergence of the latter by way of reaction. Rather, modern anti-Semitism was itself a reaction to Jewish proto-nationalism, to the incapacity and unwillingness of Jewry to divest itself of all the characteristics of national life except that of religion. True, once anti-Semitism—until then a mere undercurrent—erupted as a full-fledged movement in the 1870s and eighties, it gave a tremendous push to Jewish national aspirations. Yet this was already the second phase of a dialectical process. The starting point of the process was not anti-Semitism, but the perseverance of Jewish qualities.

There was no need for Zionism to deny that it shared a common historical ambience with anti-Semitism. Indeed, in the course of their twin histories up to the present day it has looked at times as if they might not only be reacting to one another but be capable of evolving identical objectives and even cooperating in their realization. Theodor Herzl, for one, hoped to reach an understanding with anti-Semites, who, he imagined, would appreciate his attempt to solve the Jewish problem. Ivan von Simonyi, Istoczy's colleague in the Hungarian parliament, in fact approached Herzl upon the publication of the latter's *Judenstaat* ("The Jewish State"), expressing sympathy for Herzl's scheme. Practical support later seemed forthcoming from the Czarist government, and Herzl had no hesitation in negotiating with the minister Viacheslav von Plehve, who was held responsible by Jewish public opinion not only for a series of anti-Jewish measures but even for the bloody Kishinev pogrom of 1903, a few months before Herzl came to see him in St. Petersburg. A similar attitude was later displayed by Vladimir Jabotinsky, who in the 1930s sought the support of the anti-Semitic government of Poland for the planned "evacuation'" of Jews to Palestine.

Such contacts between the representatives of the two movements remained the exception. During the course of its venturesome history, Zionism received moral and material support from various non-Jewish quarters, but none from anti-Semites. These as a rule conceived of Zionism as no more than another variation of the perennial Jewish conspiracy against the Gentile world, an evaluation that arose out of the very nature of anti-Semitism. For the actual difficulty of coping with the Jewish presence within Gentile society was only one reason, and not the deepest one, for its virulence. Behind the rational arguments lurked the historically conditioned image of Jews and Judaism. Indeed, the more articulate and radical anti-Semites, like Bruno Bauer and Eugen Duehring, denied even the possibility or the desirability of a Jewish state, the former because of the alleged incapacity of Jews to live except as parasites, the latter because he regarded Jews as a particularly pernicious species that ought not to be tolerated anywhere, under any circumstances.

It was because of his unqualified denial of the right of Jewish existence that Duehring was retrospectively recognized as a kind of ideological precursor to Hitler. The Nazis, too, toyed with the idea of establishing a separate Jewish province or protectorate in Eastern Europe or in Madagascar, but even if established, it would have been a mere stopover on the way to the planned Final Solution. For according to the more radical version of anti-Semitism spelled out consistently in Nazi ideology, there was no room for Jews anywhere on earth, whether spread among the nations or concentrated among themselves.

Theodor Herzl's vision of liberating Jews and Gentiles alike from the curse of anti-Semitism can be said to have erred on two counts. First, he identified the ingathering of Jews in their homeland with the elimination of the Diaspora, assuming that with the establishment of a state, Jews would either join it or disappear in their social surroundings. Second, he attributed anti-Semitism exclusively to the actual strain suffered by Jews and Gentiles when living in social symbiosis; he ignored the historical roots of anti-Semitism, which were in need only of the slightest stimulation to begin anew their poisonous growth.

It has been the paradoxical result of the Zionist endeavor that instead of removing the external stimulus to anti-Semitism—namely, the social entanglement of Jews in non-Jewish society—it has added a new dimension to it. The Jewish state, being the outgrowth of the perennial Jewish predicament—the retention by Jews of their national existence without the possession of its physical basis—is beset by many of the same problems and perplexities. Thus the clash between Israel and its neighbors is not simply one of conflicting political interests. At stake also is the issue of the definition of Jews as a nation. Not unexpectedly, perhaps, the positions are now reversed, with Israelis claiming for themselves the status of a nation, characterized by historical ties to a country, while their opponents deny it to them. Arab propaganda has also shown itself ready to adopt ideological weapons that include stereotypes of Christian background, from the arsenal of traditional anti-Semitism. The most discredited anti-Jewish writings of Europe, such as the *Protocols of the Elders of Zion*, have been widely disseminated, read, and believed in the Arabic speaking countries.

The post-Zionist variation of anti-Semitism is hardly restricted to Arabs. Since the partial realization of the Zionist project left most of the Diaspora communities intact, social friction between Jews and Gentiles remained endemic to the Jewish situation. Moreover, since the Jewish state has become a subject of international debate, and since Jews everywhere are inevitably associated with its fate, a new occasion for possible friction has been added. There is no anti-Semitic movement of intensity in evidence anywhere today, but occasional outbursts in the West and a steady pressure by Russia and other Communist countries are intimately linked with the real or putative allegiance of Jews to the Jewish state. The charge of divided or dual loyalty, which is of course of long standing—in fact, it is but a variant of the accusation of Jewish international cohesion—has now received some semblance of substantiality.

If Zionism has failed to eliminate the determining factors of anti-Semitism, it nevertheless has succeeded in changing the climate within which anti-Semitism operates. As the proverbial Jewish passivity has given way to active self-defense—sometimes called excessive or overactive—the traditional image of the Jews has undergone a transformation. Similarly, the reconstruction of a full-fledged Jewish society has given the lie to the notion of an inherent Jewish parasitism. If it had had the opportunity to exercise its full potential, the Zionist enterprise might well have undercut anti-Semitism altogether—not so much through a change in the Jewish situation as through a rehabilitation of the Jewish character and mentality. As things stand, the rehabilitating effect of Zionism is balanced by the continuing controversy not only over the acts and deeds of the Jewish state but over its very right to exist. The passion with which this issue is debated even in circles uninvolved in the problem makes it clear that the stand taken by people on this question for better or worse is strongly influenced by their attitude toward Jews and Judaism. Thus in our day the anti-Semitic tradition has found new sources to thrive on and new subterfuges with which to cover itself.

In view of all this, one may say that in the struggle of the Jewish state for a peaceful and tranquil existence, the fate of anti-Semitism too hangs in the balance. The continual wrangling over Israel is apt to keep alive and even to exacerbate anti-Jewish sentiment, while a catastrophic termination of the struggle would throw world Jewry back into a condition of pre-Zionist deprivation, and worse. By contrast, a comparatively tranquil resolution would alone hold out the hope of the gradual receding of the perennial tension between Jews and Gentiles. Whether the realization of this hope is to be granted us is the fateful question hovering over Jewish—and in a sense also over Gentile—destiny.

Israel and the Messiah

The prayer for the well-being of the state of Israel, which is recited on Sabbaths and festivals in most synagogues in Israel and the Diaspora, calls the state *"reshit geulatenu,"* the commencement of our redemption. The formula implies that the creation of the state of Israel is to be viewed as the initial fulfillment of the messianic expectation cherished by past generations.

The text of the prayer was written by the Hebrew novelist S.Y. Agnon at the request of Isaac Herzog, chief rabbi at the time the state was founded. It has since had to be repeatedly defended by Orthodox authorities against those who find it inappropriate or even sacrilegious.

Some who are opposed to the formula, like the sect of Neturei Karta in Israel and their supporters abroad, deny any legitimacy at all to the Jewish state. Others, like the Orthodox party Agudat Israel and the heads of noted *yeshivot*, cooperate with the agencies of the state, accept the benefits derived from its institutions, and at times support the government in return, but still withhold fundamental spiritual approval. Where the more radical regard modern Israel as the very antithesis of the messianic redemption promised by Jewish tradition, the less radical declare the issue irrelevant. But for either camp, to use messianic vocabulary in praying for the welfare of the state borders on desecration of a hallowed religious concept.

This theological and ideological controversy obviously cannot be settled except in its own terms. The question that a historian may address is not whether the state of Israel is worthy of association with the traditional messianic concept but whether a connection can in fact be drawn between the messianic hope entertained by Jews through the ages and the modern national movement that led to the founding of Israel. In order to approach this question we have to inquire first into the nature of traditional messianism.

Although the term itself is biblical in origin, messianism is a universal phenomenon. Tribes and na-

12

153

tions of disparate cultural traditions and differing levels of civilization in many parts of the world have cherished the idea of a savior who will deliver them from their present physical or spiritual circumstances. But within the orbit of the immediate influence of Judaism, and especially in Christianity and Islam, the idea of messianic deliverance assumed a novel significance, albeit one that was to differ sharply from the Jewish prototype.

The specific historical conditions that lay behind the biblical image of an anointed ideal king (the original meaning of "messiah") need not concern us here. Probably as early as the Babylonian captivity, but certainly after the destruction of the Second Temple, the plight that required redemption was mainly not that of the Jews of Palestine but that of the Jews in exile. And the plight was not economic scarcity, social degradation, or spiritual decadence, although all these at times may have been experienced as adversities to be overcome by the redeemer. Once in exile, the Jews tended to understand these sufferings as mere byproducts of a basic deficiency, namely, exile itself, the condition of banishment.

Now, being removed from one's birthplace or country of origin is a misfortune only if one's commitment to that birthplace is so intense that any other place is experienced as a physical and spiritual trial. Uncounted numbers of people in human history have changed their dwelling through voluntary or forced emigration and in the fullness of time have accustomed themselves to the situation and adopted a new fatherland. It is one of the peculiarities of the Jews' fate, conditioned by many complex religious and historical factors, that despite the lengthy passage of time the consciousness of exile did not disappear. On the contrary, duration intensified rather than mitigated the subjective experience of calamity.

Messianism was both the cause and the result of the Jews' segregated existence throughout the centuries of exile. Initially the messianic belief may have strengthened their will to resist absorption by a foreign environment. Once the Jewish community established itself as a segregated socio-religious entity, its pariah-like situation nourished expectations of an ultimate return to its own homeland.

This dependence of Jewish messianism on the concrete situation of exile sets it apart fom the millenarian fantasies of other socially or nationally suppressed groups. At the same time it distinguishes it from the purely spiritual longings of the Christian Second Coming. Jewish messianism has a point of reference in the factual history of the Jewish people. Jews had at one time lived in their own country, their own commonwealth; it was there they hoped to return in the messianic age.

In fact, a residue of the former national existence continued to play an active role in the cultural and mental life of every Jewish community. Acquaintance with the geographical scenes and contours of the homeland through constant reading of the Bible lent tangibility to the longing for return. More important perhaps was the fact that Jews continued to study and adhere to the laws of the Mishnah, which reflect the realities of life in the period of the Second Temple (when they were codified) but served long thereafter as a guide to important aspects of individual and communal conduct. The intellectual elite dedicated itself to the study of a body of law which, taken as a whole, would function once again when the nation was living under its own government in the projected messianic age. Various elements in the life of the community thus linked the memory of the past with the expectation of the future, keeping the vision of the messianic era in contact with historical reality.

Although it was exceptional in its concreteness, Jewish messianism did share with all forms of millenarianism an imaginary conception of the means to be employed in bringing about the redemption. Having failed to restore independence through military action in Roman times (the last serious attempt was the Bar Kokhba revolt in 132 c.e.), Jews ceded their fate to the unfathomable wisdom of divine Providence. This shift in the mental attitude of the nation was not the consequence of a mere ideological development. The circumstances in which Jews lived in the Middle Ages restricted their freedom of action to sporadic interventions on the local level. Any attempt to alter the basic situation of a scattered and barely tolerated people was simply inconceivable. No wonder, then, that Jewish faith in an ultimate redemption became interwoven with a belief in su pernatural agency. What the human partner could contribute was, at most, intercession with the celestial power in order to hasten the redemption.

There were in the main two avenues for inducing heaven to bring about salvation. (We may disregard the purely magical machinations of kabbalists.) One was to gain divine grace by complying perfectly with the obligatory religious duties as these were interpreted by Jewish tradition. In this approach, redemption would follow not upon any one particular religious or spiritual undertaking but upon the achievement of total religious perfection by the community at large. Others, however, found indications in the authoritative sources of some special deed or procedure that might avail. Thus in 1538 the scholars of Safed made an abortive attempt to reestablish the ancient Sanhedrin as the first act in the messianic drama; in doing so they were following a suggestion of Maimonides as to the sequence of events preceding the appearance of the messiah. A similar phenomenon was the hasty marrying-off of young couples during the feverish excitement occasioned by rumors of the impending messianic revelation of Shabbetai Zevi in 1666. (According to a saying in the Talmud, all the souls yet to be born have to reach their destiny before the messiah can appear. Mass marriages were meant literally to fulfill this condition.) As late as the 1830s Rabbi Zvi Hirsh Kalisher, later to become a steadfast advocate of Jewish settlement in Palestine and as such a veritable precursor of modern Zionism, was still addicted to this pattern of thought. Kalisher wished to obtain permission from the Turkish authorities, as well as the consent of his rabbinical colleagues, to institute a certain kind of animal sacrifice on the site of the Jerusalem Temple; on the basis of his scholarly research he believed that the restoration of animal sacrifice was a precondition for initiating the messianic process.

In the concept of supernatural redemption, as these examples suggest, human initiative was consistently restricted to spiritual or ritualistic devices. The possibility, or for that matter the permissibility, of a national restoration through human means was hardly ever discussed or debated. At most it was referred to in a homiletic or exegetic context (not always negatively). At bottom lay an acquiescence in the passive role Jewry was supposed to play as a nation in exile, at the mercy of others.

The spell of this state of mind was broken in the eighteenth and nineteenth centuries when the Jews acquired citizenship owing to the revolutionary changes in some of the nations in which they lived. Citizenship meant an end to the condition of exile in an absolutely unforeseen and therefore most confusing way.

Accepting citizenship in a non-Jewish state was regarded both by the Jews and by their emancipators as incompatible with the messianic belief that was an uncontested article of Jewish faith. Jews were more or less explicitly requested to renounce this tenet—no easy thing to do, although the impediment was not so much dogma as the role the idea had played in Jewish history. Indeed, there was a minority opinion recorded in the Talmud that confined the notion of the Messiah to biblical times alone and denied its significance for the future. This talmudic authority was cited by Lazarus Bendavid, a spokesman of the radical Enlightenment in late eighteenth-century Berlin, to refute a Catholic missionary who had observed that the Jews, having thrown away a cornerstone of their religious system in return for their emancipation, ought logically to accept the Christian redeemer. Bendavid retorted that the Jewish religion remained intact even without the messianic belief. As if on second thought, he added that Jewish messianism had anyway found its fulfillment in the liberation of the Jews by the rulers of contemporary states.

Bendavid's convoluted argument can be said to reflect the intellectual predicament in which Jews found themselves in the wake of their changed situation. Their political status may have required them to abandon the messianic tenet, yet other, less conspicuous, considerations militated against it. The need to meet the Christian challenge in a positive way, rejecting the Christian messiah while retaining a Jewish version of messianism, was one such consideration. The main reason, however, was an internal one: the messianic ideal was deeply ingrained in the Jewish mentality. Simply to try to eradicate it because of the changed political circumstances would have been a futile enterprise. What was possible was a reinterpretation, which is what Bendavid proposed.

His response to the historical situation became typical for succeeding generations. Although the Jews' integration into the modern state was not the result of an internal Jewish development, it still represented a decisive turn in their destiny and they were inclined to understand it in terms of traditional concepts. Emancipation seen as the fulfillment of the expected messianic redemption was admittedly a forced interpretation, but understandable in light of events. It is astonishing how many Jews who experienced emancipation from the ghetto almost instinctively described the event in terms drawn from the vocabulary of traditional Jewish messianism. Such emancipating rulers as Napoleon and the Emperor Joseph II of Austria were compared explicitly with the biblical Cyrus, and the dawning of the Enlightenment was frequently portrayed as the equivalent of the Messianic Age.

Still, when reform-minded theologians drew the practical implications and proposed omitting references in Jewish ritual to the future return to Zion, they met with fierce opposition. Not only the Orthodox but also the exponents of the so-called historical school objected. Granting the quasi-messianic significance of Jewish emancipation, they were still reluctant to repudiate the idea of a possible national redemption, even if projected into a remote and hazy future.

By the early 1860s political emancipation in Western countries could already be taken for granted; at the same time it could be transcended, at least by those of broader vision who, although they welcomed Jewish emancipation, were reluctant to see in it the consummation of Jewish history. Two such thinkers were Rabbi Kalisher and Rabbi Yehuda Alkalay.

Kalisher was an outstanding Ashkenazi talmudist, Alkalay a Sephardi preacher. Both were at the outset imbued with traditional messianism; in the course of time both integrated the historical experience of their age into their thinking. Jewish emancipation, really the antithesis of the traditional messianic expectation, came to be seen by them as the initial phase in an evolving process of redemption. The social elevation of the Jewish individual became a precondition for collective national liberation.

By dint of this rethinking, the very definition of redemption underwent a change. The human initiative destined to usher in the messianic age was no longer seen in spiritual or ritualistic terms. The establishment of the Alliance Israélite Universelle and the tangible political influence of Jewish notables like Moses Montefiore and the Rothschilds were taken to suggest that the resettlement of Jews in their ancient homeland by human means was not impossible. Such attempts at resettlement were regarded as necessary to the messianic enterprise; it was expected that a divine response would follow and complete the process.

That this reinterpretation of the messianic tradition was no mere idiosyncrasy is demonstrated by the fact that it was advanced independently (with some variations) by different people and, once published, found a following. In 1862, when Kalisher published a tract setting forth his views, he seems not to have been acquainted with the writings of Alkalay—no surprise, in view of the geographic distance and the difference in background that separated them. (Kalisher lived in the East Prussian town of Thorn, Alkalay in the town of Semelin near Belgrade.) Kalisher was not even aware of the existence of an Ashkenazi preacher, Natan Friedland, who pursued a similar trend on his own, although he presented it in a more homiletic fashion. It was Friedland who detected the affinity between his own thinking and that of his more famous contemporary and, encouraged by the coincidence, gave his thought a more direct and daring expression. More important perhaps for Kalisher's own self-confidence was the unconditional approval he received from his rabbinical colleague Elijah Guttmacher. A secluded scholar and kabbalist, Guttmacher was reputed to be a miracle-working saint; when he announced unequivocally that the appropriate means to pave the way for the coming of the messiah was to repopulate Palestine, it could not fail to impress many Jews.

We thus have here a new development in Jewish thinking, of which the main characteristic is the permission or even the demand for the partial realization of the messianic vision by human effort. Obviously this development did not occur in a vacuum but had to do with the impact of historical events: the unexpected and in traditional terms inexplicable emancipation of the Jews as well as the contemporaneous resurrection of the European nations. But there was equally a dialectical development within Jewish messianism itself. In particular it is impossible to ignore the deep emotional dimension that accompanied the emergence of the ideas we have discussed.

In the thought of Moses Hess, who joined the group of these early Zionists as a secular outsider, we find a similar melange of cognitive and emotional elements. A socialist ideologue estranged from Judaism since his youth, Hess at the age of fifty recovered his Jewish commitment and evolved a theory of what Judaism could still signify beyond the two contemporary variations of Reform and Neo-Orthodoxy. He advocated a national restoration in the ancient homeland and was strongly convinced that such an ingathering would release the spiritual energy embodied in petrified religious institutions. The national revival of Italy and contemporary intellectual trends that encouraged the revitalization of dormant historical sources obviously had an influence on Hess. But there is also no missing his messianic sentiments. A vision of a redeemed and rehabilitated Judaism had been implanted in Hess's mind as a child, when he observed his grandfather mourning for the destruction of the Temple in Jerusalem. His messianic vision drew its emotional power from that long suppressed childhood experience. Thus, although they differed over what would happen once the first stage of the redemptive process was accomplished, Hess and the Orthodox messianists were partisans of the same cause. And they also agreed about the immediate task: the ingathering of Jews in Palestine.

Despite remarkable exertions by Alkalay and Kalisher, very little, if anything, was accomplished on this score. Nevertheless, the concrete history of the Jewish national movement has to be dated from the appearance of this group. The vestiges of their influence can be traced in the years up to the emergence of the Hovevei Zion movement in the wake of the 1881 pogroms in Russia.

That movement, which defined its objective as the restoration and rehabilitation of the Jewish nation in its historical homeland, crystallized under the impact of the pogroms, but it could do so because the idea of a national revival had been adopted by at least certain sections of the population. The dissemination of the nationalist idea owed much to the expansion of the Hebrew press, headed by the weekly *Ha-Maggid*, which catered to a widely scattered Hebrew-reading public, especially in Russia and Rumania. Traditional yet open-minded, it appealed to a new type of Jew who transcended traditional attitudes.

The example of emancipated Western Jewry, as well as the repeated attempts by the Russian government to extricate Jews from their traditional cultural and occupational patterns, made people aware that changes in their situation were possible through their own initiatives and efforts. A readiness to act in the public interest was often combined with an Enlightenment vision of a future based on the Western model: political emancipation, social acceptance, and cultural accommodation. But this projected ideal stood in stark contrast to reality; the Jewish community in Russia and for that matter in Rumania was a politically underprivileged, socially segregated, and culturally self-reliant minority. As it happens, however, the vision of Jewish integration as the ultimate destiny of the community had already been discarded by thinkers who were in direct contact with Western countries where it had originally emerged.

The chief exponent of the new trend was the novelist Peretz Smolenskin. A militant critic of social and religious conditions especially in Russia, the land of his birth, Smolenskin fought for his convictions through his literary creations and his journalistic writings, both appearing in the monthly *Ha-Shahar*, which he edited in Vienna from 1868 on. Attacking the rabbinical as well as the lay leadership of his time, Smolenskin laid the blame for all shortcomings on the Berlin *Haskalah* (Enlightenment) and the subsequent Reform movement in Germany. The erosion of Jewish national unity and of the intrinsic link between social life and religion derived from these early developments, in Smolenskin's view. The mechanical tampering with religious tradition, especially the excision of symbols connected to the future rebirth of the nation, had sapped the vital forces of the community and let to the present dismal state of affairs. At the same time, the "reward" for these reforms, the integration of the Jews as equals in the surrounding society, never stood a chance of realization.

Erroneous and unjust as this criticism may be historically, its significance for its time cannot be overrated. It amounted to a repudiation of all that the *Haskalah* stood for, namely, the hope that Russian Jews could improve their status by emulating the ways of their brethren in the West.

Smolenskin had no alternative proposals for either the religious or the political problems of the community. Opposed to Reform, he was at the same time scandalized by the traditional rabbinate; he believed that by turning away from assimilation the community might somehow dispense with the excesses in its tradition and retain only the essentials. As for politics, Smolenskin lacked a substitute for the *Haskalah* belief in civic emancipation. When he first unfolded his views, the idea of settlement in Palestine did not yet occupy his mind. He strongly recommended the reestablishment of national unity and the regaining of trust in the national future as the basis for any collective action, which would then automatically follow. These ideas laid the groundwork for the political program of national revival in the homeland, which emerged in the wake of he pogroms of the 1880s. Smolenskin himself then became an active supporter of the Hovevei Zion.

Others had made this transition before the pogroms broke out. The assistant editor (and from 1880 the chief editor) of *Ha-Maggid*, David Gordon, impressed both by Rabbi Kalisher and by Moses Hess, and like Smolenskin opposed to the anti-nationalism of the Reform movement, defended Jewish nationalism on the modern principle that each nation should adhere to its own customs, language, and laws. How much weight in this scheme would be given to each attribute could not be authoritatively prescribed. Indeed, with the spread of the national ideal, different configurations evolved, with some assigning religion a central role and others restricting its scope or giving it up altogether in favor of other components in the national heritage.

Traces of this intellectual development became evident during the first flowering of the national movement after the pogroms of 1881, when there arose a broad consensus that at least a certain part of Russian Jewry would have to leave the country. America was the obvious goal of emigration: it was a country known to be prepared to absorb newcomers, and a contingent of Russian Jews had already settled there in the years preceding the pogroms. But Palestine was suggested as an alternative, and a prolonged and passionate debate went on for years over the relative merits of the two.

That a land lacking all the attributes that made America attractive could enter this competition at all was testimony to the previous spreading of the idea that only there could the Jews pursue their national destiny. This in turn was clearly a derivation of the messianic vision of *Eretz Israel* as the locale for the miraculous reestablishment of the ancient Jewish commonwealth. The emotional commitment to Palestine was all the stronger for having undergone a process of secularization.

The choice of Palestine may reveal still another indebtedness to traditional messianism. So little was known about the difficulties of life there that the decision to settle in Palestine must be taken as an emphatically irrational act. The only compensation for ignorance was belief in the predetermined destiny that tied the Jewish people to the Holy Land, a destiny that guaranteed the success of the enterprise. For the secular pioneers, the notion of historical inevitability replaced the faith in divine promise held by the Orthodox thinkers. In both cases, however, we see the operation of what may be called messianic determinism.

The messianic impulse did not exhaust its momentum with the first wave of emigrants. On the contrary, subsequent events contributed new stimuli that worked in the same direction. The awareness that Jewish life was being restored in the Holy Land almost automatically evoked images from the Bible that lent themselves to explicit messianic interpretation. In July 1882 Marcus Lehmann, the editor of *Israelit*, the organ of German Orthodoxy, convened a group of rabbinical and lay leaders of southern Germany to discuss how to assist Russian Jews who had left their country in the wake of the previous year's pogrom. Lehmann opened the session with these words: "It is a wonderful token of the time that a general yearning for the Holy Land has seized a countless multitude of our co-religionists especially in Russia . . . We must heed the hints of divine Providence and pave the way for a Jewish future of the most far-reaching consequences." He cited the biblical examples of Zerubbabel, Ezra, and Nehemiah, who, though facing immense difficulties, brought about the establishment of the Second Commonwealth.

Messianic overtones permeated the lives of the early settlers. As the historian Azriel Shochat has argued, even the choice of names for settlements—such as Petah Tikvah (The Door of Hope) or Rishon LeZion (First in Zion)—was guided by a wish to connect the present enterprise with the prophets' vision of Israel's future. Striking biblical passages of unequivocal messianic intent, like Ezekiel's vision of the valley of dry bones brought to life, became a recurring motif in Zionist speeches and writings. This passage appears as the motto of an association founded in Jerusalem in 1882 by Eliezer Ben Yehuda and Yehiel Michael Pines and appropriately called Tehiyat Israel, "revival of Israel." Two years later the prophets' vision served as the text for a moving sermon by Rabbi Shmuel Mohilever at the closing session of a Hovevei Zion meeting in Kattowitz. The revival of the dry bones became a Zionist *topos*, occurring independently to many people who were engaged in the revitalization of their nation.

The compelling messianic associations aroused by the national enterprise are also forcefully demonstrated by the negative reaction to them in some Orthodox circles. Secularized Jews could oppose Zionism out of political or other reasons and possibly remain indifferent to the messianic issue. An Orthodox Jew had no such middle course. The explicitly messianic discourse of Kalisher and his circle elicited much resentment in rabbinic circles. Once the movement got under way, it had either to be embraced or rejected.

The rejection by some Orthodox and especially some hasidic authorities was emphatic indeed, assuming almost the character of religious anathema. The notion of independent human action, which struck at the heart of the traditional supernatural definition of messianism, was denounced as bordering on heresy. Whatever other motives may have been involved in shaping this attitude of total censure—simple conservatism, disquiet over the religious conduct of the settlers, the anticipation of possible failure—central to it was the impulse to protect the sacred concept of messianism from secular trespass.

The leaders of the Hovevei Zion attributed their failure to attract the Jewish masses, especially in hasidic districts, to the almost universal antagonism of the hasidic courts. The non-hasidic authorities were divided among themselves: some belonged to the Zionist movement, others supported or condoned it, still others objected to it or condemned it outright. Yet even the supporters evinced a reservation concerning the messianic interpretation of the movement. Almost to a man, they advocated resettlement of the Holy Land on the basis of the preference given by traditional religious sources to life lived there as opposed to anywhere else. To this formal religious obligation—the positive commandment of settling in *Eretz Israel*—they sometimes added other considerations of contemporary relevance: the advantages of an agricultural life and the like. These had already been adduced by Kalisher as subsidiary props to his main argument, which was, of course, his messianic concept. His successors in the Hovevei Zion generation ignored the messianic aspect altogether. Abraham Jacob Slucki, who in 1891 published a collection of opinions by noted rabbis on the religious status of the movement, apologized for the fact that there were members of Hovevei Zion who regarded developments in the Holy Land as "the beginning of the redemption."

This neutralizing tendency among official spokesmen of Judaism hardly reflected the popular sentiments that nourished the movement even in its periods of relative stagnation. Those engaged in keeping the Hovevei Zion alive referred to it in correspondence as their "sacred assignment." Such quasi-religious attachment to the idea must have persisted in all the circles that followed the vicissitudes of the movement sympathetically.

The appearance on the scene of Theodor Herzl quickened these latent sentiments. Lending the movement an unhoped-for dimension, he provided the necessary incitement for popular imagination to run high. Herzl possessed all the qualities of a charismatic leader and was often identified with the messiah in his meetings with the Jewish masses. Such an identification, which amazed Herzl himself, was just as often criticized by the intellectuals in the movement.

The next opportunity for messianic sentiments to emerge was the traumatic experience of the second wave of pogroms starting in 1903, bloodier by far than the first. With the subsequent failure of the 1905 revolution, the hopes for Jewish integration in a reformed Russia were finally dashed.

These events set in motion the greatest exodus of Jews from the country, with the majority of the emigrants once again heading for America. A fraction, however, consisting of young men and women with strong convictions, chose to join the early settlers in Palestine. Thus began the period of the Second Aliyah, which added to the foundations of the first an entirely new social and ideological dimension. The newcomers shared with the old-timers the quality of messianic determinism: they were convinced of the historic necessity of Jewish national regeneration. But while the First Aliyah had been content to leave the contours of the national revival to the future, the new pioneers came with a set of preconceived social and religious ideas. These ideas gave expression to another feature of messianism: utopianism.

Messianism in its "supernatural" form held that the future would be shaped by the hand of Providence; thus it ought to have had no room for utopian fantasy. This was in fact the position of Moses Maimonides and other medieval Jewish philosophers. The popular imagination, however, projected into the messianic age a glorious image, the inverse in every respect of Jewish existence in exile. Zionism too, in the course of time, evolved a multitude of utopian blueprints. The Second Aliyah was especially given to them.

The most influential of these scenarios was a variant of Marxian socialism transferred from the pioneers' Russian background. It is associated with the names of Ber Borochov and, in its elitist version, Aharon David Gordon. Disassociating himself from other socialist ideologies, Gordon made the national revival of the Jews dependent on a return to manual and especially agricultural work—an ideal he himself consistently lived up to despite far-reaching personal sacrifices. The theories of both Borochov and Gordon seem rather removed from any special Jewish connotations. Borochov's dependence on Marx is explicit, Gordon's indebtedness to the example of Tolstoy has often been remarked upon. Yet both theories centered upon the contention that the goal could be achieved only in the Jewish homeland—a condition lacking all logical consistency and hence, in the final analysis, messianic. Similarly, the Zionist theorist Ahad Ha'am postulated that the revival of an original Jewish ethic, which he claimed to be the essence of Judaism (religion was only its outer expression) would take place with the return to Palestine—an idea which once again makes sense only on the basis of an irrational conviction that renewed contact with the ancient homeland would have a revolutionary impact on Judaism.

Although they differed in what they demanded of Jews, these three utopian blueprints were united in neglecting or even directly excluding traditional Jewish religion from their vision of the future. They thus conformed to the prevailing tendency to shape the life of the new society apart from or in opposition to Jewish tradition. Still, the tradition also had its representative, in the towering figure of Rabbi Abraham Isaac Kook, whose vision was built on messianic foundations proper.

An outstanding talmudist and student of Kabbalah, Kook demonstrated his adherence to the national movement by joining the emigrants to Palestine at the outset of the Second Aliyah in 1904. Impressed by the renaissance of Jewish life in the country, Kook took it to be an indication of divine grace, opening the process of redemption. In his enthusiasm and with his exceptional gift for literary expression he produced in his writings a profound interpretation of his time, pregnant with kabbalistic connotations and metaphysical overtones. Kook's writings left far behind the thought of his timid rabbinical precursors, who had defined the spiritual significance of the resettlement in the Holy Land purely in terms of Jewish religious law. He returned to the explicitly messianic conception of Kalisher and Alkalay, the first apostles of national revival, but surpassed them in depth and intellectual daring.

Kook differed from all his predecessors on one crucial point. All the rabbinic authorities who supported the Palestinian enterprise had made their consent to it dependent upon the settlers' being observant Jews. Kook, no less conservative in principle, nevertheless lent an overriding significance to the rebuilding of the country, even if accomplished by nonobservant agents. This did not impair his ultimate vision—a reconstructed traditional life based on Jewish religious law but highly spiritualized, as would befit the generation chosen to see the dawn of the messianic age. But for the present, Kook's messianic scenario condoned and even justified the lives and work of the secular pioneers. It thus secured a measure of unity between the camps of traditionalists and innovators—an indispensable precondition for the creation many years later of the state of Israel.

Messianic determinism played a part in several different phases of Zionist history. The conviction, permeating all ranks of society, that the underlying forces of Jewish history would inevitably culminate in a Jewish commonwealth imparted energy and a willingness for sacrifice to many people who might otherwise have been apathetic. But if this quality of dedication provided, and continues to provide, the Israeli enterprise with boundless energy, it has also tested the ability of Israel to adapt to changing circumstances. Any action taken under the rubric of messianic determinism is necessarily limited in its rationality. It is based on the assumption that the individual is responsible only for the preliminary steps; their completion is assigned to the messianic power or, in secular terms, to hidden historical forces. Activities undertaken in line with such conceptions may at times achieve what seems impossible; at other times they meet insurmountable difficulties and are defeated or frustrated. The history of Zionism is replete with both kinds of experiences; a contemporary example is that of Gush Emunim, the Orthodox "bloc of the faithful" who are vociferous champions of Jewish sovereignty in the occupied territories of Judea and Samaria.

The messianic drive behind the activities of Gush Emunim is blatantly apparent. Its quasi-political goal, the annexation of the full extent of the Holy Land as defined by religious tradition, is predicated on the belief that this is the precondition for the divine redemption—similar to what Zvi Hirsh Kalisher had believed for the more modest goal of establishing Jewish settlements in the country. Indeed, with the emergence of Gush Emunim this line of thought has come full circle, returning once again to a definition of the national objectives not just in religious but literally in fundamentalist terms. At any rate, the activities of Gush Emunim are characterized by feverish intensity and by inflexibility; only time will tell what their ultimate fate will be.

Less acute than messianic determinism but no less problematic is the other legacy of Zionist history, utopianism. The ingathering of the Jews, an achievement due to the belief in messianic ideals, has exacted a price: the results are often measured against utopian standards of judgment, and are inevitably found wanting. Aside from the gap that exists between every ideal and its fulfillment, there is the additional problem that the various Zionist utopias (social, cultural, religious) are mutually exclusive. Each could be realized only at the expense of the others; the outcome is disappointment for all parties concerned.

Zionist reality as embodied in the state of Israel is measured by a host of yardsticks, not only by outsiders but even more so by those who have created that reality and participate in it daily. This is perhaps the lot of all pluralistic societies. Yet Israelis critical of their society today tend to draw more far-reaching conclusions than used to be the case. It is not uncommon to jump from criticism to, if not the negation of the state, then at least to a renunciation of one's allegiance to it, thus justifying emigration from the country. It sometimes seems as if the very existence of the state has yet to be taken for granted, that even its *right* to exist depends on the fulfillment of an unwritten contract with one of many utopian visions.

The dangers inherent in the intimate connection between Zionism and messianism are thus palpable. To meet them, some have argued that Zionism can and should be vindicated without resort to such irrational backing. Arguments of this kind have been marshaled to counter the growing claims made by movements like Gush Emunim, but the arguments themselves are not new. As early as 1929 the great scholar of Kabbalah, Gershom Scholem, protested on behalf of "thousands of Zionists" against the blurring of boundaries between the political aims of Zionism and the religious expectations of Jewish messianism. Since then, Scholem repeatedly confirmed his profound opposition to such enterprises—an opposition that comes with special point from one who has dedicated his life to the study of the irrational dimensions of Judaism and has even been motivated in his scholarship by his personal attachment to the project of national revival. Aware of the misguided potentialities of irrational messianism as demonstrated by the seventeenth-century false messiah Shabbetai Zevi, and by the movement bearing his name, Scholem warned of similar dangers to modern-day Zionism.

The parallelism between Shabbateanism and Zionism was and is a recurring theme in the historical evaluation of Zionism, especially among its opponents. For the late Rabbi Joel Teitelbaum, the most consistent antagonist of Zionism in the last generation, Zionism and Shabbateanism were veritable synonyms. Since the ingathering into the Holy Land and the regaining of Jewish political independence had taken place without divine intervention or confirmation, as prescribed by traditional messianic sources, Zionism for Rabbi Teitelbaum represented an even greater usurping force than had the movement of Shabbetai Zevi.

The danger of messianic encroachments on politics will in the end have to be met politically. It is the test of statesmanship to channel popular sentiment toward politically defensible objectives. Indeed, the continued welfare of the state may depend on success or failure in this regard. But the neutralization of messianism can certainly not be achieved by denying its role in the history of Zionism. Attempts to banish the messianic ingredient may seem ideologically necessary to some, but the spontaneous sentiments of the Jewish people suggest the futility of the effort. The news of the Balfour Declaration in 1917; the conquering of Palestine by the English in World War I, and the inauguration of the first High Commissioner, Herbert Samuel; the 1947 United Nations decision on the establishment of a Jewish state; the declaration of independence; the victory of the Six-Day War in 1967 were all experienced as momentous and predictive occurrences for which, in Jewish cultural tradition, the messianic vocabulary is the only appropriate one. To blot out the points of reference contained in the messianic myth, even if it were possible, would impoverish the national consciousness.

Rabbinic legalists, secular ideologues, and scholars have for their various reasons tried to separate Zionism from messianism, but popular sentiment will have none of it. And this is as it should be. In every generation Jews have prayed for redemption, and never failed to include in their prayers the hope for a return to the homeland under independent Jewish rule. When this petition seemed to have been answered in our day, it was only natural to identify the momentous event as a partial fulfillment of the messianic hope. Thus the term "the commencement of our redemption," included in the prayer for the state of Israel, is highly appropriate. Holding out still the hope for a total messianic consummation yet to arrive, it is at once an article of faith and an accurate reflection of historical reality.

Notes

CHAPTER 1

1. Arthur Rupin, *Die Soziologie der Juden* (Berlin, 1930), 1, 67–100; and *The Jews in the Modern World* (1934), 21–30.
2. S. Dubnow, *Weltgeschichte des jüdischen Volkes* (Berlin, 1925–1929) 8, 83–212.
3. Ibid., vol. 9.
4. Jacob Katz, *"Die Entstehung der Judenassimilation und deren Ideologie,"* Ph.D. diss., Frankfurt-am-Main, 1934.
5. B. Offenburg, *"Das Erwachen des Deutschen Nationalbewusst-seins in der preussischen Juden-heit,"* Ph.D. diss., Hamburg, 1933.
6. Rupin, *Soziologie der Juden,* 1, 101–127, 315–499; and idem, *The Jews in the Modern World,* 130–226.
7. N. Leven, *Cinquante ans d'histoire: l'Alliance Israélite Universelle, 1860–1910* (Paris, 1911).
8. I. Ellbogen, *A Century of Jewish Life* (Philadelphia, 1944), 141–223.
9. Julius Guttmann, *Die Philosophie des Judentums* (Munich, 1933), 303–317.
10. Katz, *"Entstehung der Judenassimilation,"* 46–71.
11. Guttmann, *Philosophie des Judentums,* 317–345; Max Wiener, *Jüdische Religion in Zeitalter der Emanzipation* (Berlin, 1933), 114–164.
12. Wiener, *Jüdische Religion,* 87–113.
13. Ibid., 69–80, Isaac Breuer, *"Samson Raphael Hirsch, "* in Leo Jung, ed., *Jewish Leaders* (New York, 1953), 163–177.
14. Ellbogen, *Century of Jewish Life,* 92–103.
15. S. M. Dubnow, *History of the Jews in Russia and Poland* (Philadelphia, 1918), 2, 111–139, 206–227.
16. Josef Elias, *"Israel Salanter, "* in Jung, ed., *Jewish Leaders,* 199–231.
17. Guttmann, *Philosophie des Judentums,* 342–345.
18. Ibid., 345–362; Franz Rosenzweig, *"Introduction,"* Hermann Cohen, *Jüdische Schriften* (Berlin, 1924) 1, v–LXIV.
19. Leon Simon, *"Introduction,"* Ahad Ha'am, *Essays, Letters, Memoirs* (Oxford, 1946).

CHAPTER 2

1. Voltaire, *Essai sur les moeurs et l'esprit des nations* (Paris, 1963), II, 66–67.
2. On Voltaire's attitude toward Jews and Judaism, see Jacob Katz, *From Prejudice to Destruction: Anti-Semitism, 1700–1933* (Cambridge, Mass., 1980), chap. 3.
3. Jacob Katz, *Out of the Ghetto: The Social Background of Jewish Emancipation* (Cambridge, Mass., 1973), 42–50.
4. Alexander Altmann, *Moses Mendelssohn: A Biographical Study* (University, Ala., 1973).
5. On the history of the term *secularization,* see Hermann Lübke, *Säkularisierung, Geschichte eines ideenpolitishen Begriffs* (Freiburg, 1965), and Wilhelm Kamlah, *Utopie, Eschatologie, Geschichtstheologie* (Mannheim, 1969), 53–70.
6. Jacob Katz, *Jews and Freemasons in Europe, 1723–1739* (Cambridge, Mass., 1970).
7. Jacob Katz, *"Kant Ve-Ha-Yahaduth, Ha-Heksher Ha-Histori"* [Kant and Judaism—the historical context], *Tarbiz* 41 (1972), 219–237.
8. *Ibid.*
9. Katz, *Out of the Ghetto,* 104–123.
10. There are some studies on nineteenth-century conversion. Johan Le Roi, *Judentaufen im 19 Jahrhundert* (Leipzig, 1899). A differentiation between the types according to their motivation is offered by Michael A. Meyer, *The Origins of the Modern Jew* (Detroit, 1967), 85–123.

11. The data on Theodore Ratisbonne's life are based on his own confessional autobiography, included in Louis Bautain, *Philosophie du Christianisme; correspondance religieuse* (Paris, 1835), I, XXXIII–LXII. Additional information is contained in Theodore Ratisbone, Mes souvenirs, published by the Congrégation de Notre-Dame de Sion, Rome (no date of publication). The book is not for sale and I received a copy by courtesy of the Order in Rome.
12. On Alphonse Ratisbonne, see Jean Gutton, *La Conversion de Ratisbonne* (Paris, 1964).
13. William James, *The Varieties of Religious Experience* (New York, 1929), 219–222, 252.
14. On Drach, see Paul Louis Bernard Drach, *Lettre d'un rabbin converti aux Israelites ses frères, sur les motifs de sa conversion* (Paris, 1825). On Liebermann, Pierre Blanchard, *Le vénérable Liebermann* (Paris, 1960). On the Lemann brothers, P. Théotime de Saint—Just, *Les frères Lémann Juifs convertis.* Paris 1937.
15. Leon Poliakov, *Le dévelopement de l'antisémitisme en Europe aux temps modernes (1700–1850)* (Paris, 1968), 351–391.
16. Simon Bloch, *Ueber die Bekehrungs-Geschichten des Herren T. Ratisbonne, J. Goschler und I. Lewel,* Strassburg 1835, 63–64. This is a rare book; the only copy known to me is in the Jewish National and University Library, Jerusalem.
17. Heine's case is well known. On Riesser, see my analysis in "The Term 'Jewish Emancipation': Its Origin and Historical Impact" in Alexander Altmann (ed.). *Studies in Nineteenth-Century Jewish Intellectual History* (Cambridge, Mass., 1964), 21–25, reprinted in Jacob Katz, *Emancipation and Assimilation: Studies in Modern Jewish History* (Westmead, England, 1973), 42–45.
18. Jaacov Fleischmann, *Baayat Ha-Nazruth be-Filosofia Ha-Yehudith shel Ha-Meah Ha-Teshaesreh* [The problem of Christianity in nineteenth-century Jewish thought] (Jerusalem, 1951).
19. Jacob Katz, *Exclusiveness and Tolerance: Studies in Jewish-Gentile Relations in Medieval and Modern Times* (Oxford, 1961), 116–148.
20. Moses Sofer, *Teshuvot Hatam Sofer,* VI, no. 89.
21. Jacob Katz, "Contributions towards a Biography of R. Moses Sofer," *Studies in Mysticism and Religion Presented to Gershom G. Scholem* (Jerusalem, 1967) [Hebrew].
22. See "Sources of Orthodox Trends", following.
23. The best, albeit somewhat partisan, account of the Congress is still that of Leopold Loew, *Zur neueren Geschichte der Juden in Ungarn* (Budapest, 1874).
24. This has been observed already by Isaac Heinemann, Mehkarim al R. Shimshon Rafael Hirsch, *Sinai* XII (1949), 259. See now the paper by Michel Meyer in this volume.
25. See "Sources of Orthodox Trends", following.
26. Surprisingly enough, one, if not the main, reason for the radicality of the Frankfurt reformers lay in their connection with the Freemasons. See J. Katz, *Jews and Freemasons in Europe* (Cambridge, Mass., 1970), 54–72.
27. Hirsch's memorandum (*Denkschrift über die Judenfrage in dem Gesetz betreffend den Austritt aus der Kirche* [Berlin, 1873]) appeared anonymously. It was later reprinted in his collected essays: Samson Raphael Hirsch, *Gesammelte Schriften.* Frankfurt am Main 1908 IV, 239–253. When the memorandum was criticized in a pamphlet by an opponent of the idea of separation, Hirsch published a most polemical rebuttal—this time under his own name—pointing in the very title of the publication to the principle of freedom of conscience. Samson Raphael Hirsch, *Prinzip der Gewissensfreiheit und die Schrift des Rechtsanwalts und Notars Makower über die Gemeindeverhältnisse der Juden* (Frankfurt am Main, 1874), reprinted in the Gesammelte Schriften IV, 254–294.
28. See the article "*Rückblick auf den-ungar.-israelitischen Congress*" published in Hirsch's *Jeschurun* XV (1869), 153–154. See also below, "Sources of Orthodox Trends."
29. Jacob Katz, "*Mishnato Ha-Leumith shel Ha-Rav Yehuda Alkaly*" [The national doctrine of Rabbi Yehuda Alkalay], in Ben Zion Dinur (ed.), *Shivath Zion,* IV (1956), 9–41.

CHAPTER 3

1. Cf. J. Katz, "The Vicissitudes of Three Apologetic Passages" (Hebrew), *Zion* 23, nos. 3–4 (1958): 174–181.
2. *Exclusiveness and Tolerance* (Oxford, 1961).

3. Cf. "To Whom Was Mendelssohn Replying in *Jerusalem?*" *Scripta Hierosolymitana* XXIII (1972): 214–293.
4. Cf. J. Katz, "Freemasons and Jews," *Jewish Journal of Sociology* 9, no. 2 (Dec. 1967): 137–148. For a full treatment of the subject see J. Katz, *Jews and Freemasons in Europe 1723–1939* (Cambridge, Mass., 1970).
5. Cf. "Samuel Hirsch—Rabbi, Philosopher, and Freemason," *REJ* 125 (Jan.–Sept. 1966): 125.
6. The following remarks constitute a summation of the discussion that ensued at the original presentation of this paper.

CHAPTER 7

1. The literature on nationalism is extensive. See C. Hayes, *The Historical Evolution of Modern Nationalism* (New York, 1931); Fr. O. Hertz, *Nationality in History and Politics* (London, 1945); H. Kohn, *The Idea of Nationalism* (New York, 1946); E. Kedourie, *Nationalism* (London, 1960). Most stimulating is the classic essay of Lord Acton, "Nationality," included in his *Essays on Freedom and Power* (New York, 1955).
2. See the literature quoted in note 1.
3. The best summary of the history of Jewish nationalism is B. Halpern, *The Idea of the Jewish State* (Cambridge, Mass., 1961).
4. G. Scholem, "Zum Verständnis der messianischen Idee im Judentum," *Eranos-Jahrbuch* 28 (1960): 193–198.
5. S. Stern-Täubler, "The Jew in the Transition from Ghetto to Emancipation," *Historia Judaica* 2 (1940): 102–119.
6. B. Ottenburg, *Das Erwachen des deutschen Nationalbewusstseins in der preussischen Judenheit* (Hamburg, 1933).
7. On the social ideals of rationalism in Jewish society see J. Katz, *Tradition and Crisis* (New York), chap. 24.
8. H. G. Duker, "The Tarniks," *The Joshua Star Memorial Volume* (New York, 1953), 191–201.
9. See my article (in Hebrew) in B. Dinur (ed.), *Shivath Zion* 4 (1956): 9–41.
10. On Kalisher, see my article in Dinur, *Shivath Zion* 2–3 (1953): 26–41.
11. On Hess, see his recent biography by E. Silberner, *Moses Hess, Geschichte seines Lebens* (Leiden, 1966).
12. S. W. Baron, *History and Jewish Historians* (Philadelphia, 1964), 266, 271.
13. Silberner, *Moses Hess*, 395–403.
14. On the Messianic idea in the transition period see B. Mevorah, "The Problem of the Messiah in the Emancipation and Reform Controversies, 1781–1819," Ph.D. diss. (in Hebrew) (Jerusalem, 1966).
15. K. Mannheim, *Ideology and Utopia* (New York, 1946).
16. See N. Sokolow, *History of Zionism* (London, 1919); N. M. Gelber, *Zur Vorgeschichte des Zionismus* (Wien, 1927); F. Kobler, *The Vision Was There, A History of the British Movement for the Restoration of the Jews to Palestine* (London, 1956).
17. Kobler, *The Vision Was There*, 89–93; L. Stein, *The Balfour Declaration* (London, 1961), 15–16.
18. A. B. Makover, *Mordecai M. Noah* (New York, 1917); J. Goldberg, *Major Noah, American Jewish Pioneer* (Philadelphia, 1936).
19. Kobler in his above-quoted book confessedly intended to write the history of the movement "as an integral part of British religious, social and political history" (p. 9) and not as an annex to the history of Zionism, but he cannot be said to have lived up to his intention.
20. I. Kolatt-Kopelovich, "Ideology and the Impact of Realities upon the Jewish Labour Movement in Palestine, 1905–1919," Ph. D. diss. (Jerusalem, 1964).
21. T. Herzl, *Der Judenstaat, Versuch einer modernen Lösung der Judenfrage* (Leipzig, 1896); English translation *A Jewish State* (London, 1896).
22. A. Bein, *Theodor Herzl, a Biography* (Cleveland, 1962).

CHAPTER 8

1. Following Karl Mannheim and Martin Buber, I use the term "utopia" not in the negative sense of some illusory future that can never be realized, but in the sense of a vision that guides its adherents to their desired goal.

CHAPTER 10

1. This thesis is argued with particular reference to German Zionists in a book by Stephen M. Poppel, *Zionism in Germany 1897–1933: The Shaping of a Jewish Identity* (Philadelphia, 1976).

INDEX

Abuhab, Samuel, 43
Agnon, S. Y., 153
Agudat Israel, 153
Ahad Ha'am (Asher Ginzberg), 19, 41, 133, 147
Aliyah ideology, 108, 125
Alkalay, Yehuda, 32–33, 93–96, 99, 111–114, 123, 157–159, 164
Allgemeine Zeitung des Judentums, 32, 120
Alliance Israélite Universelle, 9, 100, 114, 120, 148, 157
Altmann, Alexander, 22
America. *See* United States.
Anomie, 23–24
Anti-Semitism, and Jewish assimilation, 3–6, 10–11, 26–27, 73, 124, 132, 136, 138, 160
    as reaction to Jewish emancipation, 132, 136
    as social reaction (1880s), 10–11
    as unchallenged tradition, 4
    culmination of, in Holocaust, 61, 150
    disillusionment with liberalism and, 124
    emigration movement and, 4, 138, 162–163
    Freemasonry and, 72–73
    historical past and, 61–62
    in Imperial Germany, 10
    of rationalists, 20–21, 50–51
    particularism as accusation in, 17–18
    pogroms and, 32, 101, 103, 125, 138, 141–142, 149–152, 159–161
    social segregation and, 3–6, 11, 17, 26–27
    theological rationales and, 40
    Zionism vs., 141–152
Apologists, Jewish, 7–8, 18–19, 37–42, 47, 84, 103
Arabs, 151
Aramaic, 3
Ararat (proposed Jewish state), 98, 109, 128
Arendt, Hannah, 61
Ashkenazi Jews, 26
Asiatic Brethren, 45, 71–72
Assimilation, Jewish. *See also* Emancipation.
    anti-Semitism and, 3–6, 10–11, 26–27, 73, 124, 132, 136, 138, 160
    as secularization. *See* Secularism (secularization).
    as social transformation, 5–8, 11, 13, 36, 37, 47

Assimilation *(Continued)*
    Jewish, as utopian dream, 5–8
    cultural, 23–27
    emancipation goals and, 7–8, 22–23, 25–26, 29–30, 32, 109–110, 119–121
    equality as precursor of, 5
    French Revolution and, 5–6, 26, 49, 77
    hazards of, 48, 81–82
    nationalism as coeval with, 7
    obstacles to, 7–9, 23–24, 49–60, 70, 80, 144–146, 148
    political vs. social aspects of, 8
    psychology of, 26, 27, 37
    Reform Judaism as expression of, 49
    social emancipation in Germany and, 68–74, 94–95
    socialism and. *See* Socialism.
    Zionism vs., 94–95, 97, 100, 135–137, 143–144, 156–157
Atheism, 45, 50
Auerbach, Berthold, 112, 120, 121
Aufklärung, and rationalism, 12
Aurore Naissante, 72
Austria, Jews in, 6, 10, 76–78, 143
Austrittsgesetz, 31
Austro-Hungarian Empire, 6
Auto-emancipation. *See* Self-emancipation.
Auto-Emancipation (Pinsker), 141

Babylonia, captivity of Jews in, 154
Baden Landtag, 66
Baeck, Leo, 41
Balfour Declaration (1917), 121, 139, 166
Bar Kokhba, Simon, 127, 155
Batei Din, 117
Bautain, Louis, 25
Benamozegh, Elijah, 28, 40
Bendavid, Lazarus, 156
Ben Yehuda, Eliezer, 125, 161
Berlin, Jewish community in, 21, 53, 59, 68–69
Berlin Congress (1878), 9, 146–147
Berliner Revue, 145
Bible, 3, 83, 96, 116–117, 134, 154, 161
    Christian, 40, 44–45
    critical studies of. *See* Historical criticism.
    Jewish, 45, 98